S0-BIP-197

THINKING IT OVER

THOMAS F. WOODLOCK

THINKING IT OVER

EDITED AND WITH AN INTRODUCTION BY

JAMES EDWARD TOBIN

THE DECLAN X. McMULLEN COMPANY

NEW YORK 1947

The Declan X. McMullen Company, New York

Printed in the U.S.A.

ACKNOWLEDGMENTS

An expression of gratitude is due to all whose kindness has helped in the initial preparation of this volume, especially: Dow, Jones & Co., Inc., proprietor of the *Wall Street Journal,* for permission to reprint the copyrighted material which first appeared therein; Miss Elizabeth M. Byrne, sister-in-law of Mr. Woodlock; John Patrick Walsh, Esq., attorney for the Woodlock estate; and Mr. Justice Edward S. Dore.

Permission to reprint copyrighted passages has also been granted by the following publishers:

Creative Age Press, Inc., for quotations from Salvador de Madariaga, *Spain* (1943).

Doubleday & Company, Inc., for quotations from *The Problems of a Lasting Peace* (1942) by Herbert Hoover and Hugh Gibson.

Houghton Mifflin Company, for quotations from Irving Babbitt, *Democracy and Leadership* (1924).

Alfred A. Knopf, Inc., for quotations from Robert H. Jackson, *The Struggle for Judicial Supremacy* (1941), Beryl H. Levy, *Our Constitution: Tool or Testament* (1941), and Thomas Mann, *The Coming Victory of Democracy* (1938).

Little, Brown & Company and Atlantic Monthly Press, for quotations from Walter Lippmann, *The Good Society* (1937).

Longmans Green & Company, for quotations from Mortimer J. Adler, *What Man Has Made of Man* (1937).

W. W. Norton & Company, Inc., for quotations from Everett Dean Martin, *Liberty* (1930), José Ortega y Gasset, *Invertebrate Spain* (1937) and his *The Revolt of the Masses* (1932).

ACKNOWLEDGMENTS

G. P. Putnam's Sons, for quotations from Guglielmo Ferrero, *The Reconstruction of Europe* (1941) and Fritz August Voigt, *Unto Caesar* (1938).

Charles Scribner's Sons, for quotations from Hamilton Vreeland Jr., *Twilight of Individual Liberty* (1944).

Sheed and Ward, Inc., for quotations from Christopher Dawson, *The Judgment of the Nations* (1942) and Peter Wust, *Crisis in the West* (1940).

CONTENTS

SOCIETY: ISMS AND IDOLS

DEMOCRACY: DEFINITION AND DEBATE

CONTENTS

ECONOMICS: ORDER AND DISORDER

CRISIS: WAR AND PEACE

CONTENTS

INTRODUCTION

To read the columns of Mr. Thomas Woodlock, published day after day in the Wall Street Journal *for some fifteen years, is an amazing and an exciting experience. It is one which leads inescapably to the conclusion that here was a man who stood still, while the world raced by to sag into a deeper morass or to whirl wildly in a typhoon.*

It is the current opinion, of course, that men should never stand still. This blithe forwardness may result in plunging with both feet into deep mud, instead of encircling the bog and pausing to post signs. It may mean that those who are touched by the mad pressure of changing winds scorn with romantic defiance the hurricane cellar of solid conviction. To be anything but modern, progressive, independent, liberal, they hold, is to be insignificant.

The poet Blake said that anything which stands still dies in stagnation—and he used a forest pool as illustration. But this, too, is a revelation of modern intellectual weakness. Mr. Woodlock would have said that those who sink in the mire become petrified wood; those who swirl in the maelstrom, porous flotsam; those who ride on the wind, mere dust. And surely, even Blake's imagined pool, standing still, does not of necessity stagnate. Good pools remain fresh and sparkling, fed by underground springs; their water is pure and drinkable. So it is with good minds.

The mind of Thomas Woodlock was a great mind, rooted in tradition, fed by the springs of century-old thought, sparkling under the true sun, fresh and satisfying to the taste. What it saw in books and men, current problems and ancient ones, it thought about for months. The resultant published opinions did not please all. Nor could they have. For Mr.

Woodlock did not believe in false tolerance, in accepting every passing fancy, every incomplete solution, every beckoning meander, every novel definition of life, of civilization, of justice. He strenuously opposed such weather-vane awareness of mere existence under heaven. He clung to one set of definitions, and measured society by such standards, as he trod the path he chose. Perhaps it is this oneness of vision and of expression which made his mind not painfully unique, but wondrously refreshing, in an age which so actively dislikes sameness.

Mr. Woodlock was convinced, of course, that he was making progress—no sane man talks the same way for fifteen years unless he is convinced that he has hearers. And that he had hearers is evident from the enormous pile of correspondence which reached his office desk every week. He knew that in one sense he was not standing still, for, while he believed in 1945 what he had believed in 1931, he believed it more firmly. His wide reading during that period strengthened his conviction, carried him over one mountain to another, ever enlarging his horizon. This is progress; this firm faith in the best things is independence; this search for freedom from monstrous shibboleths is liberalism—by his own definition of the term; this awareness of the ills of our day is intelligently modern.

He wore his views as a mediaeval monk wore his religious garb. In a phrase which is a mediaeval pun, his habit and his habits were the same: woven of the same texture, cut to the same pattern, making the same outward impression. The point is that both to the old monk and the modern editor the habits were more important than the habit. To some critics, it is a great offense not to change the base of one's mind as often as to change the base of one's wardrobe. Mr. Woodlock did not object to the repetition of a truth, but he fought vigorously against the repetition of an evil. Like the medi-

aevalist, he made no pretense about saying anything new; like him, he said the same thing on many different occasions. If there is objection to this, it can come only from those whose minds are so unformed, whose convictions are so unstable, and whose nature is so thin-skinned that they seem always to be touched to the quick.

A casual reading of his nearly three thousand columns may suggest that Mr. Woodlock said nothing but the same thing over and over again. But anyone interested in civilization has to say the same thing day after day. Civilization is like health: and a doctor does not write a hundred totally different prescriptions for a hundred patients who consult him for the same kind of ulcers.

His approach is made clear by his remarks on three-dimensional thinking, a paper which serves as a key to the subsequent columns, even though he may not have written it with such a purpose in mind. Mr. Woodlock has observed that those who think in one dimension are merely carried by the wind or the waves; they accept impressions, prejudices and "ideas," far from truth, but firmly intrenched, against which they measure passing notions or sound opinions. The true thinkers, who admit the existence of standards, who measure the transience of the now against the permanence of the timeless, go beyond these planes to a third dimension. They are the only ones who are "in complete touch with the common experience *of mankind."*

In another sense, too, Mr. Woodlock was himself a three-dimensional thinker. He could not pass comment on modern education, for example, without defining it, exposing its purpose, recording its causes, shuddering at its effects. Its causes took him into the past; its effects kept him aware of the moment. The subject matter of education, as of all human knowledge, is man. Hence he considered education in relation to those affected by it. He noted its impress on the so-called leaders of the day, its bearing on attitudes toward the state, law, justice, social needs, science, and public morality.

Thus, a casual reading of the selections made for this volume may also suggest that Mr. Woodlock never kept to the same topic, that his conversation spilled over into philosophy when he talked of the state, into politics when he talked of education, into science when he talked of war, into justice when he talked of economics. This was not carelessness, however, but the alertness, as well as the charity, of a full mind.

Life, surely, is at least three-dimensional, and the thinker cannot observe one surface without becoming aware of the others. He cannot merely glance at an action without recognizing it, comparing it, and putting his conclusion to some intellectually practical use. What Mr. Woodlock saw from his watch tower were armed hordes of barbarians, massing under banners of liberalism, instrumentalism, utilitarianism, humanitarianism, Marxism, Communism, or Fascism. Against these enemies of the best society he warned constantly. He noted their origins in false approaches to democracy, in propagandistic panaceas for the masses, in oracular admiration for Rousseau, Bentham, and Spencer, in the myth of individualism, in the impetus given to the relativity of truth. He saw their effects in government without freedom, justice without equality, education without morality, investment without reward, a world without peace.

This collection does not pretend to contain the cream of his columns. At most, the papers are representative, indicating the variety as well as the basic sameness of his outlook, as many facets as possible of the three-dimensioned world he looked at.

The steady throb beneath most of his pulsing paragraphs, however, was his defense of democracy. He had faith in democracy, as he had faith in America, and he sought to bring it about that neither was sullied or changed. His final paper, published the morning which printed his death notice, reaffirms his convictions and re-echoes his insistence that the Declaration of Independence and the Bill of Rights are, together, a priceless heritage. Of them men in public life, high and low, should speak as a creed. In them is a statement of conviction about truths. By them we should be enabled firmly to withstand the increasing inroads of totalitarianism. Because of his love of freedom and justice, of democracy as mankind, he fought earnestly in defense of the Supreme Court—possibly his most significant group of columns.

It is impossible, however, to choose one column above another, for they are all of a pattern—just as it has been somewhat difficult to arrange them under arbitrary section headings. They will not remain within such confines, they cross-index themselves, whether he talks of society and its ills, democracy and its enemies, law and its mastery over the individual, tyrannical freedom in the schools and laboratories, interference with initiative, or the course of the era which began in blood in 1932.

The title which Mr. Woodlock used for his masthead has been retained for this volume, for it is a significant one. He did not believe merely in talking, merely in reading, merely in writing. Thought came first. His conversational powers were great; his writing facile, logical, pointed; his reading range enormous. He was at home in many languages, and their fruit was offered to his readers' taste. All subjects interested him; all views stimulated him. The result of such reflection gives his statements a striking timelessness—a pertinence and a soundness which could not be if he had been blown with the winds.

It is significant to record that, when Mr. Woodlock read a book, he paused to pencil the margins. Any stimulating book, owned by the reader, should be treated in this way. If it comforts the mind, it needs these marginalia of agreement; if it errs, it needs the monitory objection at one side; if it forces comparisons, these, too, deserve recording. Books are composed of quotations between connectives; they are meant to be linked with other typeset ideas. From such phrases come the links which shape the chains of remembrance, of argument, of intellectual advancement. There is no better way of thinking it over than with a pencil at hand for scoring the impressions reason must make.

JAMES EDWARD TOBIN

THINKING IT OVER

SOCIETY: ISMS AND IDOLS

THREE-DIMENSIONAL THOUGHT

For years inventors have been seeking a way to get three-dimensional effect on the silver screen—so, at least, this writer is informed. It occurred to him while listening the other day to a scientific discussion of this problem (little of which he understood) that there was another place where introduction of the third dimension would be of enormous value, namely, into men's thinking and talking. For it seemed to him that the analogy of extension might be applicable to the process of mind, slender as might be the thread that supported it. To the three dimensions that characterize extended matter in space might be compared three dimensions in thought about things, for instance:

The one-dimensional thinker may be identified as a person who has never troubled to frame for himself any theory as to what human life is all about, that is, a man who has never exposed himself to philosophy (i.e., metaphysics) of any kind whatsoever, or troubled himself concerning the consistency of the views that from time to time occupy his mind. He is impatient of logical processes, which he dismisses as technicalities, and treats as an insult a request for definition of terms. Mostly, he will go with the majority of his class, but sometimes (as a consequence of something lying within the domain of psychoanalysis) he will go squarely against it. The leftist group has quite a representation of the latter variety. So, too, has current literature in both book and newspaper form, especially among the columnists living and dead.

The two-dimensional thinker is distinguished from his one-dimensional brother by his possession of at least some metaphysical slants or prejudices ranging from a few elementary negations to a more or less complete set of denials, all directed against one thing, namely, the existence of any permanent truth of any kind in a universe whose complete relativity and flux are its only reality. As a consequence of this, whatever is old is for them wrong, whatever was true yesterday is not true today, but may be true again tomorrow. There are no standards of any kind and all questions are always open. Truth is something that does not really exist, yet must be sought, though with the certainty that it can never be found. Not that these men are necessarily more logical or even consistent than are one-dimensional men, but they have formulated for themselves or have instinctively assumed certain definite metaphysical notions which, as already said, deny the reality of anything but change. Here, also, the leftist group is abundantly supplied, as is also literature and journalism, particularly in the case of daily newspaper book-review columns, which rather give the lie to the common charge that there is no opportunity for the young man in these days.

Finally, there is the three-dimensional group of thinkers, who differ from the one-dimensional kind in having a definite metaphysical slant or instinct (which may be and is at the top a complete philosophy), the essence of which is recognition that there *are* some things which remain true, some standards which remain standards; that what is new is not therefore better than what is old; that underneath the appearance of flux and change there is reality, and that this reality can be known as reality though not completely—thus differentiating themselves from the two-dimensional group. The main characteristic of the three-dimensional thinker is that he is in complete touch with the *common experience* of mankind.

Men in all their ordinary relations with each other have no doubts whatever of certain elemental realities; for example, that a thing actually *is,* that it is *what* it is and not something else, that a statement cannot be at one time both true and false, and that one can judge a thing, compare it with another and conclude to something certain as a result of the comparison. The negation of two-dimensional philosophy is in reality nothing more than an unpacking of elementals. This is why three-dimensional thinkers are the only ones who are in full accord with reality and why they have a swift and sure instinct for the humanist decencies in everyday life.

December 8, 1937

REVOLT OF THE MASSES

It is to be hoped that Ortega's *Revolt of the Masses,* now available in an English translation, will receive wide circulation and attentive reading in this country, for a large part of its analysis and argument is emphatically to our address. Our country is, as Ortega himself points out, the "paradise of the mass-man"—the *hombre medio*—and it behooves us to ponder the significance of that fact.

It is worth while to recapitulate his main argument and it can best be done in a few simple propositions. These follow:

(1) Every human society organized for any purpose is a dynamic union of "mass" (majority) and "minority," the latter being composed of those individuals who are by nature

especially qualified in respect of the purpose for which the society is organized.

(2) It is the function of the "minority" to direct, and it is the function of the "mass" to be directed.

(3) Within the last century and a half the population of the civilized world has trebled and at the same time the general "level" (material) of life has been raised in extraordinary degree.

(4) This has resulted in a tremendous increase in the number of "mass-men" whose living conditions have been improved enormously, and have had opened to them advantages hitherto exclusively enjoyed by the "minority."

(5) This change in conditions is the work of the exceptional few who have developed science, technics and industrial organization.

(6) But this is not recognized by the "mass-men" who regard the fuller life at their disposal as the result of an automatic natural process for which they owe no thanks to anyone.

(7) The "mass-man" of today recognizes no "superior," regards himself as the heir of all the ages, and perfectly competent to direct the world's affairs, and he has seized the reins of power. He is in fact a "primitive" type which has risen up in a "civilized" world, and is not interested in the principles of "civilization." It is a case of "barbarian" invasion, but invasion by "barbarians" from within.

(8) In these facts lies the great danger to civilization today, for that civilization is an extremely complex and fragile thing which can quickly wither. The "revolt" of the "mass-man" is a deadly threat to its life.

That in barest outline is the main thesis of Ortega's book. He develops it in simple direct language, avoiding abstractions and at all times making clear his exact meaning. The whole argument rests upon a biological fact, namely, that no two men are alike qualitatively or quantitatively in the matter of capacities. "Nature" has thus far stratified the human race in hierarchic fashion with respect to all capacities, and has definitely established "aristocracy" as the rule for human organization. The very essence of "liberal democracy" lies in recognition of that fact, and the "revolt" of the "mass-men" is a revolt against "liberal democracy" itself—although made in the name of democracy!

Ten years ago Ortega published a smaller volume entitled *Espana invertebrada,* in which the germ of the present volume is to be found (as he himself says), and it is very desirable that this should also receive English dress, for there is much in it which supplements and illuminates the later work. In particular there is a chapter entitled *"Ejemplaridad y docilidad,"* which deals with the much discussed matter of "leadership," and is a biting commentary on the present fashion of deriding the "superman."

This writer has more than once suggested that the one thing necessary to make "popular government" work successfully is "intelligent humility" on the part of Demos. It is the lack of this virtue which is at the heart of the "revolt" of Demos, and the great merit of Ortega's analysis is in the flood of light that it throws upon the consequences of that rebellion.

August 31, 1932

THE FRENCH REVOLUTION AND US

It has for a considerable time been a cherished hypothesis with this writer that the revolution in which this country is engaged is in reality the second phase of the French Revolution, expressing itself in accordance with our own national psychology. The French upheaval's motto was expressed in three famous words, *Liberté, Egalité, Fraternité*. The ideal enshrined in *Liberté* was realized, or rather was supposed to be real—in what we call democracy, that is, political equality —of sorts. That was the Revolution's first phase. We are now aiming to establish economic equality and thus give effect to the ideal *Egalité*. In this attempt we are doing a good many things which suggest interesting analogies in the matter of method with events in France a century and a half ago.

De Tocqueville points out that when the French Revolution broke out it found a "privileged" class—the nobility—which, although stripped of its political powers of feudal days by the Crown, had managed to retain and even increase its feudal privileges, exemptions and so forth, and was completely without any kind of social contact with the people at large. It was against this class in particular that the popular fury was directed. Our modern analogy may be found (at least for purpose of argument) in our "business leaders" against whom the main revolutionary attack has been directed. It has been a simple matter—dialectically—to lay the entire depression to their charge, and build a picture quite similar to that painted of hated French aristocrats by the popular orators of that day. Large profits, indifference to the public interest and incompetence make quite a persuasive combination for a tribune of the people to put before his hearers!

Another interesting analogy is that of "brain trusts." De Tocqueville tells us that the enraged people found ready to their hand elaborate political blueprints which philosophers had long been preparing and that these were put into effect just as they stood for the good reason that nobody else had other programs to offer, the people having had no political experience of their own. Also, the theories of these philosophers had long been discussed in fashionable salons in which the intelligentsia of the day were welcome guests, and in which it was the *dernier cri* to profess advanced opinions.

We, too, have our philosophers with their theories hatched in college cloisters and our millionaire and *rentier* intelligentsia who have taken kindly to parlor radicalism—and our legislators have swallowed whole many if not most of their ideas, and have passed laws without much time or thought spent on finding out what they were all about.

Nor is it too extravagant a flight of fancy to see yet another analogy between the progress of the French Revolution and our own in the case of "big business" during the last few years, and that of Louis XVI and Marie Antoinette, when after the abortive attempt at flight they were returned to the Tuilleries and there kept as virtual prisoners, although still King and Queen. In place of the jack-booted, scarved and cockaded sans-culottes who stamped at will through the royal apartments, ransacking wardrobes, desks and closets, and invading the most private recesses and affairs of their prisoners, we have our "investigations" at the hands of "committees" which have done a similarly complete job on "big business" so far as privacy is concerned, and with quite as little regard for the personal comfort of their investigatees!

Finally, as is the case with revolutions, our own follows the rule *Vires acquirit eundo.* The severity of the revolutionary measures increases with time. Two years ago we were talking in terms of "recovery"; we enacted, indeed, the famous National Industrial Recovery Act. Gradually the true character of the political process emerged, and it has now become apparent that *egalité*—by expropriation—is the goal. In the circumstances it seems to this writer that this theory concerning that process has a sound pair of feet on which to stand.

Liberté accomplished: *Egalité* well on the way—about *Fraternité?* It is to be hoped that we shall not too closely follow precedent in this matter. "Be my brother or I will kill you!"—Irving Babbitt reminds us—was the way in which the Revolution expressed its concept of the Brotherhood of Man.

How shall we express *Fraternité*—especially when the principal visible bond of unity among our various groups is a common hatred of "wealth," and a common desire for a share in its expropriation? After we get it—or after we find out that it is not there to be got—upon what basis shall *we* build our Brotherhood of Man?

July 5, 1935

POLITICAL ROMANTICISM

I

The late Irving Babbitt, in his book *Democracy and Leadership*, published some fifteen years ago or thereabout, remarked, apropos Rousseauism and some of the episodes of the French Revolution, that "the last stage of humanitarianism is homicidal mania." Babbitt was an uncompromising foe of romanticism in all its manifestations, and *Democracy and Leadership* is a biting criticism of that movement in social and political life, which has especial point for the days in which we live. In the quoted phrase he sums up a very important truth, which is seemingly a paradox, but, as Chesterton has shown us, we live in times of talk and thought so warped from truth that truth perforce must appear paradoxical.

The essence of romanticism in all its forms is in its substitution of emotion or passion for reason, and its revolt against standards and principles, often conducted in the name of the very standards and principles against which it revolts. Take, for instance, the political romanticism of today as exemplified by our left-wing intellectuals, who call themselves liberals. They fight under the banner of *liberty*, yet they are all at heart—consciously or unconsciously—for the totalitarian state, which is liberty's most deadly enemy. They are all for *justice,* yet who are more unfair in their concepts of what is just? Consider, for instance, Senator Norris' theory of what should be value for rate-making purposes in the case of public utilities—"Whichever is lowest"—and the arguments by which he supported that theory. (See the *Congressional Record,* May 26, 1933). It is a perfect monstrosity of unfairness. Yet Senator Norris is admittedly the high priest and *censor morum* of present day liberalism! To crown all, we have but to look at the controversy over the Supreme Court which exploded a year ago and note where the liberal forces stood in the fight. Have we yet at all realized the tremendous significance of that phenomenon?

With the political romanticist, too, the end will always justify the means. As readers will no doubt remember, that prominent liberal Mr. Richberg told the New York bar (in a prepared address) that Bassanio, begging the Venetian court "to do a great right, do a little wrong," spoke for "democracy"! Not all liberals have been so honestly outspoken as was Mr. Richberg but, nevertheless, he spoke their real mind. The same spokesman two or three years ago flatly rejected the fundamental principle of our political system, when he told us (in a prepared article) that every right and privilege the citizen enjoyed came to him as a gift from the State! In which pronouncement he has the approval of practically all our liberal intelligentsia!

Romanticism is a *centrifugal* phenomenon. A good analogy in the domain of physics would be found if the force we call gravitation, which keeps the planets in their courses, were gradually to diminish; the result would be that the heavenly bodies would "go romantic." Planetary orbits would become eccentric, circles would become ellipses, ellipses would ultimately become open curves and order would disappear. Similarly in the domain of art, literature, music and conduct, the forces which in the past held all these in something like order have so weakened in these later days, that in all cases there is evident an increasing eccentricity of performance. At the bottom of it all there is a philosophy which is barren of all fixed principles, and at its heart is the denial that there can be any such things—which, of course, is pure dogmatism and no philosophy at all.

It is a pity that Babbitt is not writing today. If he were, he would probably tell us that Rousseauism is at the bottom of all our difficulties, that this prophet of romanticism is wrecking the order of human society and he would show us how and where his influence is at work. A careful reader of *Democracy and Leadership* could no doubt deduce the story for himself, but Babbitt could have given us the picture in full color, and it would surely do us much good.

February 11, 1938

II

When the Declaration of Independence was signed Jean Jacques Rousseau had still two years to live and his works, notably *Emile,* were already brewing the revolution in France. The spirit of the Declaration and the spirit of Rousseau represent almost a perfect antithesis. In that antithesis, perhaps, lies the fundamental difference between the revolution which gave the American system of government to the world and the revolution which toppled the old regime in France. No writer in America has written more illuminatingly on Rousseauism in modern life than the late Irving Babbitt, and it is a pity that his works are not better known to that part of the public which reads books other than fiction. For the fact is that Rousseauism has deeply infected our left-wing thinking.

Babbitt rated Rousseau as "the most eloquent and influential of the sentimentalists," and that the sentimentalist "always has some lovely dream that he prefers to the truth." In the last year of his life Jean Jacques admitted that his whole life had been one "long revery." Babbitt called him the "very type of unadjusted man," and one who took the world for a picnic ground instead of a battlefield. He was a very prince of romanticists, a prophet of "humanitarianism."

Rousseau hated cold reason, which he said had never done anything illustrious. Primitive man, he said, was good until corrupted by civilization; let man get rid of civilization and return to the simple impulses of his nature and all would be well with him. The Social Contract would do the job. Every individual under this would transfer all his rights to the community and subject himself to the general will expressed by the numerical majority. The general will would be good because it was the general will and it could not decree anything that was not for the good of the individual. Thus absolute sovereignty of the majority is good and justifies itself. (It may
no power to find a statute duly enacted void because "un-
be noted that in the French Constitution the High Court has
constitutional.")

This romantic mood coupled with a belief in majority absolutism is the bone and sinew of our left-wing thinking, and the determinant factor in its social and political policies. The essence of the romantic mood is its centrifugal expansiveness and repugnance to control. It is the "noble savage" idea applied to society. Applied to a circle it would transform the circumference held in place by the centripetal force transmitted through the radii into a tangent headed for points unknown. It turns conscience, as Babbitt said, from an "inner check" upon impulse into an "expansive emotion." Expansiveness unchecked is synonymous with explosion. What Babbitt said of the last stage of humanitarianism applies to all the "urges" of romanticism; they all end in their contraries. The Rousseauist "conscience" is in fact the contrary of "virtue" as the Greeks conceived it, and it could produce no other result.

The romantic mood is appealing to two classes of men. One of these includes people whose hearts are naturally soft and sensitive, but whose heads are softer. A head is "soft" when it is intolerant of fixed truths, rooted principles, and all ideas which seem to stand in the way of some generous impulse of an altruistic nature. The other class includes the "unadjusted" of whom Babbitt regards Rousseau as the type. To be soft-headed is not to be unadjusted nor is unadjustment necessarily soft-headedness, for one can be unadjusted and have fixed ideas—plenty of them. Both are romanticists, actual or potential. When a society "goes romantic" the soft-heads usually far outnumber the unadjusted, but it is the latter who usually lay the course and lead the team. In this they find support from what might be called camp-followers, sutlers, scavengers or what not, who are not unadjusted, not soft-headed, not soft-hearted, but intent only upon personal advancement, and without illusions, principles or altrustic emotions.

November 6, 1940

RATIONALISM AND THE LIBERAL

Some years ago, Everett Dean Martin, in his book, ***Liberty***, gave us a very neat definition of the nineteenth-century liberal. He is "*a rationalist who walks by faith in the wisdom of an irrational majority.*" (Mr. Martin himself is responsible for the italics.) That remark carries a good deal of meaning when unpacked. Mr. Martin handed us the keys to the portmanteau when he pointed out that the liberal was a compound of eighteenth-century rationalism with Rousseauistic romanticism. The essential point of eighteenth-century rationalism was that no truth existed which was not accessible to and demonstrable by human reason, operating upon sensible phenomena. Of Rousseau and his romanticism the late Irving Babbitt had much to say. The essence of Rousseau's philosophy, if it can be called a philosophy, was a flight from realities of life into an ideal society. As Babbitt says, he was one of those men who take this world to be a picnic ground, and Emile Faguet (whose *Cult of Incompetence,* like Babbitt's *Democracy and Leadership,* is extremely useful reading nowadays) said that the image Rousseau left on the mind of the public is that of a gentleman up in a cherry tree tossing down cherries to two maidens below. On which Babbitt remarks that "This, after all, is Rousseau's essential attitude. He sought to develop the mere dalliance of an extraordinarily rich imagination into a complete scheme of life."

The blend of these two interesting compounds produced the paradoxical thing that we strangely call Liberalism. It is paradoxical because the rationalism of the eighteenth century has become the anti-intellectualism of the nineteenth, and the expansive humanitarianism of Rousseau has, as Babbitt pointed out, culminated in something like homicidal mania as its final stage. Finally, in the name of human freedom it is attempting to transfer the concept of *personality* from the individual to society. Hence the deification of the majority. Of this, Babbitt said ("The Political Influence of Rousseau," *The Nation,* January 18, 1917):

> In the most austere democracy the individual is to have no rights against the numerical majority at any particular moment, because this majority expresses the general will and the general will is ideally disinterested. It cannot have any interest contrary to that of the individuals who compose it, so that the individual needs no guarantees against it.

Comparing this theory with our political structure, it is not difficult to see where our liberals get their dislike for the principles laid down in the Declaration of Independence and embodied in the Constitution. These gentlemen are all at heart totalitarians. They hold that the sovereignty of the majority is to be absolute and unlimited. "To limit sovereignty is to destroy it," so Rousseau said; also, "The sovereign, by the very fact that it is, is always what it ought to be." As Babbitt points out, Rousseau went further than did the defenders of the divine right of kings. They at least held that the king was responsible to God, but for Rousseau the sovereign people *is* God. But all this is subject to qualification in one respect. Only one kind of totalitarianism is good, that of the proletarian; the fascist kind is all wrong. A proletarian majority is always right; any other is necessarily *ipso facto* bad and not to be tolerated.

An anti-intellectualist intelligentsia, a liberal, whose idea of freedom is freedom for a society in which the individual is submerged—that is the thing which Mr. Martin has defined in the phrase above-quoted and that is the picture of the liberal of today who swallows Stalin but regurgitates Mussolini and Hitler, and, as someone has said, is a pacifist who hates war but is willing to make civil war. Where in any civilization prior to our own can we find anything like him?

It is interesting to note that *The Nation* article from which quotation has been made was published twenty years ago, before we entered the World War. In concluding it, Babbitt said: "The combination of formidable scientific and material efficiency with spiritual and moral inefficiency is turning life into a hell right before our eyes. . . . No more decisive experience indeed can be imagined short of the suicide of the planet." What a pity he is not here to describe the world-picture today!

March 19, 1937

COLLOQUIES ON SOCIETY

I

To those who are acquainted with the work of Guglielmo Ferrero over the last forty years, a book recently issued at Lugano entitled *Colloqui con Guglielmo Ferrero,* by Bogdan Raditzka, should be particularly interesting. It consists, as the title indicates, of a series of connected "interviews" by the author with Ferrero, and a generous selection of *grandi pagine* taken from his works. It is, in fact, an excellent introduction to Ferrero for those who are yet unacquainted with his work, as well as having a special interest for his many disciples. These conversations, as Raditzka says in his foreword, contain "the quintessence of Ferrero's thought, its first origins and its ultimate development." Readers may be interested in a general outline of this thought, for it amounts to a fundamental analysis of the causes that have brought our civilization close to total wreck.

At eighteen years of age Ferrero met Lombroso, who interested him in a study of *justice,* its origins and development. The next six years he spent in travel—Europe—and in the accumulation of a mass of facts concerning civil institutions, ancient and modern, as material for study, in the hope of reaching some fundamental conclusions on the whole subject. At this point, he tells his interviewer, "I was struck by the resemblance that penal institutions presented in certain periods of decadence and confusion; for instance, in the fourth and fifth centuries of the Roman Empire, and the closing years of the reign of Louis XIV. These resemblances suggested to me the idea of a book on the decadence of states and nations which should be a prologue to the book on Justice." The result was his great work on Rome, and from then on the theme of civilizations and why they die has been the subject of his thinking and of his judgments on the state of things as they are today.

His studies of Rome led him to two discoveries. One was that the things which the ancients—Sallust, Livy, Horace, Virgil and Cicero—called "corruption" in the days when Rome was decaying the modern world calls "progress": material enrichment of life, universal desire for gain ("easy money"), for luxury, for ease, and a general restlessness in which all classes become more and more exacting in their demands. The other was Caesar (the type of the "savior-tyrant") whose career started Rome toward its final ruin, which was delayed only by the patient attempts of Augustus toward a reconstruction of the old civilization. A series of visits to North and South America (1907-9) crystallized his thought on the whole matter of civilization and left it resting upon a broad distinction, the distinction being that of *qualitative-quantitative.*

He told Raditzka,

> The old qualitative civilizations set before themselves a certain moral or esthetic ideal of perfection, certain constituent elements or forms of beauty. Modern quantitative civilization, on the other hand, drives for the maximum increase of riches ("the abundant life"), putting all the forces of nature to man's service and creating productive instruments capable of producing in the same time an ever greater quantity of goods. Science, steel machinery turned ever faster by steam, electricity, oil, etc., are the great instruments of the quantitative civilization. On the other hand, the forces of qualitative civilization were the artists, the jurists, the moralists, the philosophers, the creators and the apostles of religion, the lawmakers and the warriors. Prior to the French Revolution and the nineteenth century, the human race had created only qualitative civilizations; the quantitative civilization appeared in Europe during the nineteenth century. An enormous revolution, the greatest since Christianity that the Western world has seen.

Now "quality" cannot reach its due perfection without sacrificing quantity; "quantity" cannot multiply without sacrificing "quality." A quantitative civilization is a corrupted and a dying civilization—not progress. That is the heart of Ferrero's judgment on the history of mankind, and all his writings since the Roman volumes appeared nearly forty years ago are a development of that theme. There is an architectonic unity in his work that is rare in the case of men who have been so prolific as has he, but it is the inevitable result of having at the base of it all a definite standard of human value.

August 11, 1939

II

There are two other important ideas in Ferrero's concept of civilization. These are the principles of *limits* and *legitimacy.*

A qualitative civilization will be limited to a certain goal, which goal will be fixed by its ideals of *beauty* and of *good.* Here Ferrero definitely asserts ultimate absolute standards of the good and the beautiful—a most important affirmation—and explains the variety in the conception that men form of both at various times on the ground not of relativity, but of the necessary imperfection or partialness of these concepts as compared with the "vast whole." These concepts impose a limitation, and the danger that threatens qualitative civilizations is a freezing, so to speak, of those concepts against their enlargement by development of their content to a greater share of the underlying absolute. But standards of beauty and of good are the essence of the qualitative civilization.

The essence of the quantitative civilization is its lack of limits and this results from its lack of standards of value. It has no fixed goals; it must always move on, the farther and the faster because of this very lack, always sacrificing quality to quantity. This, Ferrero says, is to lose itself finally in moral and esthetic anarchy. Social life is impossible for man in such conditions. He must have at least a minimum of certainty that there is something fixed, unchanging and eternal about beauty, goodness and truth. In a quantitative civilization this certainty disappears; it cannot tolerate fixed and clear definitions or ideas. In summary, he says: "A quantitative civilization is not a true civilization, but a disorderly transition, a parenthesis, long or short. A civilization cannot be other than qualitative; progress consists in creating qualitative civilizations that will avoid the danger of crystallization in primordial definitions devoid of the power of development."

It is to be noted most carefully that it is *development* and not *change* of which Ferrero speaks; the distinction is fundamental, for he expressly rejects the notion of relativity in connection with the ideals of beauty, good and truth. Thus, he separates himself sharply and completely from the main modern current of metaphysics, which is definitely anti-intellectualist and relativist in its assumptions.

The second point of distinction—*legitimacy*—is less fundamental, perhaps, but nevertheless highly important. It is finely developed in Ferrero's small book *La Rovina della Civiltà Antica* (1926). The essence of legitimacy is *continuity*. Quoting Talleyrand, Ferrero points out that an equilibrium and a stable peace are not possible between European states if they are not all governed by *legitimate* authority, that is, authority accepted, obeyed and respected by their respective peoples. A violent or sudden change in the form of spirit of that authority, however it comes, must produce instability until it gradually attains acceptance. The chain of legitimacy was broken in the middle of the third century A.D. when the Emperor assumed the throne without the Senate's assent. It was broken again during the Great War when three empires passed away overnight. "Reading Talleyrand," Ferrero says, "it occurred to me that what he called principles of legitimacy are limited and partial definitions of civil authority analogous to the [above described] definitions of esthetics and morals. Suddenly the meaning and the importance of Talleyrand's doctrine became clear to me."

The sum and substance of Ferrero's life work is, as he says himself, a study of the struggle between what he calls the "constructive" spirit (i.e., quality, limitation) and the spirit of "adventure" (quantitative, limitless), between the innate folly of man and the necessity for man to control that folly—the struggle which he calls both the law and the enigma of human life. And his concluding words to Raditzka are: "Anyhow, of one thing I am sure; whether it comes soon or late the world will not recover order, peace, the possibility to live and to think, until the day when it shall rediscover the principles of all civilization; quality, limitation and legitimacy."

August 18, 1939

III

Published today is *The Reconstruction of Europe—Talleyrand and the Congress of Vienna, 1814-1850* by Guglielmo Ferrero, of which this writer has no hesitation in saying that it is of equal interest and importance and both in a very high degree. The translation is by Theodore R. Jaeckel.

Let the book's jacket describe its contents:

The Reconstruction of Europe . . . retraces the events in Europe and particularly in France which led up to and included the Congress of Vienna in 1815, at which the great European powers attempted to bring order out of the chaos created by Napoleon and the French Revolution. . . . It is a book of vital significance to the world today, for the author discovers the origins of the present catastrophe in the failure of the Congress to reach a permanent solution of the problems created by the Napoleonic Wars. Although the Congress managed, due to the genius of men like Talleyrand and Alexander the First, to create a European power that lasted for a century, the seeds were planted that came to fruition in 1914 and 1939.

Since Hitler's invasion of Europe much has been said of the parallel between 1812 and 1914, between Napoleon and

Hitler. There is indeed a parallel, and Ferrero describes its elements. This writer will leave to the reader the picture as Ferrero presents it rather than offer his own reproduction of its outlines, and will merely say that it is complete and convincing, and that it discloses the nature of the terrible political problem that now confronts the world. Particularly illuminating is the discussion of Talleyrand's famous principle of "legitimacy" and the difficulty of successfully correlating it in practice with the ideal of the French Revolution—which ideal, by the way, is far better expressed in our own Declaration of Independence than in its French paraphrase, the Rights of Man. There is abundant food for reflection here by our moderns who count themselves the only true guardians of "democracy." *August* 29, 1941

IV

In a little volume entitled *La Fin des aventures* there is included a short essay on "Paganisme et Christianisme" which is penetrating and illuminative in high degree. Ferrero points out that in the last three centuries the Western civilization has been undergoing a paradoxical experience. There have been two currents, one "paganizing," the other "Christianizing," each working in different spheres, but still meeting in conflict. The paganizing current aroused the admiration of the men of the later Rennaissance for the political and war-making genius of the ancients which resulted in a divinization of the state. (This process is well described in his *La Palintenesi di Roma*, published nearly twenty years ago.) Against this was the rise of the "common man" and the notion of Personal Rights, of which our Declaration of Independence is so perfectly an expression, because it bases wholly upon a Christian concept of man. The fantastic growth of commerce and industry, however, was a strong paganizing influence, war, politics and "science" working with them, and the result was to push the concept of the "free man" to extreme limits, with the result that "Christian humanism" became the laicized "humanitarianism" of the nineteenth century and modern "liberalism" was the result of the Christian notion of the "free man."

As Ferrero put it: "Thus we live in a state of perpetual contradiction. The family, social life, manners and morals keep a Christian imprint; politics and war breed of the classic and pagan tradition; law, literature, philosophy, art and history are taught in both the opposing currents." Hence the prevailing confusion as to meaning, means and ends in which we are wrapped. We do not understand the dualism within us. We are not even fully aware of it. But all our aberrations are pagan in origin. If we could realize that, we should be on our way to the solution of our problem.

The great merit of *Reconstruction of Europe* is that to the thoughtful reader it will be helpful toward that realization.

September 5, 1941

MAN: INDIVIDUAL AND PERSON

In the third of his course of six lectures on "The Defense of the Individual," now being delivered weekly at the New School of Social Research in New York, Ogden L. Mills discusses "A Free Society," and this writer likes much his approach to the subject. It goes to the bottom of the matter, because it seizes the essential principles, and because, by implication, it lays bare the fundamental defects of the philosophy which has brought the whole idea of democracy as commonly entertained in the Nineteenth Century to something like complete wreck.

The nineteenth-century notion was that human liberty was the ultimate goal of human society, and that (as, indeed, Aristotle said) liberty was possible only under a democratic form of government. Mr. Mills accepts that general premise. Liberty implies competition and, therefore, inequality in results inasmuch as individuals are quantitatively and qualitatively unequal. He accepts that. Liberty also implies a minimum of government control over individual acts. He accepts that. Finally, the nineteenth century went upon the principle that human instincts, activated by individual capacities, acting through competition (i.e., conflict) would in the long run, restrained by right reason, produce the greatest good of the greatest number. The field of reason was whatever could be *proved*; the transcendental lay outside its scope and was treated as unknowable and therefore negligible as a general form of conduct. Reason working upon proved knowledge would provide the necessary rules of morals.

It is here that Mr. Mills parts company with the nineteenth-century idea, and it is here that his view is most interesting. He quotes with approval from Ross Hoffman's *Will to Freedom* the following passage:

> When we come to set down a statement of the conditions necessary to the prospering of human nature, the first condition to be named is liberty. . . . The first political principle then will be the philosophic doctrine of the freedom of the human will, and the state will find its whole *raison d'être* in securing to men that freedom which is required for the exercise of all the faculties of their nature. Because man is a rational being, the state will secure his intellectual liberty; because he is a moral being, the state will protect his freedom of conscience; because he is an economic being, the state will safeguard the ownership of productive property; because he is a social being, the state will protect his right of association. . . . Because private property is a necessary foundation for individual liberty, it will be defended. . . . because the family is a necessary training school of liberty, it will be protected in every possible way; because religion is a necessary discipline for liberty, it will not

merely be tolerated, but the freedom of all forms of it which actually serve that end will be most scrupulously respected.

The difference between the nineteenth-century concept of the "individual" man and Mr. Mills' concept is that he conceives a man as a *person* and the nineteenth century conceived him mainly as an *individual.* The difference between a person and an individual is that, in the case of an individual, the important thing is the *species* to which it belongs, while in the case of a *person* the reverse is the case. His importance is dominant; his value is unique precisely because he is a person. The medieval schoolmen used the word *persona* to mean that which is highest in all nature. The essence of personality consists in reason and freedom to determine his destiny. The nineteenth century did not in terms deny man's possession of reason or his autonomy, but it emphasized the material side of his nature and slighted the importance of his personality. It is the merit of Mr. Mills' discussion that by implication at least he emphasizes man's personality and therefore the spiritual side of man's nature. A really free society is necessarily a society of persons rather than of individuals; only persons can make a really free society.

Given a community of human beings all uniform in instincts and desires, with an unlimited inequality in qualities and capacities, it is evident that to preserve each personality in a state consonant *with* personality some factor or principle other than those merely natural (in the sense of physical) elements must be introduced to prevent the stronger personalities from oppressing the weaker. That factor must be supra-natural—that is, in the non-material order and one not arising normally or automatically from that order. The nineteenth century relied upon reason for this necessary restraint upon instinct and passion, but reason alone never has sufficed for this task nor is there any present basis for hope that it ever will. Something more is needed; and that something must be in the order of religion. The great mistake of the nineteenth century was its failure to recognize this. Mr. Mills clearly does not make that mistake.

May 10, 1937

MR. LIPPMANN AND TRUE LIBERALISM

In *The Good Society,* Walter Lippmann delivers a crushing attack upon the whole theory of planned economy. In summary, his thesis is, first, that planned economy is not necessary as a consequence of technical progress; second, that all forms of collectivism lead to the totalitarian state and are opposed fundamentally to democracy and lead inevitably to war—total war at that.

His argument is closely knit and lucidly stated. For many people, this part of his book will be of most interest, because of the wholesale slaughter it wreaks upon our modern "intellectuals" of the pink variety. The present writer finds, however, of greatest interest and importance Mr. Lippmann's diagnosis of the disease which killed the Liberalism of the nineteenth century and of the conditions necessary to reconstruct the true liberal philosophy as the principle of social life.

Liberty is that principle and liberty is the goal of true Liberalism. In what does liberty consist? Mr. Lippmann's argument is that it has its roots in the recognition by society of a "common law" protecting the inviolable rights of human personality. Here is a striking passage (under the sub-caption "The Degradation of Man") which at one and the same time explains the crash of the old liberalism and the rock on which the new must rest:

The great reaction in the latter part of the nineteenth century was ushered in by men who had little use for the traditional ideas in which the inviolable essence of the human personality was affirmed. Their intentions were, of course, excellent and they imagined that they were attacking only superstition, bigotry and obscurantism, but, in their battle with the theologians and the clerics, their zeal outran their insight. They brought down the humanist ideal in the crash of the supernatural order and from it man, who had fancied himself a little less than the angels, emerged as much less than a man. The iconoclasts were too smart to be wise, too rational to be reasonable, too much enchanted with an immature science to hold fast to tested truths. They could not find the human soul when they dissected their cadavers; they could not measure the inalienable essence. So, in the high realism of intelligence there prevailed a radical disrespect for men and the human ideals of justice, liberty, equality and fraternity were relegated to the limbo of old superstitions along with God, the soul and the moral law. What could a mere physico-chemical system or bundle of conditioned reflexes have to do with such glamorous nonsense? In the fury to explain men rationally, there was explained away their essence, which is their manhood.

"The inviolable essence of human personality"—here Mr. Lippmann touches the heart of the whole matter. The bankrupt liberalism of the nineteenth century went bankrupt because it denied the nature of man. That word *person* contains tremendous implications. Among them are *"God, the soul and the moral law."*

The Liberalism of today repeats yesterday's denial, but, instead of the extreme *laissez-faire* of its predecessor, it offers a controlled collectivism, thus jumping from one extreme to the other. As Mr. Lippmann says:

Collectivist Regimes are always profoundly irreligious. For religious experience entails the recognition of an inviolable essence in man; it cultivates a self-respect and a self-reliance which tend at some point to resist the total subjection of the individual to any earthly power. So it is no accident that the only open challenge to the totalitarian state has come from men of deep religious faith.

In brief, Mr. Lippmann's argument leads to the conclusion that liberty and religion are indissolubly linked, in that liberty depends upon recognition of a religious principle as its very life. That is the end of Mr. Lippmann's long journey in search of a philosophy, and the thing that makes his book a real event.

It cannot be emphasized too often or too strongly that the totalitarian state is the real archenemy of man as a person and it makes little difference whether that state be communist or fascist in form. Either form is equally deadly in the long run.

It is the *totalitarian state under apparent democratic forms* that America has to fear. That is the objective of all fronts that call themselves popular, united and the like; it is the objective of our so-called liberals and it *can* happen here.

October 20, 1937

HUMAN PERSONALITY IN ACTION

Synchronizing with the publication of Walter Lippmann's *The Good Society* is another extremely interesting book, *What Man Has Made of Man,* by Professor Mortimer J. Adler, of the University of Chicago. It consists of four lectures on psychology delivered to students of the Institute of Psychoanalysis at the University, with abundant notes bearing on the subject matter and an introduction by Dr. Franz Alexander, Director of the Institute.

Dr. Adler's discussion is orderly and lucid in unusual degree and of great value to all interested in the whole subject of metaphysics and, particularly, psychology. The essence of Mr. Lippmann's book is its recognition and defense of human *personality;* Dr. Adler's lectures are devoted to an analysis of human personality *in action.* He dissects the powers and their use which give to man the position that Mr. Lippmann describes and, taken together, the two books constitute a liberal education on the roots of the present trouble.

Metaphysics, as Dr. Adler observes, deals with knowledge derived originally through the senses and developed by abstractive reflection. There are only four possible metaphysical positions logically open to anyone seeking to know the nature of existing things in the world of change and of these four only one can be right. These are:

(1) *Absolute materialism,* which recognizes extended matter as the only thing existing in the universe;

(2) *Absolute idealism,* which either denies the existence of matter as existing independently of mind or treats both as "illusions due to an incomplete experience of reality";

(3) *Dualism,* which asserts the separate substantial existence of both matter and mind, neither being involved in the other's existence; and, finally,

(4) *Formal materialism,* which sees reality in all existing things as a union of matter (extension) and form (thought), neither (the case of *man* alone excepted) being capable of existence independently of the other.

In viewing the universe one must, if he concerns himself at all in understanding its nature, adopt one or other of the above positions. They cannot be mingled in a compromise, for they are mutually exclusive.

Now, as Dr. Adler points out, all men have a certain "common experience," by which he means "the whole set of experiences which men have naturally through the ordinary operation of their senses, their memories and imaginations." This sort of experience has nothing to do with special experience resulting from special investigation, as by scientific experiment.

It needs for its materials, as Santayana says, "only the stars, the seasons, the swarm of animals, the spectacle of birth and death, of cities and wars." The data of metaphysics are those furnished by this common experience. No one has ever denied that it is a fact. In all their dealings with things and with each other, men at all times have relied unquestionably upon its reality.

If that reality be a fact and not an illusion, no metaphysical system which does not accord with the facts of common experience can be right. Testing each of the four possible systems of metaphysics by common experience, Dr. Adler points out that only the fourth—formal materialism—can give an account of that experience and that each of the other three fails at an essential point.

Absolute materialism cannot account for either ideas or sensations. Absolute idealism cannot account for matter. Dualism cannot account for the interaction of mind and body. Formal materialism alone can account for mind, matter, ideas and sensations.

Formal materialism, is of course, the Aristotelian metaphysics. It is interesting to note the new and intense interest developing in philosophic circles in this school of thought in the last few years.

Last year, Professor Etienne Gilson's lectures at Harvard *(Unity of Philosophical Experience)* created a veritable sensation, and the *démarche* of Dr. Hutchins of Chicago in his lectures at Yale *(The Higher Learning in America)*, not to mention other instances of lesser importance, have given added impetus to this resurgence of real metaphysics.

The importance of the thing for the future of society can hardly be overestimated, for at the root of the world's troubles there lies a great metaphysical apostasy, started (unwittingly) by Descartes in the seventeenth century and culminating in the nineteenth century with the denial of man's personality, so vividly described by Mr. Lippmann in *The Good Society*.

It is this which makes Dr. Adler's book—like Mr. Lippmann's—a real event. It happens, moreover, by a most fortunate accident, that Dr. Alexander's "Introduction" is a perfectly priceless example of the kind of thinking into which modern men have fallen. His view of the Aristotelian metaphysics as "a sterile form of deductive thinking" and a series of "playful deductive meditations starting from the accepted and prescribed dogmas as premises" must be seen to be believed.

It was a cruel thing for Dr. Adler to tempt him to write it. But it does unquestionably both complete the book and give it a distinctly humorous touch. *November* 17, 1937

LEWIS MUMFORD AND LIBERALISM

I

Lewis Mumford's impassioned indictment of modern "liberalism" in the *New Republic* (April 29th), and the *New Republic's* editorial comment in reply constitute a significant symptom of the time—and a healthy one. Both the six pages of his article ("The Corruption of Liberalism") and the editorial ("Mr. Mumford and the Liberals") are well worth the sympathetic consideration of all who are concerned with the currents of thought today, for both are in high degree revealing of change in those currents.

Of Mr. Mumford's indictment it can be said that it very nearly—but not quite—lays bare the heart of the matter. The heart of the matter is in the distinction he draws between what he calls "ideal" liberalism and the "pragmatic" liberalism which is the corruption of the ideal liberalism. It is the "universal elements that constitute ideal liberalism."

These universal elements arose long before modern capitalism: they were part of the larger human tradition embodied in the folkways of the Jews, in the experimental philosophy of the Greeks, in the secular practices of the Roman Empire, in the sacred doctrines of the Christian Church, in the philosophies of the great post-Medieval humanists. . . . what gives them their strength is their universality and their historic continuity. Confucius, Socrates, Plato, Aristotle, testify to them no less than Jefferson and Mill. Liberalism took over this humanist tradition, revamped it, and finally united it to a new body of hopes and beliefs that grew up in the Eighteenth Century.

Pragmatic liberalism of today, Mr. Mumford says, is symbolically the child of Voltaire and Rousseau in that it was a by-product of inventors and industrialists who "concentrating upon the improvement of the means of life thought sincerely that the ends of living would more or less take care of themselves." The pragmatic liberal did not suspect that there are "modes of insight into man and the cosmos which science does not possess." He "took for granted that the emotional and spiritual life of man needs no other foundation than the rational, utilitarian activities associated with the getting of a living." He took for granted the "world of personality, the world of values, feelings, emotions, wishes, purposes." He conceived liberalism as an "emancipation from the empty institutional religion, from the source, precepts, moralizings of the past." He did not believe in a world in which questions of good and evil are "not incidental but of radical importance." He kept his eyes "manfully on the mere surface of living." He did not deal with "first and last things." He was "incapable of making firm applicable judgments or of implementing them with action." His tendency is "to believe the best about everybody: to hope when there is no reason to hope, and to exhibit the nicest moral qualms, the most delicate intellectual scruples in situations that demand that he wade in and coarsely exert his maximum effort." In a word: "In a disintegrating world pragmatic liberalism has lost its integrity but retained its limitations."

In his statement of ideal liberalism and in his criticism of pragmatic liberalism Mr. Mumford has avoided saying the one word which would have gathered both into a finality so far as his case is concerned. All that he has said is true so far as it goes. But if he had said that the principles of ideal liberalism were a recognition of certain *absolute*—therefore *enduring*—truths concerning human personality, its first beginnings and its "first and last things," and that the fault of pragmatic liberalism is its rejection of these *absolutes,* he would have summed up his case in a sentence. If his statement of the "universal" elements of ideal liberalism does not mean that they are "absolute" it means nothing at all, and, if it means nothing, his criticism of pragmatic liberalism also falls. The present writer believes that it does mean "absolutes" and for that reason welcomes it for raising the fundamental issue. He is strongly influenced to that belief by phrases scattered through Mr. Mumford's article: "liberals no longer act as if justice mattered, as if truth mattered, as if right mattered"—"fatal deficiencies that go to the very roots of liberal philosophy"—"a meaningful world is one that holds a future that extends beyond the incomplete personal life of the individual"—"force and grace"—"first and last things"—"the arid pragmatism that has served as a substitute religion." All these words point to the ancestry of the thought that they express, as being in the direct and authentic line of the absolute.

So interpreted, Mr. Mumford has struck the "liberal" shield with his lance-point.

May 3, 1940

II

Of the *New Republic's* reply to the indictment made by Mr. Lewis Mumford against the modern "liberal," it must be said that it powerfully supports his case. The heart of that indictment was that the "liberal" had abandoned the ideals, the principles, universals on which the whole *liberal* viewpoint must rest, that he was a pure pragmatist in his outlook. By which the present writer understood (and understands) that Mr. Mumford meant that the modern "liberal" no longer believed in *absolutes.* Indeed he practically said so: "Liberals no longer act as if justice mattered, as if truth mattered, as if right mattered," and if these things are not *absolutes,* they are nothing.

To this charge the *New Republic* makes no answer whatever either directly or by implication. It even says: "Many a reader of the article who has classified himself as liberal will be puzzled by an apparent lack of direction in Mr. Mumford's fire" (!) There is not a word in the editorial to indicate that its writer is even aware of the charge. The burden of this rejoinder is devoted to rebutting a contention that Mr. Mumford did not advance, namely that "uninhibited or disoriented emotional reaction is the route to health and safety." And there is a most revealing paragraph which lights up the whole background:

> *Modern psychology* and especially Freud, have indeed revealed emotional depths in the personality which most people do not like to recognize, and the buried emotions include some that if unadjusted and undisciplined may seem like the incarnation of evil — such as murderous aggression. But the appeal to Freud will not bear out the conclusion that the proper remedy is a reversion to *moral condemnation of the mentally immature.* It is of course elementary that sane persons need to defend themselves against dangerous psychotics and that there are crises when force is the only possible defence. Yet no doctor would maintain that strait-jackets and iron shackles have any therapeutic value; . . . the only possible means of valuation for the *emotionally sick* is one that liberals and scientific humanists would thoroughly approve—an objective and sympathetic understanding. We have every reason to suppose that something like this is true concerning the evils manifest in modern society.

The writer of this editorial would surely deny the charge that he was an *immoralist* and he would undoubtedly be utterly sincere in his denial. But the whole content of the above paragraph leads irresistibly to the conclusion that for him "morals" are essentially *relative* and have no basis in the absolute—which is precisely Mr. Mumford's allegation. That is what is at the bottom of the modern liberal's confusion, for he is constantly rejecting absolutes in principle, yet when in concrete need he is constantly—and surreptitiously—falling back on them. As Mr. Mumford says:

> Such was the innocence of the liberal that those who were indifferent to ethical values thought of themselves as realists. . . . But the fact was that the most old-fashioned theologian with a sense of human guilt and human error was by far the better realist. Though the theologian's view of the external world might be scientifically reached, his view of the internal world, *the world of value and personality,* included an understanding of constant human phenomena —*sin, corruption, evil*—on which the liberal closed his eyes. (Emphasis supplied.)

The editorial paragraph above quoted perfectly illustrates the course of that criticism. "Sin" is something fundamentally different from "mental immaturity" or "emotional sickness" and that difference it is which separates the modern liberal's "morals" from morals *per se* as Mr. Mumford conceives them.

The trouble is not with the modern liberal's heart; it is with his head. He has swallowed whole a dogma which he fondly believes to rest upon science, a dogma that there is nothing which does not change, that there are no absolutes. William James did not hold that dogma. He admitted that there were things for which physical science did not account, but, as is always the case, the disciples have outrun their master. If there is anything reasonably clear in the world of pure thought it is that the whole pragmatic tide is on the ebb, and the modern dogmatic liberal is being left high and dry on a barren shore by the receding waters. It is a pity, for he meant—and means—well.

May 6, 1940

THINKING IT OVER

MR. MACLEISH AND LIBERALISM

I

The course of palinodes that is beginning to rise from our intelligentsia of the "left" received last week a notable addition from one of that group's most distinguished members, Mr. Archibald MacLeish, Librarian of Congress, well and favorably known to all lovers of good literature as a poet of authentic stature. Mr. MacLeish's palinode is of interest not merely for its orientation, but also for its sincerity, and the humility of its admission of past errors. He brings indictment against himself with the same ruthless frankness as that with which he indicts his fellows, and the force of that indictment is thereby immensely heightened. Its main count, moreover, goes to the heart of the matter.

He charges his class—the writers of his time, his generation—with having destroyed the faith of American youth in principles of right and wrong, and thus leaving them defenseless in the face of the monstrous hurricane of evil that is sweeping the world today. They did it by persuading them that these principles were no more than tags, slogans, catchwords to conceal selfish motives.

> Consider, for example [he said], the books upon which this generation was brought up—the books written by the writers who knew at first or second hand the last war. Books like Latzko's *Men In War*, Dos Passos' *Three Soldiers*, Ernest Hemingway's *A Farewell To Arms*, Richard Aldington's *Death of a Hero*. These and many like them were books written not only against the hatefulness and cruelty and filthiness of war but written also against the fine phrases and the rhetorical formulae by which war was made. . . . These are the honest words of honest men, writers of great skill and integrity and devotion. They say what all of us after the war would have said

if we could. They say what all of us who were in the war believed. But they are words that have borne bitter and dangerous fruits. . . . I am not undertaking to judge these writers. I have no right to judge them, and, if I did, my hands are tied because I felt as they did, and wrote, so far as I was able, as they were writing. . . . What I maintain further is this: that unless we regain in this democracy the conviction that there are *final things* for which democracy will fight—unless we recover faith in the expression of these things in words—we can leave our planes unbuilt and our battleships on paper, for we shall not need them. (Emphasis supplied.)

Here is the same note that Lewis Mumford struck in his palinode (*New Republic,* April 29th). What are the "final things" of Mr. MacLeish but the "universal elements" of Mr. Mumford; what are both but the "absolutes" which the shallow pragmatism of today has banished from the thinking of our modern literati of the left? It is that pragmatism which is at the root of things that today is terrifying its erstwhile devotees and rudely awaking them to the bankruptcy of their whole intellectual position.

A pretty thing it was to play with not so long ago, and they played with it up to the moment when the hurricane struck. There grew up a whole literature of spiritual defeatism, in which Mr. MacLeish honorably admits his own guilty part. That poem of his beginning, "We told ourselves we had liberty . . ." (in his volume, *The Land of the Free*) was an expression of this mood at its best. At its worst the mood produced a whole flood of print which culminated in a positive orgy of what can only be called mixed pornography and coprophagy of the kind that reviewers of the day were content to accept as "courageous realism." We have had best-sellers in the publishers' lists and long-run plays on the stage which were little else than examples of both—and not so long ago either! The appetite for this sort of thing is, apparently, dwindling in proportion as the wind rises, the shutters rattle more ominously, the sky darkens and the sea rises higher.

It is not an easy thing that Mr. MacLeish has done, that Mr. Mumford and others have done, and they should have honor for its doing. There will be others as the days go by to follow them. And there are few among us—very few—who have any right of our own to chide them for having been long deceived. If some of us have not gone equally astray in that particular respect, most of us have done so in others, and, moreover, when we had less excuse for so doing.

May 31, 1940

II

In the current issue of the *Journal of the National Educational Association* is printed a portion of an address by Mr. Archibald MacLeish entitled "The Hope of Every Living Heart"—the words are his own. The theme of it is what he sees as a drop in "liberal morale" and a call to liberals to rally from their seeming discouragement. He says:

> When it was, precisely, that the blinds were drawn and the lights turned down on the morale of American liberalism, I should not undertake to say. It was long enough ago in any case to produce a funerary and unventilated atmosphere in which hope goes out like a miner's candle. Liberals meet in Washington these days, if they can endure to meet at all, to discuss the tragic outlook for all liberal proposals, the collapse of all liberal leadership and the inevitable defeat of all liberal aims. It is no longer feared, it is now assumed, that the country is headed back to normalcy, that Harding is just around the corner, that the 20's will repeat themselves in a blaze of chromium sinks, glass-topped automobiles and four-color unemployment—and that the peace upon which the hopes of the world depends will not be made.

How did this come about? The fascist enemies of liberalism are not today as powerful as they were a few years ago. There is no sign that the public is really apathetic or defeatist on the peace problem. The liberal cause is as worthy as ever and is the cause of peace. It is not a case of failure of "leadership" for liberal opinion does not need to be shepherded. It is not a lack of "policies," for liberals know that peace must be made by peoples not by foreign offices. It is not a matter of "right-left," for it is not a mere political matter which divides people. What then is the dividing line between liberals and the rest? Mr. MacLeish sees on one side of that line

> those who believe in the future and on the other those who do not believe in the future. . . . It is an issue between those who believe in men, those who believe in the future of men, those who believe in the ability of men throughout the earth to work together, and to build a peace together, and those who, whatever their words, whatever their formulas, whatever their protestations, do not believe in men or their future. On the determination of that issue depends quite soberly and simply, the destiny of the world, and to that cause we who profess liberal beliefs are committed.

It would be easy, but unfair, to trip Mr. MacLeish on terminology, and it will not be done here, for his meaning is fairly but not completely clear. He appears to hold the gospel of "human progress" much as it was held in the nineteenth century. Now this doctrine is very recent in its origins and was virtually unknown in men's thinking up to some two centuries ago. It was entirely foreign to the mind of antiquity, and received its first full statement at the hands of Condorcet toward the end of the eighteenth century. The Victorian Age was completely under its spell and it was at the root of the whole liberal philosophy. Now the interesting thing about the notion of human progress is that its root is in the Christian view of life and that the modern age which has dropped the Christian part of that view took over the "progress" part of it and made it a root in itself. They secularized it.

Mr. MacLeish apparently calls upon liberals today, sitting in the wreckage of this "progress," to renew their faith in the liberal "metaphysics" described by Lord Lothian, and bravely promises them ultimate victory for their cause. One can but wonder to what cause he attributes the wreck that has made them lose heart. Whence came the evil forces that shook down the edifice in which the nineteenth century took such pride, if not from the "metaphysics" of liberalism itself?

May 26, 1944

THE JUDGMENT OF THE NATIONS

I

Chapter Four of Christopher Dawson's book—*The Judgment of the Nations*—is entitled "The Failure of Liberalism." What is *Liberalism* as Dawson sees it? And what is the "Liberalism" which has failed?

True Liberalism is an ideology and a tradition which has characterized the Western culture for many centuries, and *freedom* is the soul of both. The whole history of Western civilization is the story of man's long quest for freedom. The quest was born in Greece at the very dawn of Hellas. When the Eastern and Northern barbarian hordes overran the worn-out empire of Rome, Christianity took over the quest, gave it a soul and a philosophy, and Christendom arose. The root of all notions of freedom is the inviolable personality of man. That notion always had an ultimate religious basis, and Christianity for the first time laid bare its full nature. Man is by nature free as a creature of God, fashioned in the image and likeness of his Creator and endowed with free will even to the point of defying the Creator himself. Upon no other foundation can any theory of human freedom be logically based. Freedom, so understood, was the soul of the Western civilization whose ethos was profoundly Christian—and that was *Liberalism.* What is left of it today is "Liberalism!"

What is the "Liberalism" that has failed and how did it come about? It might be summarily characterized as *Liberalism* that has lost its soul. Its spiritual content began to evaporate some five hundred years ago, just when the Western world was on the brink of its amazing material development and a great release of human energies was beginning. The sixteenth-century religious split, followed as it was by the rapid development of trade and discoveries attendant upon the spread of the Western civilization to the new land, the seventeenth century's metaphysical departure, and the rapid advance of science, all paved the way for the extraordinary —indeed explosive—outburst of revolution—political, industrial, economic and social—that culminated in the nineteenth century in which the Western world gave itself over wholeheartedly to the single task of making the earth and its forces the slave of man. "Freedom" for man's energies, motivated by all manner of generous emotions which might be summed up in the word "humanitarianism," unrestrained by anything, was the gospel of the times. There hung around this gospel for a while the ghost of earlier Christendom. Cobden could still say (as Mr. Dawson notes) with entire sincerity: "We advocate nothing but what is agreeable to the highest behests of Christianity—to buy in the cheapest market and sell in the dearest." This was the "Liberalism" of the nineteenth century, and the "Liberalism" which failed.

Its failure was pretty complete. Under its guidance "democracy" has somehow produced the totalitarian state in its most hideous form. Its economics have given birth to proletarianism and mass unemployment on a colossal scale, its personal freedoms have largely vanished in a continually tightening net of government controls, and the whole process has ended in a war which engages the whole earth in a frenzied orgy of destruction, the like of which that earth has never before seen.

And the irony of the whole thing is that the "Liberals" of today, viewing the sorry mess, propose to remedy it by "planning" us into a rigid collectivist society, in which the last vestiges of human freedoms must inevitably vanish—all in the name of the "Four Freedoms"! If anyone wishes to see what the quintessence of modern "Liberalism" is, all he has to do is to read that amazing production of a couple of years ago—*The City of Man*—and ponder pages 80-85, where the authors discuss "what limits are set by the religion of freedom, which is democracy to the freedom of worship!" It simply defies comment.

To this parlous state has come the *Liberalism* which, as Dawson says, was the ideology and the tradition of our Western civilization, for which our "Liberals" of today think they are fighting. What they are fighting—and it is but fair to say that they are fighting with the best intentions in the world—is nothing more than the product of their own philosophy and they don't know it or even suspect it. How Dean Swift would have loved to deal faithfully with the spectacle, had he lived to see it! *October* 9, 1942

II

A curious thing about the nineteenth century is that in the very forenoon of its confidence in the future automatic "progress" of the world to the earthly paradise, of which the glistening minarets and domes seemed to loom plainly on the horizon, not a few voices were heard warning the people that all was not well: Constant, Chateaubriand, de Maistre, de Tocqueville, de Biran, Royer Collard in France, Newman in England, Cortes in Spain, not to mention many others of lesser fame who looked askance at the "Liberalism" of the time. This, moreover, was before Marx (and Hegel) had stood Utopian socialism on its head, and before Darwin had spoken. The "Liberalism" of the time was the child of the eighteenth-century "rationalist" Enlightenment and the Revolution, for the idol of "science" had not as yet been formally enthroned on the altars. It was not as yet wholly secularized, as it later became, for it was still tinctured with a pale deism of sorts. Nor were the apprehensions expressed in terms of orthodox Christianity. De Tocqueville, for instance, and Constant before him, were not, as were Chateaubriand, de Maistre, Cortes, or Newman, expressly speaking for the Christian faith as they questioned the assumptions of the age. Yet, when one reads them today, it is easy to discern a sort of prophetic charisma floating in the atmosphere of the time, and caught by a few men who were inspired by a hot devotion to *liberty*.

When they wrote, the physical transformation of the earth was just beginning. That transformation resulted mainly from one thing—transportation. When de Tocqueville visited America, he traveled much as Julius Caesar had done in Gaul. Last week Mr. Willkie told us of his journey around the earth —31,000 miles—performed at an average speed of some 200 miles per hour. Yet the whole burden of his address was *freedom.* After the century of fantastic "progress" in applied science we find ourselves in a desperate battle for the very thing which the prophets of one hundred years ago envisioned as in danger, and this when a scant thirty years ago most of us thought it had been forever secured. Yet, in 1886 the aging Tennyson, who had had in his youth the apocalyptic view of the "City of Man" (in *Locksley Hall,* 1842), had another vision in *Locksley Hall—Sixty Years After* (of which we are witnesses today) when he wrote: "Chaos Cosmos! Cosmos Chaos! Once again the sickening game; Freedom, free to slay herself, and dying while they shout her name."

To this the Enlightenment of the eighteenth century and the triumphs of "science" in the nineteenth have brought the men of today. In a world literally filled with examples of *order*

—our machines—we find ourselves engulfed in a tidal wave of disorder such as never before swept the earth. We have established firmly indeed the "law for things," but what has happened meantime to the "law for man"? And to the "freedom" which it is the business of the "law for man" to make secure? We know what has happened to the "City of Man." We have seen the eighteenth century's "reason" give place to brutal "power," and the nineteenth century's "science" provide that power with its arms, and it is plain as the noonday sun that this has happened because we forgot the "law for man"; we did more than forget it—many of us have denied it, formally and completely.

About eight years ago the late Marquis of Lothian, in a pamphlet entitled *Liberalism in the Modern World,* said:

> the ultimate metaphysical root of liberalism—and all great movements are based on metaphysics—is the conviction of the supreme value of the individuality of man, that it is the responsibility of every individual to think for himself, rather than to accept his thinking from any other human authority, however august, whether in Church or State, and to regard the purpose of life as progress in this world and not merely happiness in the next. From this primary root Western civilization has inexorably developed, after a thousand years of relative stagnation and preoccupation with other worldliness.

This is the "metaphysics," and this is the "liberalism," out of which have come the "chaos" of today. And we are invited by our Instrumentalist teachers to seek our "cosmos" in a metaphysics which denies its own existence and a "society" which is the "all" for which the "individual" exists!

November 6, 1942

ON SOCIETY

A SICK SOCIETY

Norman Thomas recently told the Municipal Forum that the solution of the problems inherent in capitalism—unemployment, poverty and recurrent crises—

> requires a high degree of social planning, a deliberate putting of the brains of engineers and managers to work for the community rather than for the profits of absentee owners. The condition of thus utilizing the skill of America is a high degree of ownership of natural resources and the commanding heights of our economic order, and it is the type of ownership and planning which I do not at all agree is inconsistent with freedom and democracy.

This is the familiar anthem of Socialism proper—as distinguished from Communism—and it is well to recognize the fact that it is not to be disposed of so easily as many people think. One reason for this is that the changing organization of human society in these modern days has, in the economic field, tended greatly to restrict the legitimate zones of individual action, and more and more to transform the individual from a semidetached organism with a life and an activity mainly its own into an organ in a much larger and very complex unit, with interaction between unit and organ largely replacing the old independent action of the former individual organism. The individual was always a part of the community, for the community, at its simplest, was at least an aggregation of individuals. Today he is a part in a different sense, for the aggregation is now more that that; it has itself become an organism.

This organism is sick; we all agree on that. We agree that it is sick because the multiple organs that constitute it are not correlating properly. We also agree that the problem is to make them correlate. We even agree that the reason they do not correlate is because they have been so rapidly transformed in relation to each other that the old instincts and habits generated in their previous existence as detached organisms have not given place to instincts and habits according with their new functions as mere organs in a larger entity. The problem is somehow to change these instincts and habits, without violating something of extremely fundamental importance to the individual. That something is his liberty.

Mr. Thomas "does not agree" that Socialism is inconsistent with freedom and democracy. That is his privilege. But those who regard both freedom and democracy as indissolubly linked to a human personality and not to an "economic man" will "not agree" with Mr. Thomas. The whole Marxian philosophy rests upon the theory of economic determinism and it is simply impossible to talk of "freedom" for a man who is bound in all his actions by an inexorable law. It is conceivable that a socialist "commonwealth" of the kind that we used to argue about before the war might provide adequate food, clothing and shelter for its denizens, but it could do so only under such a system of "planning" *from above* as is quite unthinkable in connection with even the forms of democracy, to say nothing of its substance.

Marx's historical analysis on which he based his theory of economic determinism has been effectively riddled so many times that one must class it as a superstition pure and simple. His attempt to apply the "Hegelian dialectic" to historic reality has been equally exploded and the same must be said of belief in its truth. In a word, the Marxian faith is analogous to what we have come to call "fundamentalism" in religion—which is, of course, not fundamental. That it has, incidentally, been useful as a critical force in social affairs is undeniable, but it is a faith that can no longer give a reason for itself as a faith. Communism is the logical home for all those who adopt the fully materialist view of human life. At least it has the courage of its convictions. Socialism, as Mr. Thomas preaches it, is an attempt to compromise things that cannot be compromised; it is neither fish, flesh nor red herring; it is an emulsion of oil and water with no stability, that must ultimately separate into its components.

The problem of restoring health to the sick organism of human society can be *solved* in only one way, and it is the *spirit* of man that must be somehow brought to the task. Human society has been sick from the beginning of historic time for failure of the spirit. It looks like a long road to the goal of social health, but there is only one road to the goal.

January 18, 1939

THE ABSOLUTE AND THOMAS MANN

Our distinguished guest and German exile, Thomas Mann, whose work has for many years been well known in this country and who is henceforth to make his home with us because, as he says, "here, in contrast to the cultural fatigue and inclination to barbarism prevalent in the Old World, there exists a joyful respect for culture, a youthful sensitivity to its products," has published a little book, *The Coming Victory of Democracy.* It is a slightly expanded version of a lecture which he has delivered on many occasions this year, and is rendered into English by Agnes E. Meyer. It is to this writer a very interesting book for a reason which he will attempt to show.

That reason is Mann's concept of democracy, which is well worth examining. He says of it that it is "timelessly human and timelessness always implies a certain amount of potential youthfulness which need only be realized in thought and feeling in order to excel by far all merely transitory youthfulness in charms of every sort in the charms of life and beauty."

To democracy he gives a very broad meaning, a much broader one than "the merely political sense of this word would suggest; for I am connecting it with the highest human attributes, *with the idea and the absolute;* I am relating it to the *inalienable dignity of mankind,* which no force, however humiliating, can destroy." (Emphasis supplied.)

What is the "idea"? "The idea," says Mann, "is a specific and essential attribute of man, that which makes him human," for human nature is what it is because of the idea. This is a "real and natural fact, so impossible of neglect that those who do not respect human nature's participation in the ideal—as force certainly does not—commit the clumsiest and, in the long run, the most disastrous mistakes."

What is the "absolute"? The three words, justice; freedom and truth, each express the idea. It is impossible," Mann says,

to decide which one should take precedence, which is the greatest. For each one expresses the idea in its totality, and one stands for the others. If we say truth, we also say freedom and justice; if we speak of freedom and justice, we mean truth. It is a complex of an invisible kind freighted with spirituality and elementary dynamic force. *We call it the absolute. To man has been given the absolute—be it a curse or blessing, it is a fact. He is pledged to it, his inner being is conditioned by it. . . .* (Emphasis supplied.)

The "dignity of man"—what of that? Here Mann brings us up squarely against—of all things!—original sin. Listen to this:

Man is nature's fall from grace, only it is not a fall but just as positively an elevation, as conscience is higher than innocence. What Christianity calls "original sin" is more than priestly trickery designed to suppress humanity—it is the deep feeling of man as a spiritual being for his natural infirmities and limitations above which he raises himself through spirit. Is that infidelity to nature? By no means. It is according to nature's deepest intent. Because it is for its own spiritualization that nature produced mankind.

Translating this somewhat foggy set of phrases into plain language, it would seem that Mann roots the "timeless" notion of democracy in the *personality* of man, which (as Walter

Lippmann discovered and affirmed in *The Good Society*) implies God, the soul and the moral law. Now if, as he says in his opening sentences, he feels that in bringing *this* concept of democracy to America, he is "carrying owls to Athens" (i.e., coals to Newcastle), he is going to be disillusioned in some interesting respects. If he supposes that our so-called "liberals" hold any such concept of democracy, he has but to ponder what Mr. Max Lerner says in *The Nation* (June 25). Says this scholarly (and typically "liberal") critic in a wholly laudatory critique of this book:

> Because it is a statement of faith and not an analysis of trend, Mann's book is not without its weaknesses. He is too prone to see both democracy and fascism *in terms of universals, which is the disease of the philosopher and artist, rather than in the terms of change and movement, which is the disease of the historian.* Of the two, I find the second today preferable. (Emphasis supplied.)

Mr. Lerner will have none of the "idea" or the "absolute." He very acutely puts his finger on the vitals of the matter. The democracy that he visualizes is as fundamentally remote from Mann's concept as well can be, in that it is devoid of the one thing that for Mann keeps democracy alive, namely, the very roots which Mann recognizes in unchanging truths. Severed from these roots, democracy must of necessity wither into its ultimate stage of decay, which is mob rule ending in despotism. The sad fact is that the school which Mr. Lerner so ably represents is busily engaged in severing the majestic tree planted by the Founders of this country from the very roots which have nourished its growth up to the present day.

When Thomas Mann has lived among us long enough to have fully shaken off the shattering effects of his German experience and is able to free his artistic sensitivities (for he is no philosopher) to an uninhibited reception of impressions, he will find that the "Athenians" who are now so lavishly welcoming him to their arms will not admit *his* owl to *their* aviary —not by any means! If he doubts this, let him ponder *this* dogma from no less a person than John Dewey (which this writer recently ran across as a quotation without reference in a magazine article and is requoted on the assumption that it is authentic): "I cannot understand how any realization of the democratic ideal as a vital, moral and spiritual ideal in human affairs is possible *without a surrender of the conception of the basic division to which supernatural Christianity is committed.*" (Emphasis supplied.)

Either Mr. Mann will have to modify his views on these matters very considerably or he will soon find his welcome among the pink brotherhood subjected to severe air-conditioning!

July 6, 1938

THE CHILDREN OF MARXISM

I

Of all books on the European problem that this writer has thus far seen, *Unto Caesar* by F. A. Voigt seems to him to cut deepest into the innermost heart of things, and to lay bare the disease that is gnawing at civilization's vitals, more clearly than any other contemporary study has so far done. Precisely for that reason it carries for us in the United States a warning to look to ourselves to see whether or not the same poison is in our bloodstream and our lymphatics.

The book's title plainly hints its thesis, and that thesis is stated in the simplest words. European civilization is sick unto death because it has elected to render to Caesar the things that are God's, and for the first time in the recorded history of mankind has set up what Mr. Voigt again and again calls a "secular religion"—the Kingdom of Heaven on earth—and has succeeded only in making a Hell of the World.

This secular religion is propagated in three main forms, Marxian Communism, National Socialism and Fascism. All three are, at bottom, one and the same thing, although each is in conflict with the other on the surface. All three are messianic, terroristic, collectivist, amoral and despotic; all three are destructive of human personality and human liberty; all three either deny or take no account of transcendental values. All three are organized for war and the tone of all three is hatred.

Marxism would destroy religion by force; Nazism would destroy it by corrupting it; Fascism treats it as unimportant in itself, possibly useful in a measure for the time being so long as it does not stand in the way of its plans. Fascism, unlike either of the others, is not sectarian, not even "secularly" religious. It is not typical in this sense; it is simply unbelieving.

Marxism, Mr. Voigt says, is the product of the eighteenth century Enlightenment. It is rationalist and urban, puritanical in its sectarianism, and ruthless, rather than brutal in its methods. It is based on *class*-hatred and *class*-war. Its sole test of right and wrong is class-interest; right is what helps the proletariat, what opposes it is wrong. It is international in its aims, and thrives upon international disorders. It submerges the individual in the community.

National Socialism is, its name implies, intensely national, basing itself on "race and soil." It wars on religion by corrupting it rather than by direct attack. It is likened by Mr. Voigt to a modern Islam based upon the idea of German unity. (Particularly interesting are his views on the character and results of the treaty of Versailles which will come as a shock to many.) War is its ideal, race hatred its soul. It is as ruthless as is Marxism, but more scientifically brutal and equally amoral, equally destructive of personality. Its mythology is one of pseudo-biology, as Marxism's mythology is pseudo-scientific and pseudo-philosophical.

Fascism is realistic and agnostic, imperialist and as essentially amoral at bottom as are the other two; equally collectivist, equally terrorist, equally warlike but indifferent to mythology. It is fundamentally as completely "secular" as are Marxism and Communism.

Now European civilization consisting, as Mr. Voigt reminds us, of its heritage from Athens, Rome and Jerusalem is incompatible with secular religion.—Only when secular religion has been overcome can there be a rebirth of European consciousness. Only then can there be a Pax Europaica. . . . But the problem of the Pax Europaica is, above all, a *problem of civilization,* and can never be solved or solve itself, without a renewal of the heritage that has come down from Athens, Rome and Jerusalem. The *trahison des clercs* is a betrayal of that heritage, an apostasy, an abandonment of religion in favor of secular religion, a rendering unto Caesar of the things which are God's. Even if secular religion has not yet taken *political* form in Western Europe, it has eaten deeply into Western European civilization. That is the reason why the spiritual change must come in England and in France as well as in Germany.

We in the United States are part of the European civilization if not of the Pax Europaica. How do *we* stand today? A second look at *Unto Caesar* from our viewpoint yields some ominous hint to which we may well pay attention.

August 10, 1938

II

Mr. Voigt points out that of the world's great powers the United States alone is *inviolable* and *invulnerable;* she has *absolute security.* France, Germany and Russia can be defeated in war but not destroyed. The smaller continental nations can be absorbed after defeat in war. England is the only great power which can be totally and permanently defeated; she is the most vulnerable of all the nations, for her very existence depends upon her armed strength, and upon her existence depends the existence of Holland, Belgium, and the Scandinavian nations. The *Pax Europaica* depends first, last and always upon "a strong England in association with a strong France." And England "must in all circumstances have for a friend the United States." She can always have this "if she does not try to convert that friendship into an alliance or expect the United States to take risks and make sacrifices equal to hers in defending interests that are much more hers than theirs."

So much for the *physical* side of things. About all else that Mr. Voigt has to say of us is that our inviolability makes it possible for us to "show an exalted idealism" in our conduct toward other nations and he credits us with a "natural generosity" in our dealings both at home and abroad. But what about our dealings with Caesar? Has the poison of secular religion got itself into our veins as it has into those of Europe? As to this Mr. Voigt has nothing to say.

Inviolable and invulnerable as we are in a physical sense, we are peculiarly vulnerable in a vital spot to this disease. The very cornerstone of our political structure is the personality of the citizen and the inviolability of those inalienable rights that inhere in human personality. Our government was founded expressly for their protection. Secular religion is incompatible with those rights, for it denies the thing that gives to human personality its very essence. The idea of personality is transcendental, and secular religion excludes the transcendental. It therefore defies our democracy. To what extent has it gained foothold amongst us?

As a formal cult, not much. The Marxian form of antireligion is not a popular phenomenon, much less than the Nazi variety. Positive atheism where it exists at all is little more than a variety of adolescent exhibitionism to which no one pays more than passing attention. But there are many symptoms that suggest an evaporation of definite religion rapidly proceeding among our more sophisticated classes and spreading down to the mass of our people, through tabloid, screen and radio. Our so-called intellectuals are as a class vastly more superficial and more dogmatic than the European type, and our more or less moronic mass has a tincture of semi-sophistication as contrasted with the relative *naiveté* of the European proletariat. Our philosophers have gone as far as any to detach "philosophy" altogether from the metaphysical and to banish all suggestion of the transcendental.

Perhaps the most significant phenomenon of our drift in recent times is the instinctive sympathetic reaction of our leftists toward the Russian experiment and their equally instinctive rally to the support of last year's court-packing scheme. Both are symptoms of detachment from fixed foundations. In its own small way, too, the caveat expressed by Mr. Max Lerner concerning Thomas Mann's confession of faith in "universals" is significant. It is not too much to say that our entire "left," from the intelligentsia down to the soapbox, is traveling the same road—philosophically and religiously—as are the European Marxians, Fascists and National Socialists, with the kingdom-of-Heaven-on-Earth as its goal. It has not yet developed a definite mythology as have they, but the mythology is implied in its instincts and there is no need for its formal erection, so long as these instincts serve their purpose.

Secular religion must inevitably produce a State which is the complete antithesis to that which we inherited from our forefathers. It must be totalitarian, collective, despotic, amoral, terrorist, and completely destructive of individual personal liberties; whether or not it stops short of firing squads and concentration camps depends entirely on the extent and character of the resistance that it meets as it grows. We are, let us hope, yet a long way from such things. But there is no little ground for the fear that our feet are on the road that leads to them. It is time that we set ourselves earnestly to discover whether we are not already giving to Caesar more than belongs to him.

Mr. Voigt has written a really notable book of permanent value to all who wish to see the world situation in its complete perspective, and he has put his finger unerringly upon the root cause of the crisis that now gravely threatens the Western World. It is the most gigantic apostasy ever committed by a great civilization, a deliberate abandonment of the heritage upon which it was built—a heritage that must at all costs be recovered if the West is not to go the way of Nineveh and Tyre—and take us with it.

August 12, 1938

FASCISM: GOVERNMENT WITHOUT LAW

I

José Ortega y Gasset's *Invertebrate Spain* deserves attentive reading by all who know his *Revolt of the Masses.* Both can be commended to those who do not, as extremely illuminating, not merely on events in Spain, but events everywhere in the Western world, and particularly in the United States.

Readers may, perhaps, recall that this writer has in the past referred several times to a work by Ortega y Gasset which antedated by several years the *Revolt of the Masses.* Its Spanish title is *Espana invertebrada,* which this writer ventured to render into English as "Spineless Spain." It first appeared in May, 1922, when the author was still short of forty years old. The *Revolt* came about ten years later. The interesting thing about the earlier volume is that it contains the germ—indeed the skeleton—of its successor, and that very scientifically articulated. As the translator (Mildred Adams) tells us, the first three chapters of the new volume contain most of *Espana invertebrada* (Why was Chapter V of its second part not included? It is extremely significant in its implications, especially as these are timeless and universal.) and also several interesting essays of recent date. It is these in which the application to this country (as Miss Adams notes in introduction) is most striking. To the careful reader also they will light up many obscure spots in the present Spanish tragedy, although written before the storm broke.

Two essays in particular are of especial timeliness. One is on "Liberalism and Democracy" and the other "On Fascism." Both are directly to our address. Of liberalism and democracy our author says:

> Liberalism and democracy happen to be two things which begin by having nothing to do with each other and end by having, so far as tendencies are concerned, meanings that are mutually antagonistic. Democracy and liberalism are two answers to two totally different questions: "who ought to exercise the public power?" The answer it gives is: "the exercise of the public power belongs to the citizens as a body." . . . Liberalism, on the other hand, answers this other question: "regardless of who exercises the public power, what should its limits be?" The answer it gives is: "Whether the public power is exercised by an autocrat or by the people, it cannot be absolute; the individual has rights which are over and above any interference by the State." . . . It is possible to be very liberal and not at all democratic, or very democratic and not at all liberal. . . . It would therefore be the most ingenuous of errors to believe that by means of democracy we can avoid absolutism. On the contrary, there is no fiercer autocracy than that diffuse and irresponsible kind exercised by the *demos*.

Greek and Roman democracies were illiberal. Bolshevism is illiberal. The English Revolution was liberal. The French Revolution was democratic. Feudalism was liberal and undemocratic; liberalism was a medieval concept following the introduction of feudalism by the Teutonic invaders. This rough classification by Ortega illustrates the above distinction. State absolutism (as Ferrero shows in his *Palingenesi di Roma*) is a post-medieval renascence, like the "divine right of kings." Modern mass-democracy is strongly absolutist in tendency; therefore, illiberal.

In the light of which it is interesting to look at the heterogeneous group in our country that calls itself both liberal and democratic, and test it for liberalism and democracy. Its democracy is of the mass type, and its liberalism is plainly absolutist. In short, it is precisely *not* liberal-democratic, but the very reverse. What liberalism (Ortega style) there is left in the country is in fact to be found in the group which the so-called liberal group dubs "reactionary."

The truth is that both liberalism and democracy are in a bad way with fascism and the "People's Front" (of which latter our liberal group is the embryo) as an upper and nether millstone crushing them out of life.

April 30, 1937

II

Senor Ortega's essay "On Fascism concerns itself exclusively with Italian *Fascismo.* It was written before Hitler's advent, and also before the inauguration by Mussolini of the Corporate State. As *Fascismo* is the model upon which other fascist and semi-fascist policies are fashioned and as the Corporate State is not in any way a necessary development of *Fascismo,* his remarks are not thereby rendered less interesting. Of Fascism, he says in his opening paragraph:

> Fascism wears an enigmatic face because its content is so contradictory. It affirms authority and at the same time it organizes revolt. It combats contemporary democracy, and on the other hand

it does not believe in the restoration of anything which has gone before. It seems to propose the forging of a strong state, yet it employs means which tend toward dissolution, as if it were a faction of destruction or a secret society. Whichever part of fascism you take hold of, you find that it is a thing and also its opposite—it is A and at the same time it is non-A.

Its two main characteristics are "violence and illegitimacy." By illegitimacy Ortega means the divorce of fascist theory from any theory of a *juridical* character. "Fascism," he says, "does not pretend to govern according to law, nor does it even aspire to being legitimate. This is, in my judgment, its great originality, or at least its peculiarity; I might also add its profundity and its virtue." In contrast to this, he points out that Bolshevism (Communism) "illegally smashed one legal state for the purpose of setting up another. Its supporters believe that today they exercise power in the name of legitimacy, founded on juridical reasoning as sound as any, which in turn is backed by a complete system of ethics and even by a conception of the universe." Bolshevism uses violence to enforce its law; Fascism uses violence as a substitute for law; "it fills the void where law was."

How did Fascism win so easily? "How is it," Ortega asks, "that other social forces hitherto enthusiastic supporters of the law allowed this triumph of juridical chaos?" The answer is immediate: "for the simple reason that *there are no important social forces today in which enthusiasm for the law is a live issue.* Or what amounts to the same thing, because legality takes no form among modern continental nations which at once satisfies and inspires their people. The moment there arises a new principle of political law which can win the unstinted enthusiasm of a social group, fascism will vanish into thin air." (Emphasis supplied.)

Its whole power, in short, lies in the weakness of others. It arose on the ruins of nineteenth-century liberalism and the degeneration of democracy. Had not that liberalism gone bankrupt and had not the democratic idea disintegrated into mass movement, there would have been no Fascism. It looks like a sound piece of analysis.

Now, if it be correct, a corollary of the first importance to us at once emerges. Not that Fascism is a danger in this country; quite the contrary. There is no sign whatever of its emergence here. The danger here is quite another. It is true that there is here a notable lack of enthusiasm for the law as such, also that our democracy has become in large measure a mass-movement and a class conflict. But the important fact is that that movement and that conflict are being steadily infused with a definite spirit and increasingly directed in a definite technique by a social group which has a definite philosophy, a definite juridical theory and an almost mystical enthusiasm for its ideas.

We are gradually building up here a definite United Front of precisely the kind that Dimitrov described in Moscow less than two years ago, and the element of cohesion is supplied by the Communist group. The danger is all the greater because the strategy is well-concealed, and quite unsuspected by the majority of its dupes. It is not a strategy of direct propaganda of the Communist ideology; not at all. It is essentially a campaign to produce disorder, and is aimed at destroying the remains of public faith in our system of government.

If this seems an overdrawn picture, there is a simple proof of its truth. Let the court-packing proposal furnish the test. Look at the ranks of its supporters and ask what is the bond that unites them—novelists, poets, actors, social workers, labor leaders, and the entire class of so-called liberals, parlor sans-culottes and soapboxers. They all agree on the court-packing and they all like the Russian Bolshevists. Not one in ten is a convinced ideologic Communist; perhaps, not one in fifty. Not one in ten, perhaps, even suspects that he is playing the Communists' game. That is the very cream of the United Front strategy.

Fascism is not the answer to that, even had we the will for it, and we have not. The only effective answer is in a reinvigorated faith in our institutions. It is they and not the Supreme Court that need reinvigoration, and they need it badly.

May 7, 1937

REVOLUTION AND FREEDOM IN RUSSIA

I

The National Council of American-Soviet Friendship Incorporated, whose chairman is Mr. Corliss Lamont, has been kind enough to send to the present writer an attractively printed brochure entitled *The Constitution of the U.S.S.R.* which is the "fundamental law" of "The Union of Soviet Socialist Republics" into which the "Russia" that we talk about is organized. The Council is anxious to give this as wide a circulation as possible in this country and describes it as a "vital, living document, the complete foundation which underlies the epic achievements of the Soviet Union's Red Army and people." As such they think it will aid in welding unity and closer cooperation—in war and peace—between the United States and the Soviet Union. Contributions towards expenses of circulation will be accepted by the Council.

This places the present writer in a quandary. Should he—subject to the economic position in which the war has placed him which has required a radical budgetary readjustment of his own affairs!—assist a "wide circulation" of this document with a small contribution, or should he not? He does not know. But he will, at least, requite the kindness of the Council in sending him the thing by discussing what he deems to be its nature and significance, and leaving it to his readers for such action as seems to them appropriate.

The *shape* of the Russian state, as most people know by this time, is that of a federation of "autonomous republics," sixteen in number, each equal to the other and all uniformly organized. About the only unusual feature in the whole is that each enjoys the right to secede from the Union. The distribution of powers between the Union and the constituent Republics is quite logical according to our concept of the relations. The source of all civil power is "the working people of town and country as represented by the Soviets of Working Peoples' Deputies." These constitute "the political foundation of the U.S.S.R." as the constitution itself says: "In the U.S.S.R. work is a duty and a matter of honor for every able-bodied citizen in accordance with the principle: 'He who does not work neither shall he eat.' " Thus in *form* the Constitution is completely "democratic" for theoretically, all the "people" *work* and the power is in *all* the "people," under universal adult suffrage. So far, so good. The all-important question is as to *substance* and the substance concerns the freedom of the citizen, freedom which in turn consists in the possession of *rights* against the state. Has the Russian citizen any such right? Chapter 10 deals with the "fundamental rights and duties of citizens." It enumerates the "right to work," the "right to rest and leisure," the "right to maintenance in old age and also in case of sickness or loss of capacity to work," the "right to education," and absolute equality in the possession of these rights. In addition all citizens are guaranteed "freedom of speech, freedom of press, freedom of assembly," and "freedom of street processions and demonstrations," also inviolability of person, homes and correspondence. This constitutes an impressive list. A special clause is devoted to "freedom of religion" which deserves special attention. It reads: "In order to insure to citizens freedom of conscience, the church is separated from the state and the school from the church. Freedom of religious worship and freedom of anti-religious propaganda is recognized for all citizens."

A hasty reading of this clause reveals nothing to shock the American mind for we "separate" church from state and church from [public] school. Of the "school" the Constitution says apropos the citizens' "right to education": "The right is ensured by universal compulsory elementary education, by education including higher education, being free of charge, etc., etc." There is nothing in the words explicitly forbidding private schools. But up to the present moment (as far as the present writer is aware) the Church has been rigidly prohibited from conducting *any education whatever,* in or out of schools or seminaries. Moreover, it is significant that the words "freedom of worship" imply no "freedom" of "religious propaganda" while the right of "anti-religious propaganda" is explicitly recognized. And, as everyone knows, it is only recently that the Church has been permitted to resume its full organizational form in the Holy Synod and only recently that the official anti-God propaganda has been suspended. Yet the prohibition of the Holy Synod and the anti-God propaganda were both in force under this Constitution which was in its present form ratified in 1941!

From which it is manifest that the Constitution's terms, as they stand in this brochure, do not *guarantee* "freedom of religion" as we understand that freedom in this country. This being the case, added to the fact that there is not a word in it to convey the idea that the citizen has any "rights" except those granted *by the State,* both stamp the constitution itself as *totalitarian.* And it may be noted that our own *Constitution, standing alone, without the Declaration of Independence's Preamble, would bear a similar appearance.* But our Supreme Court has *twice* warned us that while the Declaration is no part of our organic law, it is the spirit and the thought of which the Constitution is the body and the letter.

And that it is always safe to read the Constitution in the light of the Declaration. And that makes all the difference.

Which shows us how necessary it is in reading the Russian Constitution to *read* it—and causes this writer to wonder whether *wide* reading will be necessary following wide circulation, and if not, whether wide circulation will mean wide understanding of the truth. *September* 29, 1943

II

In the September issue of *Thought* (Fordham University Quarterly) N. S. Timasheff has an article "Revolution and Competition for Power" which is of timely interest. It is a study of the causes, the process and the consequences of revolutions, in general—of what the scientists would call their "etiology" and the medical men their "syndrome," which in plain speech means what starts them, what makes them "tick" and what becomes of them. At the close of his study Dr. Timasheff drops a remark which seems to the present writer of much present significance. The reader may be interested in the doctor's account of the "etiology" and the "syndrome" of the revolutionary phenomenon, which gives the significance to this remark.

In every civil society there is always some competition for power between the various social groups of which political "parties" are the expression. *Normally* this competition takes place within the general "institutional" structure of society, as for instance, in this country, Great Britain and other countries whose governmental order is more or less what we call "democratic." This state of things Timasheff calls *stability*. From time to time, however, there develops an intensity in the competitive tensions which disturbs this equilibrium, and the struggle for power threatens the structure itself. This condition Timasheff calls *plastic*. It develops when discontent upon the part of some of the "groups" reaches a high pitch, tending to generate what Timasheff calls a "revolutionary mass." This "discontent" can be dealt with in one or other of three ways: Reaction, Reform, or Revolution. Reaction in this sense means "to former methods," and Reform means "re-form" by *new* methods. When neither is successful Revolution ensues, and Revolution means attack on the governmental structure itself, as, for instance, when a republic succeeds a monarchy.

Revolution requires a "revolutionary mass," a "leader" (or leaders) and a "program." The "mass" becomes "revolutionary" when it ceases to trust the "socio-cultural elite" which normally conducts the government. The groups which seek the power to "reconstruct" society make their appeals to this mass by "programs" and the group which offers the most attractive program secures the power to reconstruct. Struggle between revolutionary groups is common in the earlier stages and gives rise to the saying that "Revolution devours its children." The French Revolution illustrates its truth. Usually victory rests with that group which promises most and is least deterred from violence.

The successful revolution results in a "new order." Timasheff describes the process thus: "Accommodation of the virtual leadership to the 'natural program' of 'the revolutionary mass'; acceptance by this mass of the offer thus formulated; delegation to the successful competitor of the authority to proceed to reconstruction on the basis of this program; gradual withdrawal of the repression and return to the original program; exertion of power according to this program of 'the revolutionary mass.'" Society returns to its normal state of *stability*, as the revolutionary tension is exhausted—upon which stage Timasheff comments thus: "Whether it likes it or not society has to endure the power structure chosen in the course of a revolutionary competition for power. Whether the nation continues to accept this leadership will be decided during the next revolutionary crisis when society once more becomes plastic." Then follows the remark above referred to. "Obviously the test of a nation's attitude towards its government receives quite another form if the *revolution results in establishing a true democracy.*" Unfortunately, this is a rather exceptional case." (Emphasis supplied.)

True "democracy" will not develop revolutionary conditions. It will not do so because it will not produce "group discontents" of sufficient depth to prevent their remedy by orderly methods. It will not produce them because, as a *true* democracy, it will be founded upon a general recognition of *minority rights,* and a *government of laws* for their protection. It will, therefore, not be *totalitarian* and will be free of "*class wars,*" and "*class domination.*" Here is the deep significance for our times of his remark. We can have a society which is *in form* democratic but is *totalitarian in substance* because of lack of respect for minority rights. We can also have a "democratic" society in which a "class" has, *as a class,* seized power and exercises it for class interests. A *popular front* "democracy" is of necessity a totalitarian "democracy" and a "class-government," and as such lacks the requisite of *stability* and is essentially *plastic*—which means that it must, sooner or later, develop revolutionary conditions.

From which the conclusion inevitably arises that of all the utopian dreams, the dream of peace, security and freedom by establishment of "popular-front democracy" is as wild as the wildest. Of which fact our liberal friends seem to be completely ignorant.

October 1, 1943

SOCIAL DECOMPOSITION

A scholarly Frenchman recently said to the present writer: "If you want to understand the success of Nazism in Germany, read Volume Five of Taine's *Origines de la France contemporaine* on the Jacobin phenomenon. It will show you how a majority can capture supreme power. Anyhow it will do you good to read some French written in the grand style, even if it teaches you a little or nothing." As the present writer's curiosity has always far outranged not only his very indifferent scholarship but also the capacity of his mental digestive powers—to say nothing of his sensitivity to "style" in foreign languages!—he accepted the suggestion. Perhaps his readers may be interested in some of the results of his foray.

Taine points out that the Jacobins took their stand upon *one* central dogma—the "sovereignty of the people." The government is even less than the people's deputy or its house servant. "We the people" create it and are always its master and can kick it out without ceremony; we are not bound to it, it is bound to us; we have to watch it jealously lest it hinder the free exercise of our supreme authority, or forget that we are its master. We must at all times reserve the right to act directly for ourselves, assemble, discuss, debate, control, distribute, appraise and weigh among our servants, keep our hands on the tiller of the ship all the time with our steersmen and occasionally throw them overboard. All this is logical; what is the use of overthrowing the despotism of the crown to replace it by a despotism of the functionary? In short, we must govern first, last and all the time. Commenting on a violent statement by Marat to this effect in his paper, Taine says:

True, among those who have still a little intelligence, Marat passed for a wild man, a crazy man. When it was the dogma's last words—in the political household, over the head of the powers delegated, regular and legal—it installed a power, impersonal, imbecile and terrible, whose decision is absolute, whose activity is continuous, and whose intervention is murderous; it is the people, a sultan suspicious and ferocious, who, having named his viziers, keeps his hands free to drive them and his scimitar sharpened to behead them.

Such a conception, Taine says, one can imagine being spun by a closet dreamer, living with abstractions and philosophic marionettes; one can also understand a madman in his cellar obsessed by phantoms embracing it, for revenge upon a social system which has rejected him. But how explain politicians, legislators, statesmen, even ministers and heads of state accepting, not only accepting it but embracing it all the more closely as it became visibly more destructive, laying in ruins the entire social order, and not only accepting the consequences but glorifying them, and in the name of liberty building a despotism worthy of Dahomey with hecatombs of victims like those of old Mexico, all the while believing in and pluming themselves on their rightness, and their humanity? Never before was there such a combination of mental operation and pride; what is the explanation?

Two things constitute the root of Jacobinism, says Taine, exaggerated egotism and exaggerated dogmatism. They are in every country and in all times; in stable societies they are driven underground but do not die, for they are in human nature. They live in students' garrets, bohemian hall-rooms, doctors' offices empty of patients, lawyers' offices without clients. They appeal to youth and to all whose self-esteem has outrun competence and self-knowledge, who resent compulsory subordination in the social hierarchy in which they live and which does not recognize their merits—in short, to all whom our modern jargon calls the "maladjusted." In a stable society most of youth grows up, gets over its scarlet fever and takes its place in the social order, but in an order that is cracking it does not, and together with the maladjusted of all kinds and ages becomes the material of revolution. Jacobinism, in short, is a product of social decomposition, but it lives by *faith* and a pride to nourish that faith.

The Jacobins governed France for a time with complete ruthlessness although their convinced adherents never amounted to 10 per cent of the population. Taine's description of the methods by which they accomplished this is uncannily fascinating to read in these days of the Gestapo and the OGPU. In summary, the thing was done by systematic organization of "clubs," each of which constituted a "cell" both for propagation of dogma and for acquisition of political power. These cells covered all the strategic centers, great and small, in France, and were intimately linked with the mother club in Paris. Espionage of private persons was a particularly strong feature of their activities. The result of the electoral laws, moreover, was such as to confuse the mass of the people and to cause a general abstention from voting, thus clearing the road for the "party." Moreover—a most interesting point—even within the party councils victory rested with the minority because they had the stronger faith and the least scruples. "Four times," says Taine, "between 1791 and 1794 the political players sat at the table where power was the stake and four times the Impartiaux, the Feuillants, the Girondists, and the Dantonists, the majority, lost the game." The reason was simple, the majority clung to the game's old rules, the minority disregarded them, its pistol on the table, and pocketed the stakes.

The second chapter of Taine's Volume Five is well worth study today, for the light that it throws upon political methods. The Nazi movement has common roots with the Jacobin phenomenon. Instead of "popular sovereignty," its dogma is "blood and soil" and it has the same *hybris* and the same methods. The only difference is that "science"—the "natural philosophers" of which Heine spoke—has given it weapons which the Jacobins did not possess. It is that which makes the threat of Nazism almost infinitely more dangerous to the world. But the end will be the same, whenever it comes, for it is not conceivable that "blood and soil" as a faith and *hybris* as a vital principle can establish itself as the world's way of life any more than could the Jacobin idea of a century and a half ago. The Jacobins succeeded only in destroying the French social order and under the name of liberty establishing an atrocious tyranny; the Nazis have imposed upon Germany a social "order" which is in conflict with all the things that make man human. The anarchy of the Jacobins did not last, and the "order" of the Nazis will not last; for both contravene human nature. *July* 8, 1940

DEMOCRACY: DEFINITION AND DEBATE

A DEFINITION OF DEMOCRACY

I

Democracy is that form of social organization in which the laws that provide for the maintenance of the social order and the administration of justice are laid down by consent of the common will of the people itself, and are executed by representatives chosen freely by that will for that purpose.

Man is by his nature social, because only in society with his fellows can he completely fulfill his earthly destiny. His distinguishing characteristic is his personality; the human individual, unlike the rest of the animal kingdom, does not exist for the sake of the *species*, but is himself a *unit* with tremendous unitary value and importance, and society is the natural means for preservation of that value and for providing the means for its full expression in the field of human activities.

The direct purpose of government is to preserve order; the

purpose of justice is to secure the necessary liberty for the human person to pursue his destiny in that *freedom* which is due to the dignity and the worth of human personality.

Personal liberty is, therefore, the final objective of democracy as a form of government. The *common good* of the community is neither *distinct* from nor *superior* to individual liberty but is that condition of individual relations which best promotes the maximum of personal liberty for all the people.

Democracy, therefore, connotes a *limitation* upon the *just powers* of government over the actions of the citizen, whose liberty of action may not justly be constrained or restricted except where necessary to prevent similar liberties of others from being violated. Personal rights are not *absolute;* they may, however, be lawfully abridged by the civil authority only where necessary to *protect* other people's personal rights of similar rank. Under certain circumstances the civil authorities may justly take from a citizen both his life and his liberty.

Democracy and *totalitarianism* are, therefore, incompatible: they are mutually exclusive terms. But a totalitarian state is possible under a democratic *form.*

In general, the common *will* of the people, as the source of law, expresses itself by the voice of the *majority* in free and orderly balloting. A simple definition of democracy would be "*Minority rights under majority rule.*" For the formation of the *common will* freedom of discussion is indispensable in every form. Men's opinions vary upon everything, and party or group opinions are a normal and indeed inevitable part of democratic government. But underneath these differences, which are mainly as to ways and means, there must be a common faith in the essential—namely in the inviolability of personal liberties.

There must be, therefore, a limitation upon the power of the majority. This limitation may be explicitly contained in a written instrument expressing a general *organic law* or *constitution,* or it may rest upon a solid tradition of the people itself. This law limits the power of the legislature in making new laws, which new laws must not infringe the principles laid down in the organic law.

The organic law does not *grant* the personal rights which it protects; it *recognizes* them as inherent in the natural dignity of the person. While the people, as the immediate *source* of the organic law, has the power to make what law it pleases and change it at will, if it departs from the principle just mentioned it violates the fundamental of democracy itself.

Democracy to be effective must work by a principle of *representation;* the people itself cannot directly legislate; a majority party representing a certain *policy* will elect men to legislative or administrative office who, it believes, will best carry that party policy into effect. The best results are obtained when the representatives are freest to exercise their own judgment as to ways and means for effectuating the party policy and are not subject to the direct dictation of party organizations.

An effective check upon majority action by a vigorous *minority opposition* party is an important, indeed a necessary, factor in healthy democratic government, which works best under a two-party system with more or less frequent alternations in office.

Public opinion, under a system of free discussion, is at all times a mixture of emotion and reason. In all important matters it is vital that common action be taken only in accord with the *considered* will of a *clear majority* of the people, and that hasty action be avoided. Hence, the desirability of bicameral legislatures differently elected and the requirement, in certain cases, of more than a bare majority vote to effect important changes in law—e.g., as in amendment to the Constitution, the overriding of an executive veto or the ratification of a treaty. Under modern conditions of intercommunication the effectiveness of the demagogue has been greatly increased, and demagoguery is one of the greatest dangers to democracy. There has never been a time when it was more necessary than now for the real *common will* to be distilled from the passing waves of popular emotion.

Mob rule is the result always of mass emotion and is a *degeneration* of democracy—one, moreover, to which democracy is peculiarly exposed. The reason is that it usually implies a class conflict involving fundamentals, and invariably results in one-man rule and a totalitarian state—either of them being necessarily destructive of democracy.

Democracy, as a "way of life" for human society, by its nature is best conducive to the preservation of men's personal liberty and is therefore the most desirable form of government. For its success, however, it demands a high state of civic morality in the people, who must be educated to a relatively high standard of intelligence and, above all, mutual tolerance. In the absence of either it is almost certain to degenerate, and in that process liberty tends to disappear. Forms alone are not sufficient for its preservation; they must be animated by a deep popular faith in principles of liberty itself. These principles, arising as they do from the fact of man's *personality*, are ultimately religious, for man's personality necessarily implies God, the soul and the moral law.

February 14, 1938

II

A correspondent, J. F. W. of Cleveland, writes:

You say (in effect), "The . . . purpose of government . . . is to secure the necessary liberty for the human person to pursue his destiny in that freedom which is due to the dignity and the worth of human personality." Does not this put the cart before the horse? In measure as human beings *have* worth and dignity, will they not procure and preserve that form of government that recognizes it? To you and to me this means democracy of a type which permits a large degree of personal freedom. But I deny that we have any right to this. It is a thing to be earned by us who want it. As I understand it, the purpose of government is to promote the greatest possible good of the greatest possible number. This purpose *may* be best served by different forms at different times and for different peoples. Whatever form serves it best is, *pro tempore,* the best form. To me, your statement suggests allegiance to the "divine origin" theory of democracy—a theory I regard as no sounder than the theory of the divine right of kings.

Our correspondent raises the final question of all, that of human rights—rights, that is, which inhere in a man because he is human, rights which are due to him because he is a *person,* regardless of the differences, qualitative and quantitative, that exist between human beings in respect of physique and mental capacity. The second paragraph of the Declaration of Independence sets forth the doctrine of human rights in all its essentials—their origin, their nature and their relation to government. Human liberty in theory and in practice consists in the undisturbed enjoyment of those rights. In so far as democracy has a "divine origin," it has it simply from the fact that no human being is *born* with the right to rule other people. Hence, the civil authority rests in *all* the people, whose right it is to choose those who are to exercise that authority and to invest them with the powers that are necessary and just to maintain civil order and justice.

The people, if so minded, might choose a king or single ruler to give and to administer laws for the community on his sole authority. (He *might* even rule in such a way that his subjects did in fact enjoy true liberty.) But he would not thereby be king by "divine right," as the phrase is commonly understood, for the people who crowned him would have the right to discrown him. His kingly power would have as its origin the "consent of the governed"; the civil power would rest in him only by transfer from its real origin, the people as a whole. The fallacy in the Stuart doctrine of divine right lies in its implicit denial of the common attribute of all men—

personality—which makes all equal in the possession of rights anterior to the civil authority itself, whose first duty is to protect those rights. The power which created that personality and ordained human society as the condition best adapted to development of personality placed the power to create human society in the control of the people in that society. In that sense democracy is divine in origin; the king's "right" is not.

One may, of course, if he please, deny *in toto* the proposition contained in the Declaration of Independence concerning human rights—as many have done, and explicitly done; witness, for example, Mr. Richberg. But whoever does so must be prepared to deny democracy *as a principle* and liberty as an equally baseless assertion. But our American democracy explicitly asserts all these things, and rests its entire structure upon those assertions as its foundation—something which our educators might occasionally remember.

Our correspondent further says:

> You say: "The common good of the community is neither distinct from nor superior to individual liberty." Fervently as I yearn to believe this, I cannot succeed. It seems to me that individual liberty almost invariably conflicts with the common good, and that democracy differs from dictatorship far less in the *degree* of restraint it imposes, than in the *manner* in which it imposes that restraint. In other words, Mr. Roosevelt's subjects still (thank God!) have much more to say as to when, how, and whether, their liberty shall be limited, than do Mussolini's; and a much better chance to foresee what will be done, and to prepare for it.

The "common good' is not superior to or distinct from individual liberty. Its true meaning is that condition of society which produces the maximum of liberty for *all* individual members, and is a *means* to that end. The civil authority may rightly invade an individual's *liberty* only to preserve the *liberty* of the group. In that sense there is a *quantitative* factor operative, but no superiority of a *qualitative* kind. This simply means that no right is absolute.

February 25, 1938

DEMOCRACY AND PERSONAL LIBERTY

In his address to the New York State Bar Association at the close of last week, Governor Lehman said:

Though the cleavage between dictatorship and democracy is sharp the steps that lead democracy to dictatorship are not always spectacular. On the contrary, sometimes they are barely discernible. The changes in government which have led to dictatorship abroad were in many instances at first hardly perceptible. It is, therefore, just as important to guard against gradual insidious change that attacks the roots of democracy as against revolution itself. Democracy is under pressure from powerful and selfish reactionaries on the extreme right and from equally powerful and selfish radicals on the extreme left. While their political and economic policies may differ, their ultimate objectives are frequently identical. In their greed for power and in their determination to gain their ends they are willing to sacrifice all democratic principles. There is no choice between them. A victory for either would mean the end of democracy.

The governor used the words *democracy* and *democratic* some fifteen times in about five hundred words, without defining either. We may take it for granted, however, that he was referring to our own political structure and its fundamental ideas, and that his audience so understood him. Those ideas were three-fold; first liberty—that is, inviolable *personal* rights; second, *representative* government—that is, the antithesis to *pure* democracy; third, choice of representatives by *majority* vote of those qualified to vote—all resting upon a fundamental organic law ordained by the people itself, together with a separation of governmental powers as a precaution against personal despotism. The sole purpose of the whole structure was to protect the *personal liberty* of the citizen. Democracy as a form of government has no other merit than this, that it seems to offer the best protection for human liberty.

The imminent danger to our democracy lies in two common popular superstitions. One is that *form* is its whole importance, and that its essence lies in popular voting. The other is that the majority is always right because it is a majority. The fact is that no matter what may be the democratic forms through which party majorities alternate as a result of voting, however orderly the voting may be, there must underlie these party differences a body of common beliefs on certain fundamentals concerning personal rights, which beliefs are unquestioned by all parties, and held by a vast majority of the citizens themselves—otherwise democracy has failed in its sole purpose. It is for this reason that a genuine class conflict is destructive of any or all democracies in which it develops.

Now it is unfortunately true that we have in this country today a large number of people who have no belief whatever in the *reality* of inviolable personal rights, but regard them as meaningless abstractions. And it is also unfortunately true that we have a definite class cleavage which is being sedulously whipped up into a genuine class conflict. There is no shorter road from a democracy to a dictatorship than that furnished by class conflict. Thus the foundations of our democracy are not only already sapped (for many people) on theoretical grounds, but are also gravely threatened in fact by a class conflict visibly growing in our midst.

Governor Lehman in the same address put his finger upon the heart of the matter when he reminded his hearers of Jefferson's admonition that freedom by law means nothing unless public opinion stands behind the law, and he called liberals and conservatives alike to the defense of civil and religious liberties. But it is the defense of the other fellow's liberties and not one's own that is what is needed—yet we have seen within a few days the amazing spectacle of a high official of the Federal Government and a governor of a great state both publicly repudiating the idea of "fairness" toward big business. Assistant Attorney General Jackson in his debate with Wendell Willkie at the Town Hall in New York was reported (*New York Times,* January 7) as saying "that he saw no reason for fairness in the competition between the government and the utility companies" and Governor Earle of Pennsylvania, speaking on Founders Day at the University of Pennsylvania was reported (*New York Times,* January 28) as saying: "From a moral point of view we should give big business fair play, but that is only from a moral point of view. Actually it isn't important to give big business fair play."

The terrible truth of the matter is that democracy American style as planned by the Founders holds its life—as do the liberties which it was designed to protect—only so long as the people have a real faith in *moral points of view, for the doctrine of human rights is a moral doctrine.* Nor is this all. To live the democratic life in the American way, the people must possess and practice in their political relations two most important virtues, and two virtues among the hardest to acquire or to practice. One is charity—the opposite to which is hate—and the other is intelligent humility—the opposite to which is mingled pride and ignorance. Does anyone see much trace of either virtue among us today?

January 26, 1938

DR. ADLER AND DEMOCRACY

I

A strikingly original contribution to political philosophy was recently made by Dr. Mortimer J. Adler in a paper read this winter, and the present writer believes that his readers will be interested in an outline of the thesis therein defended. That thesis Dr. Adler states in his own words as follows: "This paper will attempt to prove, *first,* that democracy is the best form of government; and, *second,* that it is the only good state."

Summarizing in bare skeleton form the argument, it runs as follows:

(1) Man is by nature a political animal, wherein he differs from all other animals; in this respect all men are politically equal; none is by nature another's political superior; he is by nature a member of a political society, the perfect form of which is the state; a political society requires government.

(2) There are three criteria of good government:

(a) "Rule for the common good in whose fruits the ruled participate, rather than rule for the good of the ruler exclusively;

(b) "Constitutional rule, in which some body of men is entitled to citizenship, and under which no man exercises political authority over another equal (another citizen) except through the governmental office he holds by delegation;

(c) "The suffrage or enfranchisement of all men as political equals and all therefore entitled to citizenship."

(3) The first criterion of the common good can conceivably be present under any good form of government, even though some men may participate in it passively only as subjects and others not at all because they are "managed as slaves." The second criterion of "constitutional rule" can exist in the absence of the third, for there can be "a relatively just constitutional rule for the common good, even though some men are unjustly subjected and enslaved. Here such unjust circumstances as nobility or wealth or race are made conditions of suffrage. Only when all three criteria are present, that is, universal suffrage of citizens added to the other two, can government be regarded as completely good.

(4) When all three criteria are present, the government is

correctly termed democracy, and this is necessarily the best form of government as completely according with man's nature as a political animal. No other governmental form satisfies this condition.

The originality in Dr. Adler's paper consists in his departure from the classical political theories (e.g., Aristotle, Aquinas, etc.) in recognizing a *normative* hierarchy in forms of government, as forms. The classical writers on politics have for the most part mainly or partly classified government as good or bad according to the sole criterion of the "common good." Dr. Adler squarely challenges both Aristotle and Aquinas on the point of either minimizing or neglecting the element of justice inherent in the form itself. Justice entitles the human being to the status of citizen, as distinct from that of subject, and the distinctive mark of citizenship is participation, however slight, in government. The citizen proper is both ruler and ruled. Hence, adult suffrage is in justice the right of the citizen who is neither criminal nor demented.

All this is in the order of morals, pure and simple. Starting from the notion of liberty as the natural right of the human person, Dr. Adler distinguishes between the passive liberty of the subject (who is enjoying a rule which accomplishes the "common good") from the active liberty of the citizen who participates (at least as voter) in the government, and insists that active liberty is the person's right because he is a person. Thus, the democratic form of government is in the order of morals the best form. And following the same line of reasoning, the state being the complete form of political society, the democratic state is the only completely good state.

There remains the order of prudence—that is, the domain of practical experience. On this Dr. Adler says:

> From the point of view of political prudence concerned with the best means to realize good ends, it can be seen that justice is more likely to be realized by a constitutional than by a personal rule and by a democracy than under conditions of limited suffrage; for the

rule of law is better than the rule of men, and in all matters for deliberation the judgment of the many is better than the judgment of the one or the few. If stability is a political desideratum, it will be seen that democracy is the most stable form of government, and a principality the least, because the better a government is — the more fully it is built on justice — the more stable it is likely to be, accidental circumstances being equal.

March 8, 1940

II

There is an old maxim—*corruptio optimi pessima*—"the worst corruption is that of the best." Dr. Adler makes an important distinction between the notion of perversion and that of corruption as applied to governmental forms. A form is perverted when it is turned to the injury of the common good; it is corrupted when its essential quality or factor is denied. The worst—least tolerable—perversion of government is the perversion of the least good *form* (i.e., paternal despotism), but the worst corruption of government is the corruption of the best *form* (i.e., of democracy by negation of one of its principles). Despotism of the majority is more tolerable than despotism of a monarch, but the corruption of a democracy (e.g., by negation of suffrage rights) is the worst sort of tyranny because it is the corruption of the best form and of all the principles of good government. Tyranny in any form is, of course, *per se* bad. Dr. Adler's point is that some forms are worse than others.

On this distinction, Dr. Adler observes:

> Since neither Aristotle nor St. Thomas could conceive democracy as the best form of government, they could not conceive the sort of bad democratic government which exists in the world today and which is most certainly the most tolerable of perverted types, precisely because it is the direct perversion of the best type, the least corruption of the good state.

At first sight it is not easy for us to regard the Nazi governmental structure as any more "tolerable" than was the Czarist government forty years ago, both being quite despotic in fact. Both, however, are *perversions*—not *corruptions*—of *form*. The German people formally chose Hitlerism by ballot, i.e., in strictly democratic form; the motives that drove them to do so are, from this point of view, irrelevant. Czarism was in form a paternal government; its form was not corrupted by its tyranny in act.

On the principle of majority rule as inherent in the democratic form, Dr. Adler argues for the "voice of the multitude in deliberative matters as the best approximation to practical truth and, hence, the voice of reason," and does so on the strength of two assumptions. Men are a compound of virtues and vices and the extremes of these will cancel out each other, leaving a general mean of virtue; also more men have "some rectitude of will" than entirely lack it. (On these assumptions finally rests the well-known saying that "The voice of the people is the voice of God.") The truth in practical matters depends primarily upon the rectitude of the will, and secondarily on the "careful deliberation which balances opposing counsels." Thus, when a matter has been fully deliberated by the public, the decision will tend to be right. From which one may draw the corollary that in proportion as the question at issue departs from the simple and is not subjected to pretty thorough deliberation and debate, the majority decision is less certain to be right. But the majority's voice must in democracy remain the final maker—or rectifier, implicitly and explicitly—of decisions made in the name of the civil authority, whether they be right or wrong. Dr. Adler's contention is that, given the necessary prerequisite of deliberation, they are more apt to be right than wrong. Finally the democratic form is apt to be in practice the most stable form of government because its base is broadest, like that of a pyramid.

It is important to remember that the whole thesis rests upon the concept of man as a person, rather than as an individual, and only on such a base can democracy as a principle be logically defended. As a concept of personality must ultimately rest upon a religious base, the concept of democracy is at bottom inseparable from religion, and its fulfillment, as Dr. Adler says, "depends upon the work of supernatural religon."

March 15, 1940

III

There remains one more aspect of Dr. Mortimer Adler's remarkable contribution to "democracy" which is worthy of attention on the part of serious students of the subject. Readers will remember that, in the first place, he pointed out that the democratic *form* alone of all governmental forms fully comported with the dignity of human personality, and secondly, that the democratic *state* was the only really good state. In both these propositions his argument (so this writer is convinced) was rigidly logical. In the third place, he said that *in practice* the democratic form, so long as it was not corrupted, however perverted it might be, was the most tolerable form of bad government, and more stable than any other. Finally, he laid down the necessary conditions for establishment of the good democratic state. The present writer believes that what Dr. Adler has to say on this aspect will interest his readers. They fall under five heads:

(1) Purification of the democratic idea from the modern errors which identify it with anarchic individualism, with the denial of authority as such, with egalitarianism of Rousseau, and the "rule of numbers instead of political equality and the rule of reason, etc."

(2) "Moral and prudential reformation of the economic

order in order to eliminate economic slavery so far as possible" by approximating the "corporative organization of economic activities."

(3) Improvement of "the means for government of, by and for the people," but specially by the people through a form of representation, political parties and all forms of "indirect but active participation in political life."

(4) Solution of the education problem which requires "a right solution of the problem of Church and State, not only for the adequate education of men as citizens and as children of God, but also because the fullest fruits of the earthly community cannot be realized by fallen men without the moral rectifications which depend upon Grace and Providential intervention in human affairs."

(5) "Hence, the fulfillment of democracy depends upon the work of supernatural religion as well as upon the improvement of natural education. One might also say that the latter cannot take place without the former."

These are rigorous requirements, indeed! Yet every one flows by even more rigorous logic from Dr. Adler's fundamental premise, the nature of man. Once concede that premise, and you are tightly bound to every one of the conclusions advanced in his notable paper. It is interesting to note that every modern error regarding democracy stems from a denial, in whole or in part, of his premise. The most comprehensive denial yet advanced to that premise is contained in that body of doctrines so closely identified with the "Dewey Society" at Teachers College at Columbia University in New York, which is why the present writer has characterized these doctrines as the most dangerous threat to our whole system of democracy and to our American liberties. Dr. Adler's paper constitutes a challenge *à l'outrance* to each and every one of them.

This writer will be temerarious enough to advance some conclusions as to whether conditions necessary or at least favorable for a good working democracy exist, believing that they also flow from Dr. Adler's premise, that is, from the concept of human personality. One is that the higher the state of a community's *culture,* the better the soil for democracy's fruits. Standardization is a deadly enemy of culture; therefore, the more completely the natural inequalities and variety that characterize human beings in the matter of taste, talents and capacities can find individual expression in a community the higher, other things being equal, will be the community's general culture and the better its democracy. It is in this sense that a democracy needs a *natural* aristocracy, and it is precisely because standardization is threatening to become the dominant characteristic of the mass age in which we live that democracy is undergoing such horrible perversions.

From all which it is not difficult to see why Maritain, as Dr. Adler quotes him, believes that

> progress to these ideals of political and economic democracy is a career to the end of time. . . . This progress, this escape from servitude among men, depends on the one hand, on technical progress, notably on the services rendered by machines, and on certain transformations and transferrences in the regime of property; but it necessarily depends also, on the other hand, on a progressive spiritualization of humanity caused by forces of the soul and of liberty, and the Gospel leaven at work in human history.

March 25, 1940

EDUCATION FOR SOCIAL LIVING

A scholarly correspondent (W.F.S., Washington, D. C.) writes:

Sir George Young in his book, *The New Spain,* quoted the oath of allegiance of the Gothic-Spanish nobles—essentially free men—

to King Alfonso I in 1187 A.D. at Jaca as follows: "We who are as good as you, swear to you who are no better than us singly, and not so good as us all together, to have you as Sovereign Lord, if you keep our laws, but not, if you do not." That is essentially the feudal idea of the relationship of free man to his chosen government. Could anything possibly be more essentially American? Compare it, for instance, with the Declaration of Independence, with the Virginia and Kentucky Resolves; with the sometimes inarticulate, sometimes badly expressed sub-conscious revolt of 1861-5 against the imposition of an outside will in matters legal and constitutional within a state or group of states; or—with the awkwardly expressed or unexpressed but nevertheless powerful and compelling reaction to the Court-packing attempt.

The quotation is apt and the point is well taken. In that oath we have the whole principle of constitutional republican government—namely, the existence of an organic law and the free choice of men to rule under that law. That the Spanish nobles were the only "free men" exercising that choice in 1187 is from this point of view of subordinate importance. The thing of *prime* importance is the limitation placed upon the sovereign civil power, and the nature of that limitation. With that fully safeguarded, the method of selection of the sovereign ruler is a *secondary* matter, for the end of government is order, the end of order is justice and the end of justice is *personal liberty*—that is, the condition necessary for human *personality* to achieve its own proper ends. It is a hierarchy of means and ends throughout, all leading up to the final end of man, to which everything else is secondary. Which is precisely the declared purpose of our whole civil system. If the forms and methods which it has provided do not work to that end, they are deceptive and useless.

From which it is clear that the first and last question to be answered is, "What is the final end of man?" And here we touch the vitals of the whole. Our system quite definitely places the end in the *person;* the second paragraph of the Declaration contains by implication the whole philosophy leading to that conclusion. Over against that philosophy stands the modern *naturalistic* philosophy which sinks the *person* in *society,* the philosophy which Professor John Dewey and his colleagues, Professors Thorndike, Kilpatrick, Counts and others in Teachers College have developed so earnestly and assiduously in the past forty years. And that is the philosophy of the "democracy" of the entire left-wing school, which definitely challenges the democracy contemplated by our system.

According to this philosophy, the human being is an *individual* who is merely an aspect of the *social organism,* and there is no such thing as inner *personality.* The social organism is the all-important thing. As Professors Thorndike and Gates have put it (*Elementary Principles of Education*), "the aim of life is not to stock the world as a museum with perfected specimens for man or deity to contemplate. It is to make men vital parts of an organized force for the welfare of the group. . . . Nor is it desirable, even from the point of view of individuals taken singly, that education should develop equally in all respects." Professor Dewey has laid it down that education's function is essentially *social,* not personal, for there is no such thing as personal morals as distinct from social efficiency; morals are purely a *social* affair.

This philosophy (of which the foregoing brief outlines receive complete detailed development in the writings of the gentlemen mentioned) leads necessarily to a "democracy" totalitarian in character, resting on unlimited majority rule, which is utterly incompatible with the theory and purpose of our own system, yet can establish itself upon the *forms* in which our system is expressed. Of this "democracy," Dr. Mortimer J. Adler (in a blistering review of *Democracy and the Curriculum,* published in *The Commonweal,* March 17) says: ". . . their picture of democracy is precisely the one Plato gives of the State which is but one remove from tyranny in its viciousness and which inevitably falls prey to the demagogue turned tyrant. Their democracy is a society 'full of variety and disorder, dispensing a sort of equality to equals and unequals alike' (*Republic* VIII, 558C)."

This writer is not concerned here to debate the merits of the naturalistic philosophy. All that he is concerned to do is to point out that its concept of democracy is completely antithetical to the American concept, and that its prevalence amongst us constitutes a danger to our concept far greater and more imminent than confronts it from any other "ism" or any other source. *March* 27, 1939

ARISTOCRATIC DEMOCRACY

A reader somewhat testily challenges the notion that democracy "needs an aristocracy to rule it," and says that "democracy" and "aristocracy" are mutually exclusive terms. He wants to know the answer to that. Other readers may share his mood and his views, so here is what this writer believes to be the argument for "aristocratic-democracy":

(1) All men have the same nature and, therefore, the same fundamental desires or instincts. Of these, two of the strongest are self-preservation and self-assertion.

(2) No two of us possess precisely the same qualitative or quantitative capacities to satisfy those desires. Each one of us is "better" than "somebody" at "something," and not so "good" as "somebody else" at that "something," nor so "good" at "something" as he is at "something else."

(3) Thus, human beings are stratified in a strictly hierarchical manner with respect to any and all human activities from golf, prize fighting and contract bridge to art, literature,

science—and statecraft. In all these activities a comparatively small number of individuals are naturally qualified in an exceptional degree as compared with the general body of their fellows.

(4) Consequently, for the purpose of any joint action looking toward a common end, this minority is naturally more competent to direct such action than is the general mass. In all common human activities, therefore, it is the natural function of this minority to direct, and it is the natural function of the majority to be directed.

(5) When, therefore, men unite in any society or organization for any purpose, their success in achieving that purpose will depend upon their selection of those best qualified to direct the society and their willingness to submit to direction at the hands of those men.

(6) In such case the *will* of the society consists of two elements. One is the will of the body as a whole, which expresses itself in a general desire to accomplish a given purpose. The other is the will of the directing minority, which expresses itself in the choice of means and measures for its accomplishment. Success in its accomplishment will depend in the first instance upon the choice by the will of the mass as a whole of the true objective and, in the second instance, upon the choice by the directing minority of the means and measures best adapted to reaching that objective.

(7) It is always possible that either of these "wills" may err in the choice that it makes. Inasmuch as, however, the directing minority is *per hypothesim* the better informed, both as to objective and means, it is necessary that its will should prevail whenever conflict between the two happens to arise. While it is true that in such a conflict the mass *may* in fact be right, and the minority *may* be wrong, this will be, in the nature of things, an exceptional occurrence.

(8) What we call the "democratic" (as opposed to the oligarchic or the monarchic) system of government is based

upon the principle that the people as a whole have the right to determine who shall exercise the civil authority—that is, to whom shall be entrusted those governmental powers which are necessary to produce order, secure justice and promote the safety and welfare of the community as a whole.

(9) Democracy can be either "direct" or "representative." In direct democracy the people as a whole determine both the end to be sought and the means to attain the end—that is, the "people" themselves "govern." In such case the "will of the people" is what a majority of the people desire at any given time. If all the individuals constituting the people were equally qualified to determine what was good for the people and how it might be achieved, and if it were possible to ascertain the people's views on these matters with frequency, ease and accuracy, there is no reason why direct democracy could not function with success.

(10) As neither of these conditions is present in the case of a modern nation or state, direct democracy is not a practicable or effective form of government in these days, except in very small units, and even there only in a very limited way.

(11) Democracy can, in fact, successfully function only in a "representative" form. In that form the people as a whole lay down certain broad objectives and certain broad limitations, and then select individuals to whom they entrust all the necessary powers. The essential point in this method of government is that the "representative" so chosen shall express *his own* convictions by word and vote instead of taking orders from his constituents. The latter have both the right and the power to dismiss him and elect another in his place, if they so choose; but, to the extent that they assume and exercise any other control over him, democracy ceases to be representative and approaches the direct form, with corresponding loss of its efficiency.

(12) From which it follows that "democracy" must *have* an "aristocracy" (of capacity—not merely of wealth or birth).

It must *recognize* it, *respect* it, *elect* it and *accept* its direction —otherwise it will function unsuccessfully, and democracy which functions unsuccessfully invariably decays into some form of one-man absolutism. *September* 21, 1934

THE THEORY OF EQUALITY

One reason why there is so much confused talk and thought on the subject of democracy is that the notion is full of paradoxes. The principal of these is that most people suppose that democracy and equality are, in substance, the same thing, whereas they are, in operation, not merely the same thing, but opposites. Democracy, in fact, can live as a principle of social organization only by functioning through an aristocracy. This was the thesis of Señor Ortega y Gasset in his well-known *Revolt of the Masses.* If he be discounted, we have the same doctrine from a man whose "democracy" is beyond suspicion, Harold J. Laski. He tells us in his *Grammar of Politics* (quoted by Dr. Miriam Rooney in *Pluralism and the Law*), that "to adjust the temper of social effort to average men is to crown mediocrity. Rather we must recognize that quality is the possession of a few, and we must equate function with the possession of that quality"; and in another place, "a democracy, in other words, must, if it is to work, be an aristocracy by delegation"; and, in yet another place, "that self-government means, in the last resort, that final decisions must be made by elected persons." In short, Mr. Laski's conclusion is that so far as "equality" is concerned, man's natural desire for that must be satisfied by the freedom to express his opinion and to vote for his representative. As Dr. Rooney says, "In other words, a social discipline is achieved by assent of the electors to the decisions made by the social aristocracy for whom they have been permitted to vote."

In the mouth of Disraeli, for example—who believed that the "landed gentry" of England were the natural aristocracy and the natural people to govern England—such a doctrine would be laughed out of court as the height of Toryism, but it is an English radical, socialist in fact, that speaks it. There is, moreover, behind it the voice of the modern oracle, Science. Twenty-five years ago, Sir William Bateson told the British Association in his presidential address that men vary almost infinitely in qualities and capacities, and that no form of organization of men for any purpose which did not recognize that fact could endure. Nor did we need science to tell us that, for, outside of politics, no one questions the fact or its implications. As a matter of fact, it needs but a glance around us to show that in all the social relations other than that of politics men instinctively seek to organize themselves in a manner far more closely approaching the feudal idea than the common idea that we call democracy. Processes of business and finance illustrate this fact to all but a blind man. So, for that matter, does organized labor despite its democratic forms.

The essence of feudalism *in theory* was a hierarchy of power built upon a harmony of rights and duties reaching from top to bottom of human relations. It failed in practice because the possessors of power clung to their rights long after they had abandoned the thought of their duties. We have seen the same thing happen again and again in modern social and economic feudalism, for men are so constituted that power of any kind is a corrupting influence. Nevertheless, the fact remains that in all human relations, power to direct others must rest somewhere. The essence of democracy consists in the power of the many to strip from those who misuse it—or seem to misuse it—the power committed to them and to place it elsewhere.

For democracy of this kind to work, two qualities are essential in the people who choose it as a way of life. One is a deep sense of the dignity inherent in human personality—and particularly in the "other person." The other is an equally keen sense of the natural hierarchy existing among men. Against both "human nature" constantly fights. It is more "natural" for a man to assert his own personality than to respect another's, and for a man to have a good conceit of himself than to recognize another as his superior. In business, in industry, and in finance, grim necessity forces hierarchy upon men upon peril of swift and serious penalty. Not so in politics, where penalties are apt to be so deferred and recognized only when too late to avoid them.

All which is a roundabout statement of a very simple fact, which is that democracy, so far from being a form of social organization into which men *as they are* naturally fall, is, in reality, a "way of life" to be achieved only by men striving to become what they should be, and that unless men succeed measurably in this attempt, all the democratic forms in the world will be of no avail against the despotism which democracy is invoked to prevent.

Which, in turn, is only another way of saying that the democratic concept is comprehensible only by men who realize their kinship with the spiritual, and is meaningless to those, who with Professor Thorndike, regard human behavior as "inevitable as that of hydrogen." Dr. Holmes' *Darwinian virtues* cannot make it work. *December* 13, 1939

LIBERTY AND MAGNA CARTA

A few days ago there was celebrated the 726th anniversary of Magna Carta's signing. Probably the great mass of our people instinctively regard that document as indissolubly linked to our own charter of liberties by virtue of its *substance*, notwithstanding the fundamental difference between the two in the matter of *form*. That instinct is entirely ness is understood, or even, for many, perhaps most of us, suspected. There is a reason and a solid one and it may be useful to set it in the light.

Magna Carta was in form a feudal, and in no sense whatever a democratic affair. It was an expression by a feudal lord—King John—of his recognition of certain rights on the part of his vassals—the barons—as well as of the Church which was *not* among his vassals. It was essentially a *recognition* rather than a new grant. The rights which it recognized were no new ideas. They were implicit in the spirit of the time. The time was the beginning of the thirteenth century when the great flowering of the medieval Christian philosophical synthesis was imminent. From the signing of Magna Carta to the death of Thomas Aquinas was but fifty-nine years, and in those years were laid down *in form* the basic principles upon which rest the whole question of the *personality* of man and his consequent right to *liberty*.

The notion of *personality* rested then in the Christian religion as its only foundation. It has no other foundation today. As Gordon O'Neill writes (in the *San Francisco Monitor*):

> The ancients had the word "*persona.*" They did not have the significance that Christianity gave to the word, namely, that each unique and individual human being had not only spiritual immortality, but a destiny in the next life in which his entire being, body and soul, might have supernatural enjoyment of God. This destiny

is dependent upon each man's employment of his time on earth. To use his time well, he must be free in the exercise of certain rights to do good and forego evil, which rights are inalienable from his nature. It received for the first time a full philosophic expression in Thomas' work, and, what is, perhaps, more significant for us, the foundations of what we recognize as our democracy were fully implicit and in no small degree explicit in that work, and this at a time when society was feudal. There is no trace of "democracy" in Magna Carta's clauses. But there is clear recognition of certain elemental personal freedoms which were deeply imbedded in the traditions and customs of the time. It is that recognition which is the *substance* of the great Carta, and gives it a real interest for us.

Moreover, it sets in sharp relief the extraordinary character of the American contribution to man's freedom, for that contribution was not merely fundamental, but strictly revolutionary—that is, re-volutionary, a return to something elemental but forgotten. Four centuries after Magna Carta English kings were asserting their "divine right" and in the Tudor days the administration of justice had left much to be desired for More was the first Chancellor who refused to accept gifts from litigants. Absolute monarchy was the rule on the European continent, almost to the day on which the Declaration of Independence was signed. Yet the Preamble to that Declaration in one tremendous series of affirmations went back at one step to the foundations of the matter. This with no preliminaries and no precedents in the world, with nothing in sight to prepare men for what was coming. There is nothing in political history with which it is comparable. There is not the least reason to suspect that Thomas Jefferson had any acquaintance with Thomas Aquinas. There are those who believe that he had met the views of Robert Bellarmine through Filmer's *Patriarca.* But however and wherever he found the notions of the Preamble, the fact is indisputable that its essential phrases can be matched phrase for phrase in the writings of the thirteenth century philosopher Thomas—this despite the fact that one must strain to the extreme limit the term "Christian" to apply it to Jefferson!

To many, perhaps, it is no recommendation of the Preamble to point out its correspondence with the medieval Christian and philosophic synthesis, however that correspondence may have come about. The fact remains, nevertheless, that no doctrine of personal rights can be based upon anything other than a doctrine of *personality,* and that no doctrine of personality can be predicated upon anything other than a definite doctrine of man as a creature of God made in His image and likeness. Nor can democracy *as a principle* have any other basis in logic. It is the imperishable glory of America to have for the first time taken that logic, boldly and courageously stated, as the very cornerstone of its civil order. The kinship of Magna Carta and the Declaration is in that common element, and in nothing else.

June 25, 1941

DEMOCRACY AND LIBERTY

I

Another symptom of change in our civil system is in the domain of law. There are in it potentialities perhaps even more dangerous than in the first. Both are oriented toward the same terminus or goal, absolute Statism, that is, absolute power of the State over the person, which is the negation of personal liberty. It is also the negation of the fundamental principle of all government laid down in the opening sentences of the Preamble to the Declaration of Independence. This symptom is apparent in the trend of court decisions in the last decade, and still more evident in the development of legal philosophy during the last generation in our law schools.

In a short but remarkably compact and lucid book published last year *(The Twilight of Individual Liberty)*, Dr. Hamilton Vreeland, Jr., a well-known member of the New York bar, traces the extension of Federal power over the citizen as exemplified by decisions of the Supreme Court from its creation to the present day. He discusses three stages in this growth, one from the beginning of the Court in 1790 to the death of John Marshall in 1835, the second covering the century to 1935 and the third the last ten years. He describes the three stages as follows:

> The first is the period of Federal supremacy concerning delegated powers of the Federal government and with natural law protecting individual liberty. The second is the period of a balanced and substantially equal dual sovereignty, with natural law and the due process clause of the Fifth Amendment and later due process and equal protection clauses of the Fourteenth Amendment protecting individual liberty both procedurally and substantively. The third is the period of the domination of the legal philosophy of Mr. Justice Holmes with enormous expansion of Federal power at the expense of the state and of individual liberty, and considerable expansion of state power at the expense of individual rights, and with the due process and equal protection clauses being applied little more than procedurally.

The "police power" was not among those granted to the Federal government by the several states. Today the Federal government is exercising enormous "police powers," all of which it has acquired under the interstate commerce clause of the Constitution with the approval of the Court. The point that Mr. Vreeland is emphasizing in the foregoing passage is the distinction between the substantive and the procedural (sometimes called "adjectival") clauses of the Amendments, and the distinction is both fundamental and of great importance. The simplest way to describe it is to point out that the "procedural" provisions are concerned exclusively with the equality of all persons before the law in all the forms and processes of its enforcement. It is the "substantive" content that matters. The simplest way to make clear that importance of the shift in the third stage is to point out that until its arrival the words "due process of law" were interpreted generally as expressing certain fundamental principles underlying all law, and a general concept indistinguishable from that to which the term "natural law" has been for centuries applied. The essence of the Holmes philosophy is a flat denial of the existence of any such thing, and it is the trend of the court's decision in the third stage away from its recognition that is the disturbing development which is the theme of Mr. Vreeland's study. He has closely examined the more important decisions of the last few years, and while his pages are not the easiest reading for the layman they offer no serious difficulty to anyone at all acquainted with the first principles of the subject. The whole question turns on whether or not there is a "moral" law, a law of right and wrong, a law for human nature, a law as unchanged and unchanging as is human nature, governing man's conscience to which all man-made laws would conform, or at least, should not violate.

That the High Court has perceptibly moved away from its former positions or attitudes toward the concept of this moral law is clearly demonstrated by Mr. Vreeland in Chapter 5 which concludes (save for notes) his volume. This chapter is entitled "Democratic Despotism" and deserves most careful reading. It is noteworthy that this form of absolutism he regards as the worst of all, in which opinion the present writer fully concurs.

April 30, 1945

II

On Monday last, as the reader may recall, this writer noted what Mr. Vreeland had to say (in his book *The Twilight of Individual Liberty*) of the encroachment of governmental authority upon the liberties of the citizen, reflected in the decisions of the Supreme Court in the last decade. It is worth while to look at the "philosophy" which underlies this trend of judicial opinion. It reflects a fundamental change in men's thinking upon *law* itself, which has long been maturing. This writer will attempt to describe its essential nature as simply as he can.

In a word, it consists in the substitution of *mores* for *morals* as the basis of *law*. Both terms spring from a single etymological root but differ radically in meaning, and it is the difference in meaning that is the all-important point. What do we mean by *morals* and what by *mores?*

Morals connotes the concept of *right* and *wrong* as recognized by human *conscience*. That in turn connotes the concept of a *law* establishing norms of right and wrong, which is binding upon conscience. From time immemorial men have recognized and accepted the existence of such a law. For many centuries philosophers and legislators have recognized it as the basis of human law-making and have called it "natural law"—the law for human "nature," that part of the divine law concerning human actions, recognizable in its essentials by human intelligence as an induction from man's knowledge of the order of the cosmos, received through his senses—a law, true, permanent and binding upon all men at all times, and, therefore, the ultimate basis of all human law-making.

What is meant by the term *mores*, and in what consists its relation to law in modern thinking? In the searching analysis of *Mr. Justice Cardozo's relativism* (in *The New Scholasticism*, January, 1945), Dr. Miriam Theresa Rooney quotes Judge Cardozo as follows concerning the laws of a state:

"They have neither their roots in the customary forms and methods of business and fellowship, the prevalent convictions of equity and justice, the complex of belief and practice which we style the *mores* of the day." Upon this she comments:

Holding that the whole common law system as developed by the judges has been built on the assumption that it is an expression of the *mores,* he declares that "law accepts as the pattern of its justice the mortality of the community whose conduct it assumes to regulate. . . . It will follow, or strive to follow, the principles and practices of the men and women of the community whom the social mind would rank as intelligent and virtuous." Now it is the judge's function to interpret this social conscience in formulating the rules of law. "Where shall we look for the revelations of the folk-spirit," asks Judge Cardozo, "if not in the prevailing standards of utility and welfare?" And since morals and folkways change, the judge tends to a result that attaches legal obligation to the folkways by reading the prevailing social mind, as exemplified in the life about him, says Judge Cardozo. It is in this way that manners and customs—the *mores,* are to be understood as a compelling source of law.

If *mores* are the "source" of law where is the "source" of *mores?* William James gives us the answer. In his essay on "A Moral Equivalent for War" he bids us look to men's "prides and shames" for that equivalent. Here is the heart of the matter. The "prides and shames" of which he is talking differ radically from the promptings of conscience. If man's prides and shames will speak to him in terms of what is and what is not "done"; his conscience says "Thou must" or "Thou must not"; one looks out upon an ever-changing scene for its norm, the other looks into an unchanging body of truth. "We are back with Heraclitus," says Judge Cardozo. "Nothing is absolute. All is fluid and changeable. There is an endless 'becoming.' " To sum it up, the essence of the new "philosophy" of law is its exclusion of all enduring principle from its space and it is in this that mores and not morals are the source and the norm of the "new jurisprudence" which has, as Mr. Vreeland showed in his book, expressed itself in these latter days through our courts.

In such a theory of jurisprudence there is no room for the principles laid down in the Declaration's Preamble, no sure guarantee for human rights and all the room in the world for the tyranny of the totalitarian state, the complete negation of personal liberty. If this theory shall finally establish itself in our civil system our government structure, Constitution, judiciary, legislature and executive will become at best empty forms and at worst apt instruments of ruthless despotism. And this theory is already solidly entrenching itself in our schools of law.

May 2, 1945

III

The other day this writer pointed out that it was necessary for our people to make a fundamental distinction concerning "democracy" in its relation to liberty. Now he will attempt to make clear its nature and importance. He has for a long time been fumbling clumsily with its formulation. Fortunately, he finds in Hamilton Vreeland's book recently discussed in this column *(The Twilight of Individual Liberty)*, a statement in brief and lucid terms and will borrow it wholesale.

Frequently in recent years this writer has referred to what he has called our seeming obsession with democratic *forms* and our apparent confidence that they furnished a guarantee of individual liberty and has insisted that they could be made instruments of despotic tyranny—which is perfectly true, but poorly stated. Also he has viewed the confusion in our public mind as one of "form" and "substance"—which is also in a sense true, but also imperfectly expressed. The merit in Mr. Vreeland's statement of the distinction is that it is placed exactly where it belongs and that is in the concept of "liberty." There are two kinds of liberty. One is political, and is the right of the citizen to participate in the government as a voter, and —if he can get the necessary votes—as an official. The other kind of liberty is *individual,* i.e., *personal,* and this depends upon a limitation of governmental authority over his action. Its essence is the possession by him of certain "rights" against government which government is bound to respect. It is the confusion of the two kinds that is apparently rife in our public opinion, and especially in what we call "Liberal" or "Progressive" circles.

The Greek "democracy" stopped at *political* liberty. The citizen (only a part of the population were "citizens") could vote and run for office, but the "government" (the state) was absolute; there were no limitations upon its powers. So, too, with the Roman state when the senate and the consuls ruled. We know what happened to both. The notion of *individual* liberty came into the world with Christianity and our "democracy" was built upon it and built in the most explicit and formal way. Its essence is the limitation of state power over the citizen and the possession by the citizen of "rights" which may not be violated by the state. There is, thus, the most fundamental difference between the two concepts of "democracy" and of government itself; yet there is fundamental similarity in their "forms." Both rest upon citizen suffrage as the base of all authority, and both express the public will under majority rule. Our "form" recognizes the ultimate omnipotence of that will for under our Constitution itself there is no limitation on its powers of amendment. If the "people" so willed it, it could in strict legal form sweep away legislature and judiciary and establish an absolute monarchy.

Thus, at the last, personal liberty depends not upon outward forms but upon the general conscience of the people itself, its concept of the person, his nature and his relation with his fellows. For the Greek and the Roman, the State was the "end" and the citizen the "means"; for the founders of our civil order, the person was the "end" and the State the "means"; the State exists for the sake of the person and not the person for the sake of the State. Now the plain fact is that there has long been going on amongst us a change in the *conscience* of certain opinion and especially in "Liberal," "Progressive," "Left-Wing" circles in the direction of emphasizing the importance of "society" as against that of the person. The "Instrumentalist" philosophy has gone practically the whole distance in this direction, and its logic implies absolutism of the "democratic" state. All the left-wing drift is in the same direction, that is, of sinking the person in the state. It is a drift toward the old Greek and Roman concept of "liberty"—*political liberty*—away from the American concept of *individual* liberty that is afoot on the "Left," a drift of which public opinion is as yet largely unconscious because the "democratic" *form* structure is not so far in question, and has sustained no *visible* change.

It is not in *forms* that this change has occurred but in the use to which the forms have been put and the validation by the judicial "form" of that use that is the point. The "police power" is the most important arm of the State and the Constitution does not give the Federal Government this power nor was it intended that it should. As we have seen in the last decade, and as Mr. Vreeland has pointed out, a series of judicial interpretations of the Constitution's (so-called) interstate commerce clause has placed in the government's hands police powers of a sweeping character, the dimensions of which are still quite unsuspected by the general public. Moreover, the logic supporting these interpretations has implications still less suspected, much less generally understood, implications of which further extensions of this power to a point where there would remain for the citizen but little of the "rights" that our government was founded to protect.

It is high time that our people generally should recognize

what is happening for what it is and ask themselves whether it is what they want. Their first job should be to get clearly into their heads the distinction between *political* liberty and *personal* liberty and how the same "democratic" structure can be made to produce either.

May 11, 1945

CHRISTMAS AND DEMOCRACY

Christmas finds us in the throes of a war more terrible in its potentialities than any in living memory. Yet for all its terrors we yield ourselves for a while to what we call the "Christmas spirit." Its essence is "good will," which is another name for love. There are two kinds of love, the love of desire and the love of good will. The love of desire—the medievals called it the *amor concupiscentiae*—is beyond our control; the other—*amor benevolentiae*—is purely a matter of will. There was once an abbot at the head of a monastery who was a stickler for order, for accuracy, and for discipline—a holy man, doubtless, but a good deal of a trial to his community. Among the lay brothers was a man whose piety and patience were patent—but his fingers were all thumbs and his notion of time was distinctly vague, with the result that he was frequently under reprimand by the superior. One day the abbot, having severely dressed him down, had a sudden interior light. "You don't like me, do you, Brother Anselm?" The brother with his usual happy smile replied: "No, Father Abbot, but I love you." It is that love which at Christmas times stirs in people's hearts for a little while only; the other kind moves as it lists, is fragile even though it may last, and is not very productive of good works.

One of the things that we overlook in our continuous chatter about "democracy" is that not all the elections or parliaments in the world will avail to make democracy "work" without a "soul," and that its soul must be this "good will." Not that we must all completely forget self and think and act solely for others. But the "other fellow," his rights and his interests, must have place in our scheme of social life, so that accommodation of his rights and his interests with our own shall be a natural process in our daily lives and not merely a temporary flaming up in a great emergency. What we mean by democracy will not work in the absence of that spirit. Not only will it not work, but it will necessarily degenerate into its antithesis—totalitarianism—for democracy is always in danger of that. Totalitarianism under democratic forms is the worst form of tyranny, for unlike personal absolutism it cannot be "tempered by assassination."

Do you mean, the reader probably is asking, that if we are to live in a democratic way we must have the "Christmas spirit" all year round? Yes, some of it, enough of it at least to drive out its contrary, group selfishness, group hates and group conflicts. All these things are fatal to democratic life. Out of these develops the totalitarian state. Democracy is not a stable thing; it must be continuously achieved, and its achievement is a work of the spirit and not of machinery, however ingeniously and elaborately devised it may have been.

What went wrong in the world during the last century and a half when democratic machinery was installed for the first time on a large scale on the European continent, with all the parliamentary and election paraphernalia? Something certainly did, and it is interesting to note that it was in the nineteenth century that there arose a highly significant doctrine, that of absolute "non-intervention" by one state in the affairs of another. What has that to do with the "Christmas spirit" and democracy? Just this: It is tantamount to a denial that *charity* (which is the same as the "Christmas spirit") has no place in international relations, and the logic of that applies to a nation's internal order with equal force. A few days ago Miss Dorothy Thompson inveighing against that doctrine called it—surely by a slip of the tongue!—a reversion to the Middle Ages. The fact is that it was a development of the "bankrupt liberalism" of the nineteenth century, which the Middle Ages would have summarily repudiated, as is aptly demonstrated by the fact that the "principle of nonintervention" was Proposition No. 62 formally condemned in the Papal Syllabus of Errors (1864), the "medieval" quality of which document would probably be admitted by its severest critics! What went wrong in the world in the last century and a half was precisely the formal disappearance of *charity* from the political and economic relations of men, the penalty for which we are all paying today.

We can take the message of the angels in the Christmas Gospel in either of its translations—"Peace on earth to men of good will" or "Peace on earth and good will to men"; the meaning is essentially the same, namely, the inseparability of "peace" and "good will." Both peace and good will are essential to the democratic way, which is only another way of saying that religion alone can give life to that way; for there can be no peace and no good will without religion.

December 24, 1941

LAW: CONSTITUTION AND CHANGE

THE SUPREME COURT ISSUE

I

The Civil War was assuredly the first really great crisis in the history of the United States. The crisis in which we are now landed is less sensational in its visible effects, but is in one respect even more fundamental. The Civil War controversy, whatever may have been its remote cause, social or economic, in its essence concerned the right of a state or states to secede from the Union. There have been and there are today not a few who regard the logic of the South's position as having been better than that of the North. It was, however, a debate that in theory at least was within the ambit of law, even though it was finally settled by force.

The controversy over the proposal to pack the Supreme Court contains no threat of arms. But it carries a threat to the very heart of our entire governmental structure, and in this respect it constitutes a crisis unique in our history and big with consequences of the most serious kind. Not only is that the case, but it also involves a violation of the most elementary principles of natural justice. The proposal is made in the name of a great party occupying the seat of power and elected to that seat by a tremendous majority of the voters. It is an event without precedent, so far as this writer is aware, in the history of democratic government. More than that, the proposal differs in principle not at all from one for which the signers of the Declaration of Independence indicted George III, listing it among the crimes which forced his American subjects to armed revolt.

If that seems an extreme statement, one has but to look at the facts. What difference is there between the enlargement of the Supreme Court and the appointment of additional judges with the avowed object of obtaining a desired interpretation of the law, and the removal and replacement of judges by the English king for the same purpose?

There is none. Both constitute the same violation of natural justice, the first principle of which is judicial impartiality. The first beginnings of civil law were in the submission of disputes to the arbitration of a third party. Morey's classic treatise on Roman Law says on the point, "The statement that civil jurisdiction had its origin in arbitration is verified by the earliest forms of civil procedure with which we are acquainted." The essence of arbitration is impartiality. A court's independence is the means, and impartiality is the end. The entire judicial process hangs on that principle. The Court proposal strikes directly at the heart of the entire judicial process.

In our system the Court is the guardian of the people's will against the usurpation of either legislative or executive. It is also the guardian of the people's rights. Above all, it is the guardian of the rights of minorities. Minority rights are the very ark of the covenant in our political structure. The great danger in a democratic system is that which arises from a temporary majority, expressing itself through a temporarily triumphant party. It was precisely to obviate that danger that the Constitution was framed and its amendment made none too easy. De Tocqueville, who was a stout believer in democracy, warned that anarchy would be the consequence of an unrestrained majority. *May* 21, 1937

II

It is not necessary to question the good faith of the President either in making his proposals for changes in the federal judiciary or in advancing his reasons for support of those changes to arrive at the conclusion that it is not the age of the Supreme Court justices, nor the congestion of their calendar, nor their summary treatment of petitions for review that is the matter. It is the opinions of the justices themselves—rather, of certain of the justices. The President's own words are frank enough on the point. He said: "A constant and systematic addition of younger blood will vitalize the courts and better equip them to recognize and apply the essential concepts of justice in the light of the needs and the facts of an ever-changing world."

This writer cannot help wondering whether, if the late Oliver Wendell Holmes were still on the bench at the age of say 90, the idea would have been phrased in just those words! However, take them as they stand and analyze their content. What do they really mean? Either they mean nothing, or they mean that it is the proper function of the Supreme Court to change its interpretation of the country's organic law to meet the "needs and facts of an ever-changing world." This writer submits that this doctrine is utterly incompatible with the very heart of our governmental system, and, if applied, would destroy its very essence. That essence was the *complete* separation of powers—law making, law administration and law interlocking of functions between the three departments.

In providing a judiciary, the organic law was careful to impose no limitation on the judicial power. The Constitution's makers were careful to limit that power to the natural function of a judiciary which is to declare the law as it stands, and not to make it, or pass upon its wisdom. They were well aware of the fallibility of man and never supposed that the Court would not make a mistake or reverse its judgment. But they were quite clear that, right or wrong, the Court's decisions should be the law. They provided the machinery—impeachment—for removal of an unjust judge. They provided the machinery—amendment of the Constitution—for changing the law when the people wanted to do something that the Court declared to violate the law as it stood. Having done that, they took the risks of human nature. There is no safe tampering in the slightest with the system thus set up.

Moreover, there are other risks that the Founders took. They took the risk of improper appointments by the executive power and their ratification by the Senate. They took it because they assumed that judicial appointments would be made not upon grounds of opinions on controverted questions of public policy, but upon grounds of character and capacity in the profession of the law. They assumed that the executive would appoint only men of that caliber and that, if he did not, the Senate would refuse to confirm the executive action. The risk in that assumption is, at least in theory, as great as the risk previously mentioned.

Finally, they balanced the risk of judicial incapacity from age against the necessity of complete independence assured by life tenure, and took the risk. It cannot be said that the history of the Court until now shows that they erred in this. The concept of "nine old men" is distinctly a modern phenomenon, of which we heard little in the lifetime of Mr. Justice Holmes.

This writer is not, as his readers well know, a lawyer, and he is perfectly willing to accept the assurance that what the

Administration proposes to do can be done within the framework of the Constitution. But there is a plain implication in the President's own words that it is not vigorous youth that is the envisaged need of the Supreme Bench, but a different view of the principles of interpretation by the Court of the nation's organic law. That is a most serious matter. It is difficult to imagine anything more serious than the possibilities it holds of danger to the elemental rights of the humblest citizen. When the time comes that judges are appointed for their opinions on great questions of public policy, we might as well scrap both Court and Constitution, vest supreme power in the legislature and take the consequences. The first step in that direction makes the last inevitable.

February 8, 1937

III

Among the paradoxes of democracy as represented in our system of government is that, while the majority must rule, it is absolutely necessary that its rule shall be restrained within certain limits. Without such restraint, we should have a totalitarian state both in form and fact, in flat contravention of the principles laid down in the Declaration of Independence. The only purpose of the Constitution is to prescribe those limits. Bryce called the Court

> the conscience of the people who have resolved to restrain themselves from hasty or unjust action by placing their representatives under the guaranty of the minority, who, when threatened by the impatient vehemence of a majority, can appeal to this permanent law, find the interpreter and enforcer thereof in a court set high above the assaults of faction.

We are accustomed to regard Great Britain, France and ourselves as the strictly democratic nations. Yet, only in this country is there a "conscience" such as Bryce describes. The highest court in France has no power to invalidate a law passed by the Senate and Chamber of Deputies because it conflicts with the Constitution. Nor has the highest court in Great Britain. Furthermore, the protection of the minority here is not absolute. A majority can always have its way about anything if it can persuade the people to amend the Constitution.

It is this which stamps the present suggestion of packing the Supreme Court as lacking. We are told by its proponents that the country has voted overwhelmingly for the Administration's policies. On this premise, amending the Constitution should be as easy of prompt accomplishment as was repeal of the Eighteenth Amendment. But we are told that the process is too long and difficult; there is the so-called Child Labor Amendment still hanging fire after twelve years. And on that score we are asked to change the Court so as to change the interpretation of the law, instead of changing the law.

How are we going to settle the matter? The answer we give to that question will throw a good deal of light, too, on at least one other thing, that is, the character of our public education. We shall see whether our public schools have done the most important job the law allows them to do, namely, train our future citizens in the knowledge of their governmental system, the principles on which it rests and the place of the citizen in it. It is devoutly to be hoped that these schools have done and are doing a better job than have our law schools, if one may judge from some of the things that graduates of those schools have been saying about the Constitution and the Court in these latter days. *February* 19, 1937

IV

Some days ago the National Education Convention was in session in New Orleans. Thirty-one professors, including representatives of Columbia University, New York University and Teachers College in New York, signed a long telegram to the President commending his proposals concerning the Supreme Court. In the course of this dispatch the signatories advanced some interesting ideas, among which are the following:

(1) The problem now before the country is to reconstitute the membership of the Supreme Court to make it "sensitive to the needs of the time and thus to preserve the spirit of constitutional government."

(2) The Supreme Court "is not only a court of last resort but also an instrument for the interpretation and development of the fundamental law of the land. This second and superior function confers upon the Court vast legislative powers and heavy responsibilities for shaping national policy."

(3) The legal mind is tied to the past; the Court should have some lay members representing various areas of interest and outlook, such as corporate business, farming, labor, civil liberties, humanitarian interests, national and racial minorities, international relations, social legislation, culture and education, and scholarship in American constitutional history, government and economics.

(4) The Supreme Court's rulings during the past generation are due to the fact that the great majority of the justices have been associated with the corporations. The Court should not have more than two members with such affiliations.

The signers of the telegram identify themselves as "We, a group of educators. . . ." Have we here a partial hint of an answer to the question as to what our schools and colleges are teaching with respect to our government system—a question, by the way, which this writer has put several times, and to which he would much like to have an answer? When a group of educators tells us that the "superior function" of the Supreme Court is to legislate and that this function confers the necessary powers, one is tempted to ask—"What and when *is* an educator, and what *is* education?"

Here are thirty-one professors—Columbia's own John Dewey is among them—who conceive the main function of the judiciary to be legislative. How many more professors are of the same opinion? Is it not time for us to find out? Can we have an investigation say, by the General Education Board, from which we could find out what our colleges are teaching their students concerning the elemental principles of the Declaration of Independence and the Constitution? It ought to be possible to devise a questionnaire on a not too elaborate scale (with a provision, if desired, for secret balloting on a "yes" or "no" principle) from the answers to which one could learn, for instance, whether or not college professors generally believe in the existence of the unalienable rights mentioned in the Declaration. Donald Richberg tells us that he does not. How many educators agree with him? How many educators hold with the thirty-one that the main function of the judiciary is to legislate? How many hold it proper that judges should be appointed because of their known opinions on the matters expected to be in controversy before their court?

It need not be a lengthy affair. Those three questions would do very well for a start, for the answers could contain far-reaching implications which could readily be developed from the bare affirmatives and negatives. Nor could any professor legitimately object to being polled on these points, especially as all precautions could be taken to preserve anonymity.

These are days when almost everything is being investigated. Nothing is more important in a democracy than is the education of its citizens. Next to the training of character, nothing is more important to the education of its citizens than is knowledge and understanding of the political system of which they are expected to be a part, and of the principle upon which that system is based. No government in this world is founded upon principles higher than those asserted in the second paragraph of the Declaration of Independence as self-evident truths, and our Supreme Court (see *Gulf-Colorado & Santa Fe* v. *Ellis,* 165 U.S. Oct. Term 1896) has laid down that the Declaration is the "thought and the spirit" of which the Constitution is the "body and the letter."

No language is more worthy of frequent and thoughtful consideration than these words of Mr. Justice Matthews speaking for this court in *Yick Wo* v. *Hopkins,* 118 U.S. 356, 369:

> When we consider the nature and theory of our institution of government, the principles upon which they are supposed to rest, and review the history of their development, we are constrained to conclude that they do not mean to leave room for the play and action of purely personal and arbitrary power. The first official action of this nation declared the foundation of a government in these words: "We hold these truths to be self-evident, and that all men are created equal, that they are endowed by their Creator with certain unalienable Rights, that among these are Life, Liberty and the pursuit of Happiness." While such declaration of principles may not have the force of organic law, or be made the basis of judicial decisions as to the limits of right and duty, and while in all cases, reference must be made to the organic law for such limits, yet the latter is but the body and the letter of which the former is the thought and spirit, and it is always safe to read the letter of the Constitution in the spirit of the Declaration of Independence. *No duty rests more imperatively upon the courts than the enforcement of those constitutional provisions intended to secure the equality of rights which is the foundation of free government.* (Emphasis supplied.)

March 3, 1937

V

Not a few people seem to be confused in their thinking concerning the controversy over the Supreme Court by the appeal to the analogy of Great Britain. Parliament in Britain has unlimited power to legislate without interference from the courts. Why should not Congress do the same? It may be helpful to repeat the fundamental distinction between Great Britain's system and our own. Simple as it is, many do not seem to appreciate its force.

It rests upon one fact, namely, that we have a written organic law from which Congress derives its powers, while Britain has none. Our Constitution not merely confers certain powers on Congress, but also lays upon it certain restrictions. It says in terms that it may do certain things and may not do certain other things. It may do only the things the Constitution permits. It may not do certain other things, because it has not been granted the power to do them, although it is not in terms prohibited from doing them; it must not do certain things, because they are specifically prohibited. It is the creature and the subject of the organic law of the nation—the federal Constitution.

The British Parliament, by a long evolution expressed in a series of statutes over several centuries, is the supreme legislative authority in the land. These statutes, up to and including the law which emasculated the House of Lords, are the British equivalent of our organic law, and behind them the House of Commons is absolute in its powers. What, then, is the "British Constitution" of which so much is heard from time to time?

The easiest way to describe it is to say that it consists of anything that the British voters may happen to approve at a general election, fought upon a controverted question of public policy. The House of Commons could tomorrow pass a bill abolishing the British monarchy. The House of Lords could reject the bill. The premier could force the king to dissolve Parliament and an election would follow. If the voters returned a majority supporting the premier, the Commons could repass the bill, the House of Lords would be compelled to approve it and the king would have to give the royal assent of his own deposition. That, in substance, is the British Constitution and that is the way it works.

The British courts deal with the statutes of the land in precisely the same way as our Supreme Court deals with the Constitution. Their task is to interpret and define these laws as our Supreme Court's task is to interpret and define the Constitution. The House of Lords, through its law lords, is the highest court in the land. In both cases the judicial function is the same, for it is the fundamental function of the judiciary according to its very nature. Because of that nature, the judiciary must be free from all interference or control. This is an axiom in Great Britain, and it should be an axiom in this country, for the fundamental liberties of the citizen are absolutely dependent upon its observance. The slightest tampering with the freedom of the courts in the performance of their natural function, either by the legislative or executive power, would be instantly rejected in Great Britain, as it ought to be here.

As a consequence of the British system, any Parliamentary election may be equivalent to a national convention amending the Constitution. In the last thirty years more than one election has so functioned. It is necessary to note that the last great constitutional change, the act stripping the House of Lords of practically all its *legislative* powers, was passed under a threat that, if the peers did not consent to their own sterilization, the King would "pack" the upper House with enough peers to swamp the recalcitrants. There is no analogy here with proposal to "pack" the Court. The question was one wholly in the *legislative* order, and did not in any way touch the *judicial* function. The operation was wholly within the powers of the people. Nor did it touch the judicial power of the Lords. Moreover, the act was merely the final stage of a long evolution—at least a century—in which the upper House had become gradually more yielding to the popular will as expressed by the Commons. Had it not been exceptionally obstinate in opposition to Mr. Asquith's liberal measures, the act might not have been proposed.

These are things well to bear in mind as we fight out the present battle for independence of the federal courts.

March 5, 1937

VI

As the debate over the federal courts is apparently to be brought directly to the people by radio addresses *pro* and *con*, it is well to keep in mind the one main question to which all else is subordinate. There is, happily, no dispute as to what that question is, for both sides have frankly accepted it.

That question is: Shall we pack the Supreme Court so that it will decide constitutional questions in the way that the majority party desires, so that Congress can legislate in the way that the party thinks the country needs and wants?

That that is the question is clear from the fact that supporters of the proposal demand that the Court be "unpacked." That is only another way of demanding that it shall construe the Constitution as they wish. The issue is thus plainly, in fact nakedly, joined—a most fortunate thing.

Now, the very essence of the judicial concept is impartiality —not infallibility. A judge is impartial so long as he interprets the law according to its terms as he sees them; he becomes partial when he departs from that rule, for any reason whatsoever. He is not concerned with the wisdom or the folly of the law; he is concerned only with what it means as he sees it, not what it ought or ought not to mean. When he becomes partial for *any* reason, he commits the most grievous sin that he can commit—a sin against the nature of his office. Thus, to pack a court in order to accomplish a purpose, however good, is an immoral act *per se* and, therefore, inadmissible under any circumstances.

That is the act that it is proposed to commit. The proposal is supported by various arguments all unsound.

There are those who frankly accept the immorality of the act and in so many words say that the end justifies the means. "To do a great right, do a little wrong," according to some of these, is "the voice of Democracy." We need not argue *that.*

There are those who say that the Supreme Court has usurped the power to invalidate congressional laws because the Constitution in terms did not grant that power and the Founders did not intend it to be granted. Whatever the Founders intended or did not intend, the power is plainly granted in the Constitution, which would be meaningless if it were not. The proof is that the Constitution said to Congress "That shalt not" do thus and so, and there is and can be no power other than in the Supreme Court to say whether Congress has obeyed the Constitution. The Court must be the keystone of the whole structure, or it is nothing. There is no escape from that conclusion.

There are those who say that there is a precedent for what is proposed, that the Court has been packed in the past. Even were this true, there can be no precedent to justify the repetition of an immoral act.

There are those who say that we cannot wait to accomplish the desired reforms while we amend the Constitution, and that we must take this short road to avoid a violent revolution. The argument condemns itself not only on the ground of immorality, but on the ground of common sense. If there is so great a demand for the reforms, the passage of a constitutional amendment should be accomplished without much trouble or delay. Others have been so accomplished and in the recent past—why not this one? If the election of 1936 proves the demand, it also proves that it can be satisfied by constitutional means.

The truth is that the issue before the people is one of plain right and wrong in their simplest forms. It is not a question of ways and means, of customs, conventions or traditions; it is a question of the most vital importance to individual human liberty and democracy itself, especially to our concept of democracy. Democracy is, after all, only a means to liberty. Liberty depends upon law, and justice is the object of law. Law is and must be what the courts say it is. If either executive or legislature undertake to tell the courts what to say, we have the beginning of absolutism. Our governmental system is founded upon denial of absolutism—the first government in the world's history so to stand.

If the people of this country permit the Supreme Court to be either "packed" or "unpacked" they will have signed away their ultimate protection against absolutism—whether at the hands of a majority or a dictator will matter little.

March 8, 1937

RELATIVE TRUTH AND THE LAW

As Buffon remarked, a man and his style are one, so it is natural that Mr. Justice Frankfurter's first formal opinion should have attracted wide interest as giving the public a taste of his quality. Style is very much a matter of verbal selection, verbal arrangement and of overtones, and when linked to clear thinking it results in delivery of full freight of meaning at the terminals of the reader or of the hearer to whom the meaning is consigned. But the overtones are frequently as important as the actual theme, or the descant on the theme, for they suggest backgrounds or hinterlands in the meaning left unexpressed in the theme itself. Even a single word will sometimes like a lightning flash light up those hinterlands.

Referring to the dictum of Marshall that the power to tax is the power to destroy, Mr. Justice Frankfurter characterized it as "partly a flourish of rhetoric and partly because the intellectual fashion of the times indulged a free use of absolutes. . . ." It seems to the present writer that that noun "absolutes" might suggest not a little by way of a philosophic hinterland and that the suggestion is heightened by the Justice's later reference to the comment of the late Justice Holmes upon the Marshall dictum, "not while this court sits." As everyone knows, Justice Holmes was a complete relativist who never really retracted his youthful remark that truth was what the majority thought, if it had power to enforce it. Nor is the suggestion weakened by the reference to Lincoln's phrase, "pernicious abstractions." All three phrases taken together might seem to some to exhale a definitely relativist attitude, perhaps no more than a slant, toward the Constitution and its interpretation.

Now the importance of any such suggestion, however erroneous, is that the "absolute" is the great bugbear of the modern school of philosophy in this country. By the "absolute" is meant (the word has come to have an unfavorable connotation!) *any form of unchanging truth.* That notion is fundamentally unacceptable to our American philosophers of today, for the one and only *constant* thing that they recognize in all nature is change. In this they are faithful disciples of Heraclitus, who said it all many centuries before they did. To convict a man of holding any "absolute" whatever nowadays is to exclude him from intellectual society.

This writer does not for one moment mean to suggest that Mr. Justice Frankfurter's philosophy is necessarily that, or anything like that of, say, the "Dewey Society" in all its completeness. What he wishes to suggest is that so far as both Congress and the Supreme Court are concerned (as distinguished from the people) the Constitution of the United States *contains a very definite core of absolutes, which only the people can change.* All that the Congress can do is to suggest changes. The function of the Court is to interpret and apply the Constitution's absolutes to the controversies that are brought to its bar. The principle of interpretation is essentially that of an *unpacking of the content* of these absolutes, not of either a straining or an altering of the absolutes themselves. The whole structure of the Aristotelian metaphysics, for instance, is nothing but an unpacking of the content of the "common experience" of man in the light of man's "common sense." Strictly analogous to this process is the process which the Supreme Court was founded to conduct upon the Constitution, and the first consideration in such a process must be respect for that content, absolute though it be.

That, as a matter of fact, clearly appears to be Mr. Justice Frankfurter's own view of the Constitution for, near the close of his opinion, he said: "Judicial exegesis is unavoidable with reference to an organic act like our Constitution, drawn in many particulars with purposed vagueness so as to leave room for the unfolding future. But the ultimate touchstone of constitutionality is the Constitution itself and not what we have said about it." In other words, the Court should neither read into the Constitution absolutes which are not there, nor alter or nullify the absolutes that it contains. In avoiding either extreme, there is often room for differing opinions, quite apart from changing facts, and as we all know, a dissenting opinion today may tomorrow become the Court's judgment—with or without a change in personnel. But absolutes must stay absolutes until the people change them.

Having in mind the experience of two years ago, and the disclosure that it brought of the "hinterlands" of many people's thinking concerning the Court and its functions, we will do well to keep that at all times clearly before us, for, if ever our "philosophers" have their way with the Court, our whole political system goes down and with it our liberties.

April 3, 1939

MODERNIZING THE LAW

Last week Mr. Sol A. Rosenblatt, General Counsel of the Democratic Committee, addressed the convention of the American Federation of Labor in session at New Orleans on the subject of the "Freedom of the Press," and his remarks attracted a good deal of attention by reason of his attack upon that portion of our newspaper press which opposed the re-election of President Roosevelt. With the merits and the logic of his arguments this writer will not concern himself, or invite his readers to concern themselves, but there is one passage in his speech which is deserving of attention. It did not appear in all the summaries printed in the New York newspapers and this writer is indebted to a special dispatch for the following quotation (*New York Times,* November 21, p. 27): "If our liberties are to be protected from the termites within and without, we need, too, a more modern viewpoint in the law, in the practice of which I am myself engaged."

Whether or not the word "termites" was intended by Mr. Rosenblatt to apply to newspaper editors and publishers only is not clear, but it probably included them. That is not, however, the important word in the above-quoted remark. It is the words, "a more modern viewpoint in the law," that stand out. Mr. Rosenblatt is a lawyer and presumably skilled in the use of words. It is, therefore, not only permissible, but necessary, to look closely at the words used. Let us do so.

The first thing to note is that our need, as he sees it, is not for a "new law." Indeed, in the course of his speech he said (to borrow again from the *Times* dispatch): "The freedom of the press is guaranteed by the Constitution and the Bill of Rights and nobody wants to change the Bill of Rights." No; what we need is a "more modern viewpoint" in the law. There are two departments of our government whose business it is to express "viewpoints on law." One is the Congress, whose "viewpoint" is expressed in its *making* of the law. Mr. Rosenblatt apparently did not have Congress' viewpoint" in mind, for he disclaimed wanting new law. The only other department empowered to have a "viewpoint" on law is the judiciary, which it expresses in *interpretation.* We must conclude that it is from the judiciary that we are to get the kind of "viewpoint" that Mr. Rosenblatt wants. He tells us that he wants one that is "more modern." This means—if it means anything—a change in the *interpretation* of the law by the judiciary, a "more modern" interpretation.

Since when, one would naturally ask, has it been recognized in jurisprudence that an interpretation of laws becomes outmoded by passage of time when the law itself is unchanged—that a law means one thing at one time and another thing at another time?

Unfortunately—and this is the sinister connotation of Mr. Rosenblatt's words—there has arisen here (and elsewhere, too) a school of jurisprudence which would answer that question, "Now." The new school of "realistic" jurisprudence, as it calls itself, or is called by its adherents, is new only in a relative sense, for it has been growing amongst us for at least a generation. This writer invited his readers' attention to it two or more years or so ago, and then pointed out that it was essentially *pragmatic* in its philosophy and consequently rejected the notion of enduring *principle* in law. It has been erected formally into a system abroad and a professor of law at Bordeaux named Duguit is one of its principal exponents. Its essence is, in substance, the making of law to meet what at the time appears to be the needs—i.e., the desirabilities—of a situation without regard to either principle or precedent, and *when it can be done without plain violence to the terms of a law,* to change interpretation of the law in application to the facts without regard to principle or precedent, expressed in previous interpretations to the same set of facts. Principle, in short, is "out."

It is impossible to avoid the conclusion that Mr. Rosenblatt, in demanding "a more modern viewpoint in the law," is demanding a changed interpretation of the Bill of Rights in its application to the "freedom of the press."

One thing is certain: if "realistic jurisprudence" is to rule in the interpretation of the Constitution, the Constitution might as well be discarded as the collection of "myths and folklore" that Assistant Attorney General Arnold only a few years ago declared it to be, and the Supreme Court with it, leaving the legislature supreme so far as the making and application of law are concerned.

This would be a more honest procedure than attempting to reap the same result by packing the court. That that attempt was made, that it was supported by the National Lawyers Guild, only four years ago, indicates how far some of our jurists have gone on the "realistic" road. And it is that which invests Mr. Rosenblatt's demand with so sinister a sound.

November 27, 1940

THE SUPREME COURT AND MR. JACKSON

I

It would be unfair to describe *The Struggle for Judicial Supremacy,* by Mr. Attorney General Robert H. Jackson, as merely a brief in defense to the attempt made four years ago to pack the Supreme Court. It is, however, an excellent statement of the philosophy upon which that attempt is dependent, and for that reason it is an important book which deserves the attention of all who are concerned with the nature of law, and particularly of the concept of law, as exemplified in our American civil structure. The present reviewer pretends to no more competence in the general matter of jurisprudence than has the ordinary layman. But it seems to him that the question discussed in this book involves principles far transcending the technicalities of the courts and going to the very heart of our civil life, and that the Attorney General's position is with respect to those principles in direct opposition to that of the founders of our system.

There are two and only two ultimate concepts of law. One of these regards civil law as founded in fixed and enduring truths of right and wrong. The other regards it as the expression of the sovereign will—the people, in our own case—in any time that will is formed. The former concept roots ultimately in what the medieval jurist who in the twelfth and thirteenth centuries laid the foundations of the English common law called the natural law. "The king," said Bracton, "is under God and the Law. . . . it was for this that he was created and chosen that he do justice to all." Our own common law is essentially the same as that of England and has the same roots. Both assert freedom as due to human nature. The Preamble to our Declaration of Independence enshrines the whole thing. The other concept is pure pragmatism. It denies all fixed truth and principle and stands upon the one principle of the "will of the people"—Rousseau's *volonté générale,* but not as Rousseau conceived that will. Rousseau was not—consciously—a pragmatist. He believed in a fixed law of right and wrong, and he assumed that the will of the people would always be attuned to that law because man was by nature "good." The modern pragmatist—unlike William James—recognizes no such law. In jurisprudence the "pragmatist" recognizes the will of the people as the supreme law. It is in this sense that the "democracy" of the pragmatist is necessarily totalitarian and is the common antithesis of the "democracy" of the common law, which is the "democracy"—the Republic, the founders called it—of our making.

The present writer has no knowledge of what may be Mr. Jackson's personal philosophy. But his book reeks of the pragmatic conception of law and of the judiciary. It is in the overtones of a man's speech and writing that one gets, so to speak, flashlight photographs of the hinterland of his thinking. In his preface there are many of these. The very title of his book is eloquent in the one word "supremacy." The common law jurist does not question the supremacy of *law*. The distinction implied between the *law* and the *judiciary* is highly significant. So, too, is the subtitle, "A Study of a Crisis in Power Politics." In the preface the overtones are even more perceptible. Here are one or two:

. . . the struggle has produced no permanent reconciliation *between the principles of representative government and the opposing principle of judicial authority* . . . the truce *between judicial authority and popular will* may not ripen into a permanent peace . . . That instrument [the Constitution] created . . . an appointive court, whose Justices are chosen for life, and thus set up an *over-riding legal authority completely independent of popular will* . . . [which] by 1933 had established a supremacy that could deny important powers to both state and nation on principles nowhere found in the Constitution itself . . . my generation has won its fight . . . by marshalling the *force of public opinion* against the old court through the court fight, *by trying to influence the choice of forward-looking personnel* and, most of all, by persuasion of the court itself . . . even inventing *such limitations as "freedom of contract" where none existed in the Constitution.* (Emphasis supplied.)

These may serve to illustrate the persistent antithesis expressed by Mr. Jackson between the "judiciary" and the "popular will," and that antithesis is pure pragmatism. Nor can Mr. Jackson evade the imputation by a distinction between the "judiciary" and the "law," for those words "forward-looking personnel" give him away, just as did the plea of "unpacking" the court convict the defenders of the packing scheme out of their own mouths. To put men upon a court of justice because of either "forward-looking" or "backward-looking" views on a set of laws is a violation of principles of natural justice. On the other hand, it is perfectly good pragmatism. But this writer wonders what use there is in pragmatic jurisprudence for a written constitution, beyond the job of distributing the legislative and executive powers with a judiciary to see that each stays within its proper sphere.

January 20, 1941

II

Published simultaneously with Attorney General Jackson's book on the judiciary comes another extremely interesting volume on the same subject by Dr. Beryl Harold Levy, of the New York Bar, entitled *Our Constitution: Tool or Testament!* It dovetails perfectly with Mr. Jackson's, and sets out in even sharper detail the fundamental change that is in progress in our American theory and practice of jurisprudence. Mr. Levy's book is built around four great Justices of the Supreme Court, Marshall, Taney, Holmes and Brandeis, each typifying an "attitude" toward the Court and the Constitution. The "hero" of the book is Holmes, the "villain" Marshall, and the standard of "vice" and "virtue" is at bottom a matter of pure philosophy, that is, of the philosophic concept of law itself. The "hero"—Justice Holmes—stands for a thoroughly pragmatic view; the "villain"—John Marshall—for the "natural law," the unchanging law of right and wrong, and Mr. Levy's sympathies are all with the "hero."

At the very outset of the book, he quotes Volney's definition of this "natural law" as follows: "The regular and constant order of facts by which God rules the universe; the order which His wisdom presents to the sense and reason of men to serve them as an equal and common rule of conduct and to guide them, without distinction of race or sect, toward perfection and happiness." Upon this he remarks:

> Thus when it fell to Marshall to interpret the Constitution he found considerable "natural law" abounding in terms of which he made his constructions. Since "reason" *discovered* this natural law which was *presented* to men's minds by God or nature, the rights thus disclosed were not a matter for argument for the legislations of men. The natural law discoverers on the Supreme Court were to enshrine for many a decade to follow what to us is clearly the grandiose expression of temporary and finite outlook.

Having thus summarily thrown out of court the villain and the doctrine of "natural law," Mr. Levy lovingly builds up the portrait of his hero, Justice Holmes, and sketches in touches of Holmes' philosophy. Holmes' metaphysics was "naturalistic" by which term Mr. Levy says: "I refer to that commonsensible view so current in temporary American philosophy which starts in revolt against supernaturalism and transcendentalism and which ends by being quite happily at home in the surrounding world which we can explose in more ways than one." Holmes "did not regard his truths or values as backed by God or Nature." So he saw no reason to enforce them on others. (By way of digression, why do people who disbelieve in God usually treat nature to an upper case N? Would it not be more "commonsensible" to reduce the Creator to a lower case G?) He "had a naturalistic approach to ethics and law, as well as to the cosmos. There were no 'Thou shalts' for him."

He said of John Dewey's *Experience and Nature* that "he seemed to me to have more of our cosmos in his head than I ever found in a book before," and he was not "dissatisfied because assurance is lacking that 'the ultimates of a little preacher on this little earth are the last word of the unimaginable whole.' " (Mr. Levy explains Mr. Justice Frankfurter's declination of a seat on the Massachusetts Supreme Bench on the ground that he thought "his work in turning out hundreds of well-trained law students according to his modern, factual, economic, pragmatic lights more important." A highly significant collection of adjectives! There are many more similar remarks of Holmes (and of Mr. Levy on Holmes), all of which spell one thing, namely, that in Mr. Levy's view law is entirely a matter of pure pragmatism completely devoid of any traces of the absolute.

Now if there is one thing that is clear beyond dispute it is that a government which, as democratic as you please in its forms, is pragmatic in its jurisprudence must be totalitarian in the fullest sense of the world. It must throw out of the window the Preamble of the Declaration of Independence and the Constitution's Bill of Rights, and with them all the safeguards for the liberty of the person. Both Mr. Levy's book and Mr. Jackson's amount to a purely pragmatic concept of the law as law, and that concept is tantamount to flat denial of the fundamental principles upon which we supposed the Founders to have built our government. We have, in short, apparently in progress a most fundamental revolution in our political system, the existence of which is still unsuspected by the great mass of our people. *January* 27, 1941

ON LAW

TRUSTEE OR MASTER

Speaking—as many of us are much of the time—of "Democracy's fight against Fascism," one thing is certain, that is, the need for a definition of the two fighting words, and especially of "democracy." We need that definition more particularly because those who lead (in number and volubility) the argument for "democracy" seem to use the word "Fascism" to describe everything that is not "democratic" as they conceive "democracy." As there is no school of thought—at all events no articulate school—in this country defending "Fascism," the only definition obtainable of that word is to be looked for from its opponents and that will clearly not "define." Moreover, as it is clear that this country does not want anything like *Fascismo*, the really important thing is to define the "democracy" for which we are fighting. It is important to define it, for there is abundant evidence that the word does not mean the same thing to all those who are using it. Not only is this the case, but it is evident that the difference in the "meaning" is of the greatest importance for it goes to the first principle on which our entire political order is based, and, indeed, to the first principle of all free government, everywhere and always. That principle is the distinction between free government and government that is not free, namely, whether the civil power is or is not limited with respect to the citizen.

It is, regrettably, clear that by no means all of us who are, as we believe, fighting for "democracy" are fighting for that principle. What a great many people do not seem to understand is that a democratic form of government in no way guarantees the principle's application. That form can achieve as totalitarian a regime as can any other. If the advocates of the "Popular Front" type of "democracy" recognize the principle, they have so far not only successfully concealed that fact but have given abundant evidence that they do not recognize it. The very name "Popular Front" itself implies that, as do the acts of all "popular fronts" so far observed in actual performance. Nothing in the statements of our "front" parties contains the implication of any limitation upon the power of the majority. Nor, indeed, can there be found in the doctrine of the "liberal" school of our politics any such implication; quite the contrary in fact. The only difference in the position of a civilian under *Fascismo* and under a "popular front" democracy is in the difference between one set of masters and the other.

The whole thing turns on the question—government, *trustee* or *master?* A government can be "democratic in form and yet be as tyrannous in fact as a dictator or a king; there has been such and there can be such again. Obviously that kind of "democracy" is not what we think we are fighting for. Not even our "fronters" can fairly be charged with consciously aiming at its establishment, much less our "liberals." It is not that they definitely conceive and advocate an essentially totalitarian "democracy" as the road to the "freedom" which they, like the rest of us, undoubtedly desire. It is rather that they do not fully understand the nature of the freedom itself. They do not understand it because they have lost their hold upon the truths which the Preamble to the Declaration of Independence asserted as "self-evident." However this has come about, the fact is indisputable, and it is of great importance. Some of them, it is true, openly deny these truths, even treat them with contempt. But this is not true of a great many who are emotionally "liberal" but not given to rigorous thinking, and they bulk large in the "liberal" forces.

The practical importance of this state of things is rather with respect to our policy of after-war reconstruction of the oppressed countries than with respect to our domestic situation. It is at the bottom of the North African imbroglio and is now looming large in the Italian problem. The key to both is in the "popular front" propaganda here for both countries.

There are in it great potentialities of trouble for all concerned, for if there is one thing quite sure it is that the only sure hope for peace for Europe or anywhere else is in the *extirpation of totalitarian government under any form or disguise—including that of "democracy."*

July 23, 1943

WHAT IS THE CONSTITUTION?

On Sunday next this country will observe the 157th anniversary of the adoption of the Constitution of the United States. There has been no single anniversary in all the 157 years when our people had more reason to give serious thought to that document and to its meaning than they have today, for it never has been in greater danger than now, and that at the hands of our own citizens. If that seems a wild statement it is necessary only to look at the facts to realize its truth.

In the first place, what *is* the Constitution? It is what lawyers call the "organic law" of the nation—the law which makes the American people a nation, a law made by the people for that purpose. The Constitution distributes the necessary powers of government which rest in the people themselves and are delegated by the people to their representatives, and delimits those powers in such fashion as to prevent so far as possible the lodgment of excessive powers in the hands of any one of these delegated officials. Furthermore, it delimits the powers so delegated to all these officials so as to preserve to the citizen certain fundamental rights against government itself. All these things our Constitution does, and in plain terms.

In the second place, what was its fundamental purpose? It had one great purpose. That was to "implement," as diplomatists say, the Preamble to the Declaration of Independence which laid down the doctrine of "unalienable" personal rights as the one thing that governments are primarily instituted to protect. Our Supreme Court has twice told us that the Declaration is the "spirit and the thought" of which the Constitution is the "body and the letter," and that is strictly true. Thus, its purpose was not merely to prevent too much power lodging in the hands of any one official, but also to *prevent absolute power from resting in the state itself.* The Declaration and the Constitution were the first instances in human history of a nation formally founding its existence upon an explicit rejection of *totalitarian* government, i.e., *absolute* government in any form. They remain today the most complete expression of that rejection to be found in the world.

Human freedom is incompatible with totalitarian government in any form whatever. A republic—we are a republic—can be as totalitarian as a Byzantine despot. The danger to our Constitution is in the fact that the totalitarian spirit is loose amongst us, and of that we have had in recent years damning proof. We have long had in our higher educational institutions a body of political thought which scoffs at the notion of any personal rights outside the state. We have it also in our law schools, some of them. We have a political group describing itself as "liberal," which is partly consciously and partly unconsciously totalitarian in its aims. All this is common knowledge to anyone who reads the newspapers. But we had some seven years ago a demonstration of the extent to which the totalitarian poison has infiltrated our system which should, if the other symptoms do not, suffice to bring us sharply to the alert.

That was the amazing proposal by the Administration to "pack" the Supreme Court of the United States in order to secure from that court an interpretation of the Constitution which would permit the administration to accomplish such ends which it deemed desirable. The proposal was openly made and its purpose frankly avowed. It was supported before Congress by professors of law schools, even by a professor of constitutional law, and it was backed by a national association of lawyers. Congress would not have it. The Senate Judiciary Committee majority blasted it in terms so magisterial that no reply was attempted. But in the course of a short time, as the result of death and retirement, the Supreme Court was made over, so that seven of the nine members today are appointees of the Administration. And, lest there should be doubt as to the spirit which dictated these appointments, the advocates of the court-packing plan have openly boasted of their victory, and do so still!

When it is remembered that, if one wished to destroy the Constitution and open the door wide to totalitarianism, the quickest and easiest way to do it would be by packing the Supreme Court, the significance of this episode should be plain enough for anyone to understand. Yet our people seem either to have forgotten it or never to have fully realized it.

With that fact staring us in the face, when in all its history of 157 years was there more danger to the Constitution—and our freedom—than there is today?

September 15, 1944

EDUCATION: DARWIN AND DEWEY

JOHN DEWEY AND AIMS IN TEACHING

The Committee on Teacher Education of the Association of Colleges and Universities of the State of New York has issued a report on "the responsibility of institutions educating teachers," from which the following passage is extracted:

> The first task of education is to transmit to the young the values and virtues of the social order, that way of life which represents the vitality of the state and nation or of the civilization to which a people consciously belong. This can hardly be gainsaid, since it would be suicidal for society to establish and maintain organized instruction whose aim was the destruction or the revolutionary modification of its own institutions. Through education of the young and in certain other ways, society seeks to ensure the perpetuation of its established and generally accepted traditions, customs and basic ideals.

A perfectly sound statement; it is "values and virtues" that are the soul of the social order, for they are the soul of the "culture" that creates and maintains that order. And that makes it highly important to know what are the values and virtues of *our* social order and whether our teachers are being educated to transmit them to their pupils.

There are in this country some seventy colleges for training of teachers. Among these, Teachers College at Columbia University in New York stands prominent; a good many educators would probably account it as in the top rank of such institutions. Over a year ago the present writer had occasion to examine the general scheme of "values and virtues" which had been represented at this institution by a leading group of educators generally identified with the "John Dewey Society," which, in two public addresses, he summarized as follows:

(1) We live in a universe without final ends, forms or assignable limits, either internally or externally, of which continuous evolutionary change is all that can be predicted.

(2) Man is as much a product of this process as are all other visible things, and is strictly continuous with nature. There is nothing transcendent to the visible universe and man's home is within it. His thinking is a pure product of experience and cannot transcend it. There is no such thing as metaphysics, which is merely a collection of empty dreams and idle fancies. Man has no soul, mind or reason as metaphysicians understand those words. Ideas are merely plans of operations to be performed, not statements of what is or has been. They are merely hypotheses. Experience evolves new standards and values. All human affairs, whether personal or associative, are merely projections, continuations, complications of the nature which exist in the physical and prehuman world.

(3) God as a being does not exist; He is merely that unification of ideal values that is essentially imaginative in origin when the imagination supervenes in conduct. There is no such thing as religion in any sense of relation to God. Faith in the sense in which the Western civilization understood it is

impossible for the "cultivated mind" of the Western World today.

(4) There is no enduring moral law of fixed principles. Morals are purely social. The question of "ought" is merely one of better or worse in social affairs. The only moral end is an abundant life shared by all, achieved by growth itself. There are no absolute moral standards; the moral and social qualities of conduct are identical. There is nothing absolutely and unchangingly good.

So far as this writer is aware, no one has yet challenged the general accuracy of that summary.

December 27, 1940

EDUCATION AND HEDONISM

I

Every year with the regularity of the Nile inundation and the Indian monsoon our educational institutions unloose a flood of sonorous rhetoric in the shape of baccalaureate sermons and addresses to graduates. The press selects from these such sentences and paragraphs as will support a more or less striking headline, which may or may not convey the thought that the orator really meant to express. Occasionally—not often—it will give us his remarks *in extenso*, this only when the speaker has the necessary news value to warrant it. Most of the oratory discharged in this way is blank cartridge with black powder; very little of it is smokeless and shotted. We may reasonably suppose that most of the effect is, as in the case of salutes, usually confined to a temporary titillation of the auditory nerves.

Occasionally we get something worth attention—as, for instance, from Mr. Walter Lippmann, speaking to graduates at Ann Arbor's commencement. The point that he chose to emphasize was the dependence of our civilization upon our faith in education. Our people, he said,

have believed that with opportunity there would emerge from the people leaders and thinkers, inventors and organizers who would know how to make democracy work. They would not have built these schools had they not had this faith in their fellow-men, had they not believed that wisdom breeds wisdom, that men will respond honorably to honorable treatment, that in the long run men, if they are trusted, will be worthy of trust, that when things are expected of them they will rise to the opportunity. . . . Our hopes are in free men making their decisions by open debate.

Those hopes are built upon our faith in education. Mr. Lippmann gives us a hint of the aim to which education should be directed.

I do not say that the day is over when a man can achieve great success by specializing in some field and attending strictly to one job. On the contrary, it is certain that to be effective and to be independent a man must be able to do a particular job well. But I do say that the highest satisfaction will be reserved for those who, as an old teacher of mine used to say, knew that the world is round, and knew it all the time, who can see what is under the hood of the engine and why it runs, and where the road leads beyond the next mountain range—who, starting with their job, can see the whole plant, can see the plant in the whole industry, can see the industry in the national economy and the national economy in the world.

We may safely conclude that in these words Mr. Lippmann intends to imply a good deal more than he says and that while he talks of seeing life clearly in terms of jobs, plants and industries, he has no intention of suggesting that in seeing it in these things alone one would "see it whole." He would assuredly be one of the first to deny that life had no "values" that could not be expressed in "prices." And he would probably agree that the main purpose of "education" was to equip a man or woman with the capacity to appraise all things human according to their real "values," all those values related to the nature of man himself and the purpose of his existence on this earth.

But here we bump into something of a dilemma. The "value" of anything from a human point of view is necessarily determined by the nature of man himself and the purpose of human life. It follows that one's appraisal of values will be determined by the opinion, hypothesis, theory or conviction that one entertains as to *what* man is and *why* he is here. Now we all explicitly agree that men may rightly—and that, in fact, they do—hold diverse views upon these matters. Not only that, but very many of us take it for granted that nothing can in fact be definitely *known* about them. And, furthermore, our general scheme of education—both primary and secondary—is, in fact, predicated upon leaving these matters almost entirely to individual private opinion. One of the fundamental principles of what we call "academic freedom" is the right of any educator to "teach" whatever opinion, hypothesis, theory or conviction he may happen to hold with respect to these things.

This being so, it is evident that diversity and relativity in these matters, accepted as a starting principle, necessarily involves diversity and relativity as a consequence in the derivative "values." Yet we profess to suppose—or at least we "teach" that way—that these derivatives from a relative base have a real existence of their own, and that they should appeal in an *a priori* or *prima facie* way to the intelligent mind, on their face compelling acceptance. William Graham Sumner's famous four questions—"What is it?" "Why is it?" "What of it?" "What should I do about it?"—(which were his invariable method of approaching everything) seem to be here truncated by omission of the first two. How can the last two be satisfactorily answered with the first two excluded from consideration?

The adjective "spiritual" is sprinkled all over the turbid flood of graduation oratory. If it means anything it means something other than "sensible" or "material." If there are "spiritual" values in man's life, they can arise only from a spiritual nature in man. If we are not prepared to assert and teach that man has a spiritual nature, how can we reasonably assert and teach that life has spiritual values? No matter how scientific a hedonism may be, no matter to what degree it can be refined, it remains hedonism, and there is nothing spiritual in it.

Are our colleges really "teaching" today anything more than at best an intelligent hedonism? If not, let us drop talk about the "spiritual."

June 25, 1934

II

If age is strictly honest with youth, it has to tell it things that are not altogether good for youth to take to heart. The experience of the years is largely made up of vanished dreams, deluded hopes and frustrated ambitions. But it is the very dreams, hopes and ambitions of youth that accomplish so many things that age in its wisdom knows to be impossible. Where would the world be if wisdom ruled youth and power rested in age? Most interesting is it to note that Polonius, in his "address to the graduate" Laertes, confined himself strictly to a few most canny counsels of behavior which in no way need inhibit dream, hope or ambition, even if they are with one exception pitched upon none too high a "spiritual" level—as one orator this year bitterly complained! What, in fact, *has* age to tell youth that it is good for youth to know and to remember? Particularly, what has present-day age to tell?

There is the rub! If one may judge by such samples of graduation oratory as have percolated into newspaper columns, one has an impression that the Niagara of words that has poured over the land is like the Colorado River, a very muddy flood, reflecting an enormous confusion and uncertainty of thought and emotion, and leaving in its wake a sense of almost complete futility. (One suspects, moreover, that much the same could be said of most "valedictories"!) Now what is the reason of this? It is not very difficult to discern. Let us take one example for illustration.

The word "character" cropped up, perhaps, as often as any other bit of flotsam on the rushing waters. What is "character"? If it does not mean a habit of self-control for a high purpose, it means nothing in particular. Neither self-control alone nor high purpose alone suffice; they must be joined. But what did most of our orators have to say of the "purpose" for which youth should control itself? Except here and there, where a definitely religious note was appropriate to the occasion, there was little beyond vague and unsubstantial—if sonorous—rhetoric. This notwithstanding that another word also came bobbing along frequently on the stream—"spiritual."

But what "spiritual" really meant was just as cloudy as was the meaning of "character." Yet both words contain tremendous implications as to the nature of man and the purpose of life. They imply, indeed, a whole philosophy—the philosophy of human personality.

Now it happens that it is precisely human personality that is threatened by the forces that are loose in the world today. To the medieval mind, the word "person" meant that which is "the most perfect thing in all nature." (That, at least, was what Thomas Aquinas said of it, and he did not squander superlatives.) Yet the modern mind is transferring the idea of "personality" to the state and reducing man to the status of the mere "individual" who exists for the sake of the species. And the grim joke is that, having done its best to convince men of their mere "individualism," it seems surprised that they do not perform as "persons." What room does modern psychology offer for the notion of real "self-control" or for a definite "high purpose"?

It seems as if the thing can be summed up in the statement that the colleges generally are inculcating—in some cases directly teaching—a philosophy concerning man, his nature and his destiny in which there is no room for the concept of him as a "person," while people in general are still emotionally living in the ideas (and the terminology) of an age whose whole philosophy centered in that concept. Naturally there is confusion of thought and of speech. We bandy terms such as "character" and "spiritual" as if their mere reiteration could import some helpful influence into our struggle with something that we do not understand.

We cannot make a working mixture of a metaphysics which denies human personality and a morality which depends entirely upon that as its fundamental principle. One or the other must be dropped.

June 24, 1936

PROGRESS IN EDUCATION

I

Two friends (upon whose watch chains hang the coveted Phi Beta Kappa key) have sent the present writer identically marked copies of the summer issue of the *Key Reporter*. The "marks" are against an article entitled "The Fantasia of Current Education" by Dr. I. L. Kandel, Professor of Education at Teachers College, Columbia University, in New York City; the piece is described as a condensation of an article to appear in the summer number of *The American Scholar*. It is a refreshing breeze, all the more in that it comes from the erstwhile stronghold of the "Dewey Society" group of educators, who have wrought such havoc upon our hapless youth in the last several decades and aroused the hope that a real change in the wind is in the making.

Dr. Kandel comprehensively impeaches the "modern idea" of the school. Despite the fact [he says] that educational literature is full of accounts of failures in the established routine subjects in the school, in the teaching of which teachers may be expected to have acquired some proficiency, they are now to become experts in the solution of all social problems. Children in schools are to be plunged into surveys of their community, national and world resources which are more really and vitally educative than books. The reality of ideas is to be abandoned for contact with reality.

He explains this, first, by the existence of a prevailing "contempt for knowledge and its mastery; or as the educational theorists put it, the important thing is not ideas but the thinking process. How the one is possible without the other is never explained." Next, by the notion that "education can only be made 'meaningful' as it deals with the problems of the environment in which the pupils live. Whether the pupils realize the existence of these problems, whether they have any direct stake in their solution, whether the problems and the solutions will be the same when they in turn become adults is immaterial." Next is the notion that "the process of thinking can only be stimulated by having a problem to solve when a fork in the road is reached or when the choice of action has to be made. How the existence of a problem can be recognized without a background of antecedent knowledge is not explained." Finally, underlying all these notions is a "critical attitude toward everything traditional in education and a faith that the latest is always the best. Starting with an attack on 'intellectualistic' education and stressing the part played by the emotions, the latter-day theorists, without realizing it, are promoting the retreat from reason."

If anyone were to assert that the end of technology was to produce machinery for mere purpose of motion, he would be instantly laughed out of court. Yet the analogy of such a notion with the notion of "education" entertained by the "modern" school of educators is pretty close, for their emphasis upon the "thinking" process as against the "idea" amounts to just that thing. It is Lessing's shocking statement over again—that it is the search for truth and not its attainment that is important. The difference is merely that misuse of technology brings instant retribution, whereas misuse of the intellect can go on for a long time before the penalty is enacted. It has been going on for a long time in our schools, and the penalty is only now beginning to loom into sight. Dr. Kandel's article closes with the warning that "the American public needs to become aware of what is being sold to it under the guise of progress in education." Fortunately, there are accumulating signs that it is at least beginning to suspect the existence of that need.

May 19, 1941

II

While Henri Massis' book, *Défense de l'occident,* concerns itself mainly with the orientalizing of thought in Germany, it carries a definite warning to us of the danger that lies in the spread of the "pragmatic" philosophy (so-called) as represented in the (so-called) "progressive education movement." That philosophy is as direct a treason to the Western civilization as are the oriental philosophies in Eastern Europe, for it is in conflict with the thing that most fundamentally separates East from West. That this is the Western metaphysics which centers on the idea of *being,* the most fundamental fact of all facts; *being* as contrasted with *non-being,* the fact that things *are* when they might not *be,* the fact that anything *is.* Chesterton once remarked that a man knows nothing until he knows *nothing.* It is upon this tremendous fact that the whole Western civilization's philosophy has been built up, for that philosophy is at bottom no more and no less than an unpacking of the content of *being* as *being.* The East refused to confront that task and it is not surprising that its view of existence became deeply tinctured with a fundamental and dissolving pessimism which finally came to regard existence itself as an evil thing.

Not so for the West, for the heart of its thinking was a full acceptance of life as life, a full realization of the fact that existence was a thing to be regarded with perpetual wonder as a new and exciting discovery, and the starting point of all knowledge. Upon this fact it concentrated all its intellectual powers and pushed human reason to the utmost limits of its range in the search for ultimate realities. It was for this that Dante gave to Aristotle the title "Master of Those Who Know," and it was upon this philosophy, completed and vitalized by the Christian revelation, that the civilization of the West was built—a philosophy of first beginnings and final endings, a surpassing triumph of the human intellect.

The shortest way to describe the general body of thought which is commonly called "pragmatism" is to say that it denies the Western philosophy in all its vital points. It takes no account of first beginnings, final ends or purposes; it takes *being* for granted but views it as mere *becoming,* and denies that the intellect can do anything more with it than accept it as a fact; it denies the entire metaphysical order as having no reality whatever and consequently it denies truth as having any constancy or continuity of endurance. It recognizes only *chance* in everything. Whereas the philosophy of the East sank the human person in a vague, intangible "oneness," Western pragmatism sinks him in "society"; in both cases "personality" disappears, and personality is, next to *being,* the most fundamental concept of the West, and the very cornerstone of our American philosophy of social life.

Thus, despite the violent contrast between the seething activity of Western life and the inertia of the East, the same forces of dissolution are at work under the surfaces of our society as those which have paralyzed the East for millennia, and if they shall succeed in getting the upper hand will wreck the whole structure of human liberty, under which, as a *conditio sine qua non,* the Western life has been made possible. It is this which is the most imminent danger to our American way of life, for it is attacking that life at its roots in the education of our youth.

It should not be necessary for this writer to point out that in impeaching the underlying philosophy which largely dominates the so-called "progressive education" movement — namely, the philosophy commonly identified with the "John Dewey Society"—he does not include in that indictment *all* the methods introduced by its leaders into the work of the classrooms. Methods rightly change as conditions change, but methods are one thing and principles are another. Changing conditions do not change principles, and it is principles that matter. Furthermore, this writer is not in this discussion arguing the truth or falsity of this "pragmatic" philosophy. All that he is trying to do is to show that it is in fundamental conflict with the principles on which the West and, above all, our own country, have built their way of life, and that we must choose between that way of life and this new philosophy. We cannot have both.

There is one mark by which the adherence of this "new learning" may be readily known—the fanatic hatred that they profess of "absolutes" in any form, together with a marked dislike for "definitions." It is this latter trait which makes their literature such hard reading. Of much of it, it would not be unfair to say that only its negatives are stated with something like plainness; the rest seems to slip through one's fingers as one tries to seize its meaning. But its denials are the important thing, for it is in those that its destructiveness appears. At bottom, it is essentially an irrational philosophy of nihilism.

November 24, 1939

PROGRESSIVE EDUCATION AND EXPERIENCE

"The Case for Progressive Education" is the title of an article in the November issue of the *Journal of the National Education Association of the United States,* written by Dr. William Heard Kilpatrick, Professor Emeritus of Teachers College, Columbia University. Dr. Kilpatrick has long been recognized as the leading proponent of the Dewey philosophy in connection with education, and his influence in the schools has been very great. Such, at least, is the opinion of several writers on the general subject. He has left us in no doubt as to his own views on things in general. He is an out-and-out Darwinian (nineteenth century vintage), a complete Heraclitean who recognizes change as the one law for everything; he will have no truck whatever with Aristotle or metaphysics in any form, much less with religion (as a "truth") and he holds that an individual's business is to adjust himself to the society and the culture to which he is born with no reference to a future life. For him there are no "morals" which are not "social"; experiment and experience are the beginning and the end of everything; growth is the end of life, growth and abundant "living." The doctor, in a word, is the perfect Deweyite, the complete "Instrumentalist" and believes that the proper purpose of education is to train youth to follow in the steps of his master.

"Train," however, is not the right word for training means "indoctrination" and that is anathema to all "Instrumentalists." The doctor, in this article, will have none of it. He contrasts "living" with "learning," that is, with learning of the old-fashioned type, by examination and recitation. This kind he says, "seems to the typical learner as more or less artificial and arbitrary; it does not arise out of his own felt needs." It does not offer the pupil a "situation" which he can "feel" for it comes out of textbooks and lectures, and "does little for mind or heart, and possibly even less for character, for it hardly gets into life." The true type of learning is quite different, for it furnishes the pupil with "a situation of his own, such that he feels himself inwardly called upon to face it; his own interests are inherently at stake. And his response thereto is also his own; it comes out of his own mind and heart, out of his own very self. He may, to be sure, have had help from teacher or book, but the response when it comes out is his." This is "life's kind" of education, and it "furnishes the foundation for Progressive Education."

The doctor defines this kind of learning thus: "If we take the verb 'to live' in a full enough sense, we may then say that, by definition, *learning has taken place when any part or phase of experience, once it has been lived, stays on with one to affect permanently his further experience.* And we assert that *we learn what we live and in the degree that we live it.*" Now if we substitute the word "*truth*" for the words "*part or phase of experience,*" the word "*assimilated*" for "*lived*" and the word "*conduct*" for the closing word "*experience,*" we have a good definition of the type of "learning" which the doctor rejects and the real difference between the two types appears. The essence of progressive education is, of course, its denial of fixed objective truth in all forms, which is also the essence of the Instrumentalist philosophy. This gives point to another of the doctor's definitions which reads as follows:

"We may sum up all this in the following words: '*I learn*

my responses, only my responses and all my responses, each as I accept it to act on. I learn each response in the degree that I feel it or account it as important, and also in the degree that it interrelates itself with what I already know. All that I thus learn I build at once into character."

Here we meet that interesting word "*character.*" What is *character* in the Instrumentalist scheme? We know what it is in the traditional scheme, a habit of self-control in the light of *principles.* The only principle recognized by Instrumentalism is that of *change.* Obviously, character in that system must be the opposite of self-*control,* it must be self-*adjustment* to changing conditions. The individual builds his character in proportion as he adjusts his thinking and his conduct to the society, the culture, in which he lives. By so doing he "enriches" his life; his "living" becomes "adequate." True, he is encouraged to "think for himself." He "must" understand the why of our institutions, of our system of legal rights, of moral right and wrong, for only thus can he "use these essential things adequately or change them intelligently."

"*Moral right and wrong*"? Moral? What are "morals" in the Instrumentalist philosophy? We know that they cannot be *fixed* standards of conduct. They must be floating, flexible, and experimental, and "Society" is their only possible source. Moral conduct thus becomes a conduct "adjusted" to the prevailing code of a society or a culture in which the individual lives and his "adequate" living will be the result of a complete adjustment of his conduct and his thinking to that code. The code will necessarily be that which results from the collective "feelings" of the community; whatever is "felt" to be right *is* right, and vice versa.

This, the doctor tells us, is the kind of philosophy in which our American youth should be trained. This is what "progressive education" means. It is not a question of teaching *methods,* but it is a question of fundamentals, and it is totally incompatible with the fundamentals upon which our entire civil order is based, for it leads inevitably to totalitarianism in its most dangerous form. Do we want it?

November 24, 1941

THE THORNDIKE MAN

One version in English of the test of the angels' song at Bethlehem has it, "Peace on earth, good will toward men," and the other, "Peace on earth to men of good will." This writer will not debate the question which is the correct rendering, but merely note that the words "peace" and "good will" are common to both versions, as are "earth" and "men," and that the principal phenomenon in the doings of men on this earth at this recurrent season of Christmas is the absence of "peace" and the prevalence of the precise antithesis of "good will" upon a scale nearly universal in the "civilized" world. Not only is this the case but we have the spectacle, unprecedented in human annals, of great nations which once based their whole culture upon the story of Bethlehem formally repudiating it in favor either of an *ersatz* paganism or a complete philosophy of antireligion backed by a semimystical fervor in its propagation by fire and sword.

The latter is something new in the experience of mankind. We have had many varieties of religion, each associated in its time with a great culture, but never until in our day has there been found on this earth a nation to take its stand upon a denial of all religion, vowing itself to a war upon the Creator. This is a cultural phenomenon of appalling significance to the future of civilization.

It is appalling because both the national *ersatz* paganism and the national atheism have arisen within the civilization upon which both are now making war—within Christendom itself. They have not come as invaders from without, as, for instance, did Islam and the "barbarians" of the fourth century. Both have grown like cancers upon the body of the West. Neither has appeared as a mere "heresy." Both totally repudiate the entire synthesis of faith and tradition that we call Christendom; both deny the very soul that made Europe what she was and still—partly—is. Both, united only by this gigantic denial, are allies in a war on what remains of the Europe which once was the unchallenged leader of civilization on this earth.

This writer does not believe that we in America yet grasp the meaning of the conflict that has opened abroad. We chatter fatuously of "dictators" and "democracies" as if it were merely a matter of governmental forms or, even, economic theories that is in question. It is not rival *forms* but rival *substances* that face each other—the most vital of all substances, *ideas*, and the most fundamental of all ideas, man's idea of his own *nature*, man's concept of *himself* and his *destiny*. All philosophies come to that as the end of their travels. It is of the utmost importance that we Americans should realize that at the bottom of the war beyond our borders is a conflict over the nature of man, because in our country, "peaceful" as it is —at least, untouched by active war—and giving itself wholeheartedly to the annual resurgence of the "Christmas spirit," the same debate is under way, quietly, no doubt, but actively, and in places where it touches most vitally the life of the nation— our schools, colleges and universities.

There are but two alternatives in the case. Man is either the man of the Psalmist, "a little lower than the angels" ... "crowned with glory and honor" and "set over the works" of His Creator, or he is the thing described as follows:

> Darwin taught two great principles for all human thinking and conduct. The first is the principle of evolution, of continuity. . . . The second is the principle of naturalism—that in life and in mind

the same cause will always produce the same effect, that the bodies and minds of men are a part of nature, that their history is as natural as the history of the stars, their behavior as natural as the behavior of an atom of hydrogen. If I had time I could show you how this same contribution has acted to transform our views of all human institutions, the state, the church, education, and every feature of civilization and our treatment of every practical concern of life. (From an address entitled, "Darwin's Contribution to Psychology," delivered at the University of California in 1919 by Professor Edward Lee Thorndike, long identified with Teachers College at Columbia University.)

Between these two concepts there is no middle ground, no halfway house. And here is a picture of the "Thorndike man's" moral set-up:

Man's traits, insofar as they are a part of his inheritance, owe their origin and biological meaning to their survival value. All natural traits and impulses of human beings must therefore be fundamentally good, if we consider the good as the biologically useful. Cruelty, selfishness, lust, cowardice and deceit are normal ingredients of human nature, which have their useful role in the struggle for existence. Intrinsically they are all virtues. It is only their excess or their exercise under the wrong conditions that justly incur our moral disapproval. (From an address by the presiding officer, Dr. S. J. Holmes, to the divisional convention of the American Association for the Advancement of Science, at Palo Alto, California, as reported by the Associated Press in the *New York Times* of June 28, 1939.)

It is the "Thorndike man" who is loose in Europe today. This is of no small concern to us. But of much greater concern is the fact that he has long been loose in our educational world. For in the *Teachers College Record* (XXVII, No. 6, February, 1926) Dean Seashore of the University of Iowa said (reported by Professor J. McKean Cattell) of him: "No school is uninfluenced and no humanistic science is unaffected by his labor"; and in the same publication Dean James E. Russell says of him: "In developing the subject of educational psychology and in making it a fit study for students in all departments, Professor Thorndike has shaped the character of the college in its youth as no one else has done and as no one will ever have the opportunity of doing."

This writer is not here discussing the truth or falsity of either of these concepts of man and his nature. All he is concerned to point out is that the philosophy which has plunged Europe into war has planted its roots in our educational system, that it is time that we recognized its pressure there, and that it is in complete opposition to the philosophy upon which our nation founded its whole polity. That polity is quite incompatible with the Darwinian "virtues"; it was created for the "man" of the Psalmist. We are free to choose between the two philosophies, but it should be a deliberate choice. It will not do to find too late that we have been educating our youth in one philosophy while we supposed that we were training them in the other. *December 22, 1939*

ACADEMIC FREEDOM

I

This writer has for many years heard the phrase "academic freedom" bandied around and has wondered what it meant. Not long ago he thought he had a chance to find out from a friend who, himself a fine scholar with a lifelong connection with one of our greatest universities, had repeated the words with impressive emphasis. The attempt was a failure, for all that it led to was a statement by the friend that if this writer didn't know what academic freedom meant he couldn't tell him even if he spent forty years in trying to do so, and with this remark he abruptly departed with every appearance of a badly ruffled temper. As a result, this writer's perplexity on the point was notably heightened.

Nor is it lessened by the episode at Madison, Wisconsin. President Conant's distinction between the executive head of a university and a university professor is helpful, so far as it goes. But it does not answer the question that always confronts this writer, a question that seems at one and the same time simple and serious—most serious in its applications. It concerns the nature and the purpose of a teacher and his right to teach.

A teacher is someone who says to those who will listen to him—"This is this; that is that; this is so; that is not so." We all agree that anyone has the right to teach anyone else who is willing to be taught. In that sense there is real academic freedom. What troubles us is the freedom of those who are selected by institutions of learning and paid by them for teaching something to students who pay these institutions for being taught. In general we agree—at least in practice—that a university has the right as well as the duty of selecting its professors to teach the subjects for which the selecting authority regards them as qualified. But here arises the first difficulty.

These subjects fall in two main clases. There is no trouble with the exact sciences—physics, chemistry, mathematics, etc. There is no trouble with the arts proper, including the languages and literature. Where the trouble comes in is in those studies which concern themselves directly with man's nature and his behavior—metaphysics, theology, psychology, ethics, economics, politics and, in general, with the thing we call sociology. All these things ultimately base upon metaphysics. The trouble is that metaphysical thinking, where there is any such thing at all today, is hopelessly divided into warring schools, and it follows that the same is true of the derivative subjects.

Now the university authority which selects a teaching faculty must proceed upon one of two theories or plans. Either it will elect to teach, in general, certain groups of doctrines or it will elect to teach them all. In the former case, it will choose for its professors men who in general hold the doctrines which it desires to inculcate and these professors will tell the students that this is this and that is that, and the effort will be to train the students in those ways of thinking. In the latter case it will undertake to lay before the students all varieties of thinking on disputed points, leaving them to decide for themselves what to think about any or all of them. In practice, neither theory finds complete application. What we have, in fact, are institutions of learning which by implication offer universal knowledge—that is, all varieties of thinking—yet are governed, so far as selection of faculty is concerned, by a man or men who are not really so "agnostic" in doctrine as they profess to be or as they think they are.

The consequence is that when a professor by his teaching in some subject tramples upon a sensitive corn—usually in economics or sociology—the university authority is naturally impelled to discharge him, and occasionally does so. Whereupon those who think as the professor does rise in vigorous vocal defense of academic freedom. Their claim, in substance, is that he has a right to teach at the university's expense something which the university authority does not wish to be taught in its halls.

Upon what basis does such a right exist? Is there such a thing as a right to teach at another's expense something that that other does not wish to have taught? This writer is unable to conceive such a thing. It seems to be, in fact, contrary to academic freedom itself. Freedom to teach is one thing, but freedom to compel somebody else to pay for it is quite another thing.

After all, it is students who make a university, and for that matter a teacher. The students will in the long run settle the question for both university and teacher. That is where academic freedom really comes in. Why confuse a matter which is really one of wisdom by calling it a matter of freedom?

January 13, 1937

II

Among the various learned societies which devoted the closing days of 1937 to a survey of their interests was the American Historical Association of Philadelphia. Discussion was centered on the Constitution—at least that was the peg on which speakers hung their remarks, it being solid enough to carry a large number of ideas on this and that! Dean Wittke of Oberlin selected academic freedom as his text and (so Mr. Lawrence Davies tells us in the *Times*) roundly accused the educational authorities of some states of racketeering in "piling up requirements for teacher training," while being "strangely silent" on the "larger issues of freedom of teaching and tenure rights."

The schools, he said, belonged to both sides of the class struggle and democracy was bound not only to tolerate differences, but to encourage them. The teacher's job was "to promote an understanding of what is meant by democracy rather than recruits for democracy . . . not to impose a particular doctrine, but to promote the exercise of intelligent thought." Discussion, not propaganda, was his task. "We pay teachers to support schools so that our children may get ideas in the school room which they did not have before or which they could not get so well at home. Yet, when a new idea actually sprouts in our children's heads some parents do not regard this as evidence of a fair return on their investment, but as the signal to mobilize the forces of the great American home in defense of the *status quo.*"

Assuming that the correspondent correctly summarized

Dr. Wittke's position, we have a curious picture of the educational process as he conceives it. The main job of a teacher it seems is to promote an understanding of what the word *democracy* means. He is not, however, to impose upon his pupils his own theory of its meaning. His pupils are, apparently, to be favored with the views of other teachers which do not agree with his own. This thing democracy, then, requires that people shall differ in their opinion about itself; its essence, Dr. Wittke tells us, demands that. We are all presumably committed to the *thing* so long as we are not agreed as to its *nature*—that is, what the word really means. The great aim of teaching would seem to be that of encouraging new ideas concerning democracy to "sprout" in the pupils' heads, the great virtue of which is seemingly to be measured by the degree in which they shock his parents!

We have here an interesting demonstration of the modern mind in relation to the attainment of truth. It was well expressed many years ago by Dr. Arnold, who was delighted to think that "I can come down to breakfast every morning rejoicing that every question is an open question." We start with one fundamental dogma, namely, that all knowledge is hypothetical and all dogmatism false. It reminds one of the Frenchman's remark, "All generalizations are untrue—including this one," and it is, of course, simply intellectual suicide.

Now things, as in fact they exist in our schools, are not quite so bad as all that—yet. But that they are drifting in that direction there is little doubt, for the agitation over academic freedom is a measure of that drift. What most of the loudest academic-freedom advocates really seem to want is the right to propagandize at the public's cost, resting their right to do so on the above-mentioned fundamental dogma. All the rows that break into public notice clearly exhibit that characteristic.

We all, apparently, agree that *democracy* must at any cost be preserved as the principle of our social structure. What do we *really* mean by that word? We all believe in *liberty*—at least we all profess that faith. What do we *really* mean by *that* word? If those words mean anything at all, they mean exactly what our political structure was created to secure to us, *minority rights under majority rule*. Are these ideas, either or both, to be regarded as perpetually open questions leaving to our school pupils the task of "sprouting new ideas" on them from time to time? Or are they ideas to be taught as truths—propagandized, if you will, as one "propagandizes" grammar, biology, botany, cooking, salesmanship, ornamental sewing, etc.? Are the pupils or their parents the proper people to answer those questions?

Racketeering is an ugly word, but in some of their manifestations the protagonists of academic freedom come perilously near to exciting our suspicion on that ground.

January 7, 1938

SCIENCE AND MYTH — AND MR. WELLS

I

Each year, as September comes around, Great Britain indulges itself in a perfect intellectual orgy when the British Association for the Advancement of Science opens its sessions and the newspapers tell the marvelous stories of scientific progress (in fact and in theory) during the twelvemonth which has passed. These occasions usually are marked by more or less provocative addresses by outstanding authorities and, in the past, have produced some outstanding revelations by such men as Darwin, Wallace, Rutherford, Bateson, Tyndall and Huxley.

The presidential address generally is looked to for something of the sort, but many striking discoveries in medicine, genetics, etc., are reported in the departmental meetings.

This year's president, Sir Edward Poulton (who might be described as an unreconstructed Darwinian), had been present at the Association's meetings in 1881 (this is the 106th anniversary of its birth) at which Thomas Henry Huxley delivered his notable address on palaeontology, directed against the astronomers who would not concede enough time for the earth to do the job of evolution on Darwinian lines. Sir Edward's address this year sketched the course of thought concerning evolution in general, and Darwinism in particular.

For the layman, the principal interest in his remarks, perhaps, was their strong flavor of mid-nineteenth-century optimism based upon a law of "progress," automatic, inevitable and unlimited, for in these days when the literature of despair is keeping the world's presses busy, one does not hear much of this sort of thing.

This year, the indefatigable H. G. Wells virtually stole the show. Last year, the educational department of the Association chose him as its president. In his presidential address, this month, he cut loose in a comprehensive indictment of present education and educators in his best manner. He proposed to scrap their system in the entirety of its curriculum and replace it with a totally new structure.

Taking the child at five, he would have given him at fifteen a knowledge of world history, beginning with the great civilizations of the past, leading up to the rise of the modern states and, only then, permit him to concentrate (and that not too much) on the history of his own land, instead of working the other way about. He would have the child approach geography on the principle of the earth as a unit, with enough geology to enable him to conceive the processes of its development as the home of the human race.

At fifteen, the child also should know the main story of

invention and discovery and the main elements of physics, chemistry, physiology, etc., and, especially, the structure and working of his own body. All this is to be done in ten working years of forty weeks and six hours a week—total 2,400 hours of teaching.

Tradition and "myth" are to have no place in the curriculum. Mr. Wells pointedly referred to "the little legion of Palestine" as having occupied far too much space in the history books, for nothing really happened there of importance to the world! From which statement may be unpacked a good many rather startling conclusions as to Mr. Wells' mind and method.

Among these may be noted its utter contempt for metaphysics in general and its Gradgrind-like reliance on *facts.* (Something of the same dislike of abstract thinking also underlay Sir Edward Poulton's address.) This should interest American educators not a little in view of the recently revived interest in metaphysics.

The Spectator neatly puts it: "Nothing (says Mr. Wells) began in Palestine, nothing was worked out there. Nothing began there but a people's search for God; nothing was worked out there but the discovery. Perhaps that belongs to the realm of metaphysics, not of fact."

But *does* it? *The Spectator* unkindly reminds Mr. Wells that, only five years ago "Sanderson of Oundle" (whom Wells in his book on him called "beyond question the greatest man I ever knew with any degree of intimacy"), speaking to the National Union of Scientific Workers (with Mr. Wells in the chair), said:

"One of the greatest tragedies scientific men have allowed is for others to steal the Bible from them. The Old and New Testaments, with their record of progressive revelation, form the most scientific book ever seen. Yet scientific men have allowed a certain type of men to steal it from them."

October 1, 1937

II

The annual meeting of the British Association for the Advancement of Science is proceeding this year in the appropriate surroundings of Cambridge. The last time, by the way, that Cambridge entertained the Association was in 1904, and was signalized by the fact that its president that year was Lord Balfour, who was also Prime Minister. Lord Rayleigh, who presides this year, referred in his opening address to this doubling of functions, as illustrating the vast differences in world conditions today from what now seem to be the placid days of the opening of the century.

The presidential address to the Association is always expected to make a nice blend of scientific discussion with an application more or less direct to the state of the times. Lord Rayleigh's remarks this year were divided between two subjects. One was strictly scientific, concerning the vision of the eye and the aids furnished to human vision by science. The other was a defense of the scientists against the charge that they were mainly responsible for the horrors of modern war. As to this, his point was that the application to war of the results of invention was not the fault of science or scientists. The progress of chemical science had always been motivated by an irresistible urge to explore nature's secrets and its achievements in application had always been primarily for the benefit of mankind. That urge could not (and should not, if it could) be suppressed, and its control and confinement to peaceful uses was to be sought in the order of morals.

The point of his remarks on human vision was that, notwithstanding the apparent paradoxes of science in dealing with what we call matter and what we call light, "seeing" was still "believing." That solids—matter—consisting mainly of space, with particles of something equally unsolid moving in it with incredible velocity, did not mean visual sensations were deceptive and unreliable. Nor did our failure—thus far

—to understand how light could act both as a particle and a wave belie the conclusions arrived at by our visual faculties. Our senses could still be trusted; all we had to do was to interpret more fully the indications they gave us. Commenting on this, the London *Times* says:

> Science has to some laymen become a mystery, in delightful and awe-inspiring contrast to the drab and dull knowledge provided by our senses. The late Lord Rutherford agreed with Lord Rayleigh in rejecting this view. The advice which he is reputed to have given to a young scientist eager to write a book on modern physics for the philosophic layman was: "Very well, if you must, you must; but try to avoid using the word mysterious." Lord Rayleigh has stressed the point that although "much of modern scientific doctrine appears at first sight to have an elusive and even metaphysical character . . . yet the main triumphs of science lie in the tangible facts it has revealed."

This might be translated into saying that all the discoveries of science still confine man's knowledge of material *things* within the order of sensation—the *physical* order—and that the border of the *metaphysical* remains where it has always been, that is, where the process of mental abstraction begins to work on the material furnished to it by the senses. The common delusion of the day, the "modern doctrine," as Lord Rayleigh called it, that modern science has anything more to tell us of the metaphysical than the "common experience" of mankind told Aristotle and his successors, was strikingly illustrated at Cambridge by the irrepressible Mr. Wells, who followed up his attack of a year ago on modern education with a demand that teachers should cease "trying to pickle an old world" and tackle their "primary business" of giving their pupils a picture of the world into which they have to go. We live in a rapidly changing world and education should prepare youth for the change; it should be creative, not conservative. From which it is apparent that for Mr. Wells either metaphysics does not exist or it is identical with modern physics.

It would be interesting if some president of the British Association in the near future would take for the subject of his address the delimitation of the metaphysical frontier in the light of modern science. A good text might be found in the new doctrine of "relativity" as propounded by Professor Einstein, where the transformation of a mathematical description of physical facts into a metaphysical doctrine has been widely accepted by the lay mind. The interesting fact in this case is that the Einsteinian mathematics applied to the physical facts of the cosmos furnish a visible proof of the metaphysical impossibility of an infinite cosmos made up of discrete parts—hence the conclusion to a *limited* universe.

Mr. Wells would be shocked, no doubt, to be told that he is a survival of late Victorian days and not a foremost skirmisher on the line of modern thought about to reveal to the world the "shape of things to come." His eschatology, however, differs in principle not at all from that of Professor Tyndall two generations back. *September* 26, 1938

III

That seven-point charter of scientific principles which the British Association for the Advancement of Science adopted at its annual meeting last week looks imposing, but resolves itself into a few simple ideas, none of which is new or startling. All will agree that liberty to teach, opportunity to teach, and power to understand are necessary for the extension of knowledge. So, too, no one will question that communities depend for their survival and growth upon knowledge of themselves and the properties of things. It will surprise no one to be told that all nations and social classes have contributed to this knowledge, and its influence upon human developments, nor that the basic principles of science depend on independence and cooperation. Scientists likewise must be the trustees for the world's inheritance of scientific knowledge and all scientific workers are united in a fellowship "which has the world for its province and the discovery of truth." Lastly pursuit of scientific inquiry demands complete intellectual freedom and unrestricted interchange of knowledge the world over.

Carried *nemine contradicente,* we can all say "Amen" to it. As a matter of fact, "science" has had all these requirements until very recently (and then only partially lacking) as the state of pure and applied science itself testifies. The acquisition of knowledge of matter in motion and change has not so far been notably or long interrupted in the world as a whole nor is there any danger that it is likely so to be in the future. Nobody has much quarrel with "science" as the knowledge of *why* things happen, *how* to make them happen and how to stop *some* of them from happening. What is wrong is what to do with the knowledge that science puts at our disposal and that is *not* science's business.

That is something that "science" does not always seem to understand. Not, at all events, Mr. Wells. He ought to know "science," for he has written a comprehensive "outline" of the whole subject. Yet he emitted a wail of despair at the Association's meeting that was little short of pathetic, inasmuch as it pointed to the extinction of the human race unless man "adapts" himself to the changing conditions. "The question," he said, "is whether man can adapt himself with sufficient rapidity to become either a progressive super-homo or ascendant species, or one of a series of degenerating subhuman species, or whether he would fail to adapt himself and end altogether. Record of the past is on the whole against the idea of any survival whatever of the human strain."

So, having made over the face of the earth to suit himself, having come close to abolishing time and space for his convenience, and having largely emancipated himself from muscular exertion in getting a living, man must now adapt *him-*

self to the conditions he has himself created! Shades of the "Century-of-Progress Man"! To this pass have we come after all the high hopes with which Mr. Wells has entertained us over the last forty years in those fascinating excursions of his fancy on the "shapes" of "things to come." Poor man is no more than Frankenstein, it seems, the victim of his own ingenuity! It seems to this writer that what "science" needs a good deal more than a charter of its liberties is an examination of its own position in the general order of things. As a matter of fact, it is really a very important position, and it has been well filled, well developed and deserves generous recognition as such. What the general run of scientist does not seem to understand is the limitations of that posiiton. "Science" is supreme in its own domain which is the knowledge (science) of matter in motion and change. But scientists as a class—with rare exceptions—have never been satisfied with their own domain. They have always been striving to extend it.

It is true that a scientist is a *man*. As such he is by nature meta-physical for a man cannot help meta-physicizing. What the scientist (generally) forgets is that his "science" has nothing whatever to do with his meta-physics. The two orders of "knowledge" are fundamentally different. They require completely distinct functions of the intellect. It is failure to recognize this elemental fact that has generated the great modern superstition of "Scientism," which with the closely related superstition of "Progress" are perhaps the most distinctive characteristics of the modern age. The superstitition of "Progress" has received a shattering blow in the last quarter-century but "Scientism" still flourishes. The best service that "science" could render to mankind would be to administer the coup-de-grâce to that fungus growth by a thorough examination of its own conscience and a frank confession of the resulting truth.

That truth is, simply, that all the knowledge that "science" can give us of matter in change and motion will tell us only what we *can* do with matter. It can never tell us *what* we ought to do with it or *why* we ought to do it. The fatal blunder of the modern age is in the supposition that it can so tell us and for that blunder *scientists,* and not *science,* are mainly responsible. They have mistaken a part of the story for the whole. It is only fair to say that most of our modern metaphysicians from Ockham down to the present day have made the same mistake.

October 3, 1941

SCIENCE AND CULTURE

Mr. Lawrence K. Frank's article in the June, 1940, *Scientific Monthly,* on "Science and Culture," sets forth with admirable clearness the fundamentals of the all-important question of our time upon the answer to which everything else depends, namely: What is the nature of man? Mr. Frank has his own answer to that question—as should have every thinking person. But the value of his article is mainly in his treatment of the question, for it makes clear both the vise with the two rows between which the choice must lie divided, and the principles determining that division, and that is an ideal way to approach it

Mr. Frank's starting point is one on which we can all agree, namely, the *uniqueness* of man in the visible universe. Man differs from all other living things "because, unlike all other species, he has made his adaptations [to nature] not by organic specialization and bodily differentiation, but through ideas and tools, whereby he has retained his organic plasticity, remained biologically young, unspecialized and capable of continued development." In a word, "man has attempted to live in a world of his own creation." To do this, "it has been necessary not only to forego life on a biological level but also *to create the assumptions and the concepts upon which he could build the human world.*" (Emphasis supplied.) These "assumptions" and "concepts" determine "the process by which man creates and maintains the peculiarly human world and mode of living," and this process Mr. Frank calls "culture." It is the relation of *science* to this "culture" that is the subject of his article.

All human cultures, he says, are attempts at solution of four main groups of problems or questions:

(1) The nature of the universe; how it arose or was created; how it operates; who or what makes these things happen, and why? (2) Man's place in that universe; his origin, nature and destiny; his relation to the world, whether inside or outside nature; (3) Man's relation to his group; who must be sacrificed for whom; the individual's rights, titles, duties and obligations; (4) Human nature and conduct; man's image of self and his motives; what he wants and what he should have; how he should be educated and socialized.

The answers given to these questions are "expressed in the religion, philosophy, the law and the art of each cultural group."

In all cultures of which we have knowledge, there has been, Mr. Frank says, "a theory of origins" which postulates a "super-human, supernatural source"—in other words, each culture has had a *religion.* Here we come to the fork in the road, with the entry of *science.* Mr. Frank's thesis, succinctly stated, is that modern science has eliminated the "super-human" and the "supernatural" from modern culture and remains the sole guide for man in shaping the "assumptions" and the "concepts" by which he will order his life in the world.

We are beginning to realize [he says], that our own culture has been cumulatively undermined by what we call scientific investigation, so that we can no longer accept or believe the older ideas and concepts. We have, in short, a breakdown of the older Western culture, and we must, with the aid of science, formulate new answers to the questions above listed, and in the light of those answers build a new human culture soundly based on scientific knowledge.

Science must give us those answers. "Discovery of the human origin and development of culture," says Mr. Frank, "will be recognized as the greatest of all discoveries." He quotes in a footnote from a former paper of his own on "general education" (*Social Frontier,* March-April, 1937): "We are waiting for a statement of the meaning of scientific knowledge in terms of its emotional significance for living, so that modern astronomy, geology, and biology will provide the equivalent of 'Now I lay me down to sleep,' in which the traditional cosmology, biology and psychology were expressed." He also quotes John Dewey ("Theory of Valuation," in *International Encyclopaedia of Unified Science,* II, 4, p. 66) to the effect that science "is the supreme means of the valid determination of all valuations in all aspects of human and social life."

If science is limited to the observation, correlation and classification of things and facts, which can be seen, heard, touched, tasted, smelt, measured and weighed—as it is commonly supposed to be—what answer can it make to the question: "Why *is* anything, when it *might not be?*" That things *are* is the one great fact, the fundamental and the universal fact that stares us all in the face. All metaphysics is based upon the implications that lie in that fact, and we need no "science" to assure us that it is a fact. There is no more fundamental question that one man can ask another than that "Why?" If science is as we suppose it to be, it has no answer to give to it; if it assumes to answer it at all, it ceases to be science and becomes metaphysics, in which category of intellectual functions it has no competence *as science.*

There is no way out of that dilemma. That Mr. Frank is caught in it does not rob his article of the merit of having made the dilemma's nature clear. The plain fact is that metaphysics owes and can owe nothing to science, while all cultures owe everything to metaphysics. Our Western culture has broken down because it deserted the metaphysics that made it. And it might well be pardoned for looking a trifle askance at the "science" that is now busy destroying it!

July 24, 1940

SCIENCE AND THE MORAL ORDER

Turning the pages of the Rockefeller Foundation's annual report for 1940—and very interesting pages they are (as usual)—this writer's attention was sharpened by the caption: "Science and the Moral Order" and he read with close attention the remarks which followed. They were short and may be summarized very briefly.

Science, says the report, is attacked on the ground that it has "betrayed" civilization, and that it is "degraded" because it "shirks the spiritual issues." The question is frequently asked: "Are there too many nations and too many people everywhere using the instruments of a civilization they have not achieved? Are bigger telescopes and cyclotrons needed in a world like this?" Science is a means of obtaining power and power can be used to do evil. But "possibility of misuse is not an argument for no use at all." Science is more than technology, more than the discovery of new facts; it is a method, a confidence and a faith—a perfectly honest method, a confidence that truth is discoverable, a faith that truth is worth discovering.

Science more than technology? That makes one prick up one's ears. What and how much more? Well, it has developed a "specialized set of mental procedures in a noble tradition respecting their use." The scientist sorts out "pertinent factors," discards irrelevance, describes, clarifies, correlates, constructs hypotheses, then tests, discards or adjusts these hypotheses, extending them to new fields, suspending judgment until the evidence is there, always re-examining theories and definitions, and always prepared to abandon any position however attractive, being always "sanely skeptical of conclusions" and always maintaining "complete dispassionate intellectual honesty."

An excellent description of the mental attitude not only of the true "scientist" but of the attitude of the "intelligent man" in his approach to anything in search of knowledge anywhere any time. This writer will agree with Dr. Fosdick that such an attitude "has undeniable social serviceability," for "it can be a nourishing atmosphere for the development of a factual outlook, of a healthy and flexible skepticism, of a disposition to seek for the causes of things, and of objectivity and tolerance in the appraisal of evidence." (If one is "objective" in appraising evidence, where does "tolerance" come in?) And he will also enthusiastically agree that "measurement and accuracy by themselves do not touch even the fringe of social questions. . . . *knowledge of facts does not tell us what to do about them.*" (Emphasis supplied.) Fine!

But what does? All the *knowledge* that *physics* supplies—for that is what most people understand "science" to mean—has nothing whatever to tell us about what we *ought* to do with the knowledge that it offers, and "morals" means the knowledge of "oughts." That knowledge is completely inaccessible to physics, inaccessible to "natural philosophy," inaccessible even to "mathematics." It begins in "metaphysics." Failure to understand that fundamental fact is the source of the common confusion of popular thinking today, and that confusion is neither more nor less than a gigantic superstition. The essence of that superstition is the opposition that physical science will somehow, sometime, give us all the ultimate answers, the answers to the ultimate questions—*whence? how? why?* and *whither?* of man on this earth. And, to make that superstition all the more deadly in its effects, there is the concomitant superstition that there *is* no metaphysics, that metaphysics is a pure illusion. In the light of that superstition, or rather in its darkness, the word *morals* and the notion of *ought* have absolutely no place—of which obvious fact, the superstition's victims have no recognition.

There is not a word in Dr. Fosdick's remarks on "Science and the Moral Order" that suggests that he is not perfectly aware of this fact. But it seems to this writer that the argument for the scientific *method* would have been all the stronger, if he had at the same time sharply distinguished between the *method* and the *matter* of physical science, and clearly drawn the frontiers separating the knowledge attainable by "science" and the knowledge of the "moral order."

August 6, 1941

EINSTEIN AND GOD

I

What we have grown accustomed to call "ivory towers" are not perhaps ideal vacations resorts for the young and vigorous in these troubled days, but they certainly suit the taste of an aged scribe who is no longer the concern of his country so far as his capacity for any kind of useful service goes. So much, at least, this writer will aver after spending a luscious three weeks in one of them. The main purpose of these edifices is to furnish the opportunity for one's ideals to "settle" and arrange themselves in some kind of order or hierarchy, or, to change the metaphor, to afford a sort of look-out point from which the human scene can be viewed in a somewhat wider perspective than can readily be attained elsewhere. The idea is that the contours of the landscape thus seen will disclose their main alignment and relation to each other, and the landscape as a whole take on its true significance.

That is the *idea*—but the fact is that there is nothing automatic about an ivory tower, nothing, that is, that guarantees a true perspective to the watcher. It may tell two diametrically opposite tales to two watchers, for it depends much upon what the watcher himself brings to the eyepiece of his telescope what he will take away as his map. It happens that the present writer caught—or thinks he caught—a "perspective" that may interest a few of his readers, and on the chance that he did he will venture to offer it for what it may be worth.

Some two weeks or more ago there met in conference in New York a group of men representing religion, philosophy and science, for the purpose of interchanging views in search of common ground upon which these major components of culture might unite in common action for the good of the nation. The group was representative in every sense of the word. The present writer was not privileged to attend the discussions and his information concerning them is derived from press reports. At its opening the conference achieved wide popular notice by reason of an address by Professor Einstein, the world-famous mathematician, in the course of which he informed his hearers that the idea of a personal god could no longer be entertained in the light of modern science and modern thought. This was, of course, "news," just as thirty or more years ago the late Thomas Edison's birthday thoughts on God, immortality and so forth used to be also "news." Probably for many, if not most, newspaper readers, this was all the news there was in the three-day proceedings of the conference.

But the real significance of these proceedings was that they brought clearly into view the great "superstition" of the present time, which asserts that the only *truth* within man's reach is that which modern science has discovered by its experimentation. This resulted from the challenge by "philosophy"—represented in particular by Professor Mortimer Adler, of Chicago, and Jacques Maritain—to the scientists, which was made in the plainest terms and roused the scientists to something like rage. Through these speakers "philosophy" informed "science" that both "theology" (resting on faith) and "philosophy" (resting on reason) were not merely *knowledge* (as truly knowledge as was "science"), but, as knowledge, were *higher* knowledge than the knowledge furnished by science, because dealing with higher orders of reality. In the hierarchy of reality, they said, theology comes first, philosophy next and science last—with, by the way, mathematics nowhere, for mathematics (save as a tool) has nothing to contribute to *reality*. Science, as such, has nothing to teach either philosophy or theology. Thus philosophy's challenge to science.

In responding to the challenge, science could only fall back upon its fundamental dogma that behind the evidence of the senses there is no reality within mankind's ken—nothing knowable of first causes or final ends—and that all speculation on either is pure fantasy and not knowledge. Now the interesting thing about this dogma is that it is itself a *metaphysical* dogma in its very denial that there is such a thing as metaphysical knowledge open to man. It is that which makes the dogma pure superstition. Furthermore, that this denial is made is merely evidence that man is by nature metaphysical; if he were not he would not *deny* metaphysics; he would not be interested in it. If science is asked, "Why *is* anything when it might not *be?*" it has nothing to say, for it knows only *contingent* being. Metaphysics begins with that question and that is where science ends. It seems to the present writer that in clearly setting forth the positions of theology, philosophy and science *vis-à-vis* each other, the apparent failure of the conference to agree on anything may in fact be its real success in laying bare the controversy in its ultimate. And from his ivory turret the present writer seems to see in that controversy the ultimate explanation of the appalling spectacle offered by the world. Such, at least, was a "perspective" that he thought he perceived.

September 30, 1940

II

This writer will beg his readers to allow him one more word on the subject of the "scientific superstition" to which he referred in this corner on Monday last, and its relation to the present state of the world. There are three stages of this phenomenon, all stemming from a basic truth. The truth at the bottom is that science proper, that is, the special investigation of the evidence reaching man's intelligence through his senses, can do no more than report the phenomena of change in the relations of the various forms of matter one to another as they are perceptible of observation by instruments which extend the power of the senses. It must operate upon the data given it, as to the ultimate origin, nature and end of which it can know nothing. It takes matter as it finds it, life as it finds it, just as does man in his common experience of sense, but it can add nothing to that experience in *knowledge* of these ultimate realities.

The first stage of the "scientific superstition" is the belief that science can and someday will attain to this knowledge, and this is the superstition's commonest form. The modern man would call it "faith" in science, but it is faith entirely without support in reason for which there is neither evidence nor authority. The second stage—which is, of course, equally unsupported—is that which, while admitting that man cannot now reach the ultimate realities of science, asserts that the only knowledge that is open to man is that furnished by science, and that all else is pure fantasy, which may or may not be true. The third stage is the assertion that there is no reality other than matter in motion and change; matter, motion and change being self-existent and therefore eternal. This last stage exhibits the superstition in its most extreme form, and, like the first and second, is pure dogma, and dogma without a shadow of support. It is found perhaps most completely expressed in that body of thought associated with the "John Dewey Society" and Teachers College at Columbia University in New York, and it has been erected into a "philosophy" called Naturalism.

This superstition in all its forms is a strictly *modern* development, and in fact *the* distinctively modern heresy, and it is at the root of the crisis in the Western culture and civilization of which the present war is the consequence and its most concrete expression. One way to describe that crisis is in terms of "order." No civilization perhaps ever exhibited a condition of complete order, but every civilization known to man had a conscious urge to order, and order based on some kind of definitely *moral* base, which base had a definitely *religious* character of some sort. As such it was definitely *metaphysical,* that is, outside the realm of science. Christianity, for instance, was the base of the Western civilization, now in a struggle for its life, and it gave us the basis for an *order* in human relations under which we developed a culture and a civilization, the highest of which history has record. Many factors combined over a long time to undermine that base and the order resting upon it, but the impact of the scientific superstition coming first in the nineteenth century seems to have been the most serious influence.

Man is so constituted that he cannot long endure disorder. If he cannot get order in one way, he will seek it in another. The moral base of order being rejected by him, there remains for the modern man only *force* and the totalitarian state's essential characteristic is precisely order by force, completely divorced from morals. But order by force is not an order that accords with man's nature, if he is a thing of spirit as well as matter—as most of us feel that we are. Hence the instinctive revolt against the totalitarian phenomenon on the part of people whose instincts are more *human* than their "philosophies," and we find, happily, many of these fighting against a "philosophy" in action, with whose base in the *abstract* they are more or less inclined to concur. For the scientific superstition in any form can offer little or no ground of opposition to the "philosophy" underlying all three forms of totalitarianism —Fascism, Nazism or Soviet Communism.

So long as our instincts prove stronger than our superstitions, there is hope for the civilization to which we belong, for which others are fighting, and for which we are mobilizing *force* to defend. But how long can we continue this condition to last, if our superstitions continue to exist and to grow, as the scientific superstition has grown in the last century? That we owe much, very much, to scientists in the *application* of their science, and that we revere the true spirit of scientists working in their own tremendous field, is no reason why we should accept the gratuitous dogmatizing of so many of them in fields where they not only have no competence but upon their own postulates can logically claim none. A man cannot reasonably in one breath deny *meta*-physical knowledge of truth by a *meta*-physical judgment; yet this is what the third stage of the superstition requires one to do.

October 2, 1940

ECONOMICS: ORDER AND DISORDER

MEN MUST BE PUT TO WORK

I

Some seven months ago, when President Roosevelt took office and inaugurated the "New Deal," it was literally a "sea of troubles" that confronted him. The most acute and immediately dangerous of these troubles was the bank crisis. That was happily surmounted by swift and courageous handling, even if there yet remains a great deal to do before our bank situation can be called healthy. But the most serious and persistent of all the problems that then demanded attention was that of unemployment. It was—and is—the most serious because, if it remains unsolved, solution of the other problems would not avail; it was—and is—the most persistent because there was—and is—no "short cut" to its solution. Today it looms more clearly than before, and the basic difficulty in its solution stands out in all the bolder relief for the partial clearance that has been made in other directions.

The *Wall Street Journal* deems it useful to set out in plain terms the nature of that difficulty, for, if that be done, the road by which it must be surmounted will become plainly visible. So, too, will appear the consequences of refusal—or inability—to take that road.

Statistics of "unemployment" are notoriously incomplete and unreliable; they will, therefore, be eschewed. We start with certain plain data. One is that since March last a substantial number of men have been returned to work. Another is that a much larger number are still unemployed. A third is that the one main object at present, whose importance transcends all others, is to get the latter back to work at the earliest possible moment.

Certain other assumptions seem to be valid. The first is that while a substantial number of men have already been returned to work in the "durable goods" industries, as well as in those producing "consumption goods" and "services," a further rapid and large addition to the *latter* forces cannot reasonably be expected without a considerable increase in consumption by the nation as a whole. The second is that the main hope for employment, so far as the greater proportion of those still unemployed is concerned, is a marked increase in the production of durable goods. These goods are of three general classes:

(1) Durable goods of a gradual consumption character (e.g., houses, furnishings, motors, etc.).

(2) Durable goods represented by public property for public convenience and pleasure (e.g., streets, parks, sewers, water, roads, etc.).

(3) Durable goods of a commercial or productive character (e.g., office buildings, factories, machinery railroads).

Class 1 is paid for mainly from individual savings (i.e., capital) or by creation of debt eventually to be liquidated by individual savings. Class 2 is paid for from accumulated corporate or individual borrowing eventually liquidated by current savings. *Long-term credit or permanent capital investment bulks most largely in the creation of all three kinds.*

Therefore, if production of these classes of goods is to be resumed, long-term credit or permanent capital investment must be made available.

Inasmuch as the greater part of present unemployment can only be removed by resumption of production of durable goods, inasmuch as such production requires investment of capital in some form and inasmuch as capital of this sort can only come—in the natural course—from corporate or individual savings, past or to come, *the real problem of unemployment resolves itself into a problem of enlisting privately owned capital in support of the National Recovery campaign.*

One of the most notable features of the present world-depression has been the reluctance of capital to go into long-term investment. This phenomenon is practically universal; at all events it is not peculiar to the United States. The reasons are so obvious as to require no more than mere mention. They resolve themselves into one great overshadowing complex of doubts—doubt as to safety of principal, doubt as to prospect of return and (perhaps most acute of all) doubt as to the stability of the very money units in which capital is measured. The result is that in all countries capital has sought to keep itself "safe," and its tendency to rush from one market to another in its efforts to find a haven of security has had much influence in precipitating the general chaos of the currencies.

Nevertheless, it is in the United States that our problem presents itself and it is here that it must be grappled with and solved.

Capital is always more or less timorous save in times of pure speculative boom. Its excesses, moreover, at these times make it correspondingly overfearful in times of depression. It has always before it difficult problems of costs, wages, volume of product, prices, and so forth, and all are present now. But mainly determining its present reluctance to grasp what should be—and in times past has always been—an opportunity for its active use are two outstanding fears.

There is the fear of "inflation" of the money unit. There is the fear that "return" upon investment, however small, will be hard to earn, within a reasonable time, and that under the New Deal capital's rights and profits are ultimately going to be restricted within very narrow limits. Rightly or wrongly, both these fears are present and it is the presence of these fears which is important.

If they could be removed the road to employment would be opened, and progress to the goal would be greatly facilitated. That road is the shortest and the best because it is the natural road. It is the road that has always been traveled in the past. If it can be opened now the problem will be on its way to solution. *October* 16, 1933

II

Throughout all public and private discussion of the 1929-1933 depression and the means of combating it has run the word "inflation" like the chant of a Greek chorus.

It has seldom meant the same thing to any two disputants or the same thing to any one of them twice. In the scrambled terminology of the day it has been used to mean anything from an unlimited printing-press currency to an expansion of the volume of outstanding credits and deposit money.

Some time ago we began to discuss currency inflation as a "cure" for depression, to be deliberately taken in appropriate dosage and discontinued the moment it had served that purpose. It was to give prostrate industry only the initial impulse it needed to regain its feet. Then the emphasis shifted and we spoke of so rearranging the monetary system that it would automatically raise all commodity prices enough to render an insupportable debt burden no heavier that it was when incurred.

Still more recently gossip from Washington centers around

"redefining the dollar" and "stabilizing" our currency in order to facilitate foreign trade, war-debt settlements and Government refunding and new financing. While the talk is still of "monetary readjustment" for this, that or the other purpose, it is still tacitly assumed at all times that whatever form of "inflation" may be under discussion it is always to be a "controlled" inflation.

The argument for "control" is simple. All the instances of inflation in the history books have resulted from Government's imperative need for money to meet its expenses—that is, from unbalanced and unbalanceable budgets. Ours is to be a deliberately chosen policy, undertaken for a definite and limited objective, and to end with attainment of that objective. Consequently, it can be controlled and we have the will to control it. So say the "inflationists." It sounds like fair logic.

But even as logic it does not convince capital, which is convinced that, logic or no logic, real and thoroughgoing "inflation" will follow any tampering with the money unit.

Furthermore, an unpleasant fact is emerging into sight which does not fit the logic. That is that the many and varied projects which are part of the general plan of recovery are apparently carrying the question of our "money" steadily away from the level fields of free choice to the slippery slopes of compulsion.

These are the projects which draw their life from the use of Government credit. Assume (it is a liberal assumption) that the "ordinary" budget of the Treasury is in balance; our "extraordinary" projected commitments, actual and contingent, lie somewhere between a minimum of eight billions and a maximum of twelve, and a large part of these may become actual obligations within twelve months. Already in the last three years we have increased the national debt by six billions.

What is the difference between an "ordinary" budget which is unbalanced and a balanced "ordinary" budget coupled with a huge "extraordinary" budget for which no corresponding revenue is or can be made available? And if there *is* no difference, what becomes of the logical distinction which the advocates of inflation seek to draw and to apply?

It is uncontrolled (because uncontrollable) inflation that capital thinks it sees ahead, and it is fear of that which—perhaps most of all—has induced its present emotional paralysis.

In face of that paralysis it seems almost a waste of time to examine the arguments for even a "controlled" inflation, as a means of restoring what we regard as a "normal" level of prices and thereby recreating a tolerable relation between debtor and creditor. But it is well to keep one or two things in mind.

For instance—"Money" *as such* affects prices of everything else only as a result of change either in its *volume* or the *rapidity of its turnover*. Debasement of the dollar *as such* can be effective in raising the *general* level of prices only if it increases the volume of money units outstanding or the velocity with which the outstanding units move in trade whether directly as cash or as bank credit. The only exception to this is the case of such commodities as are exchanged mainly in outside markets where prices are still measured in gold. *Standing alone*, dollar debasement does not *necessarily* increase either volume or velocity of outstanding money; it merely provides the *potentiality* for increased issue of paper money or increased bank credit upon the same quantity of gold reserve.

Innocent as would be in itself the single act of dollar debasement, capital dreads it as a first step on the fatal slope. Once upon that slope, fear, like the force which we call gravity, has its own law of acceleration, and if not checked it ultimately outstrips even the utmost speed to which the printing presses can be driven—as Germany has showed us.

In a word, it is the economic romanticism of any and all proposals to tamper with the money unit that capital (which is ever intensely realist) instinctively rejects. Economic romanticism of all sorts is an invariable product of hard times. So long as it is rife capital simply will not seek or accept its normal employment. As a matter of fact it has been abandonment of romanticism that has always in the past marked the start of recovery.

Can we suppose that our experience this time will be different? *October* 17, 1933

III

Next to the fear of inflation of the currency, which stands first among the factors driving the owner of capital into anything which looks like a "safe" hiding place, is doubt as to return of income obtainable from its employment.

No amount of hortatory rhetoric will avail to dispose of the fact that return—in plain language, profit—on invested capital is the very heart and essence of what we call the Capitalist System. Without it that system cannot exist in any form. If people are to continue to save and to put their savings to work, they must have a sufficient motive, and the only conceivable motive that will suffice is the expectation of profit. That profit, moreover, must be large enough to make the motive effective. How large it "ought" to be to accord with the principles of social justice is a legitimate subject for debate. But the immediately important fact is that if capital is to be brought into action the motive *must* be present, and that—whether rightly or wrongly, reasonably or unreasonably, is for the moment irrelevant—the motive is lacking.

It is lacking because one important part of the New Deal constitutes an inversion of the process by which in the past recovery from depression has got itself underway. That process *began* invariably with reappearance of *some* profit in industry and commerce. Under that stimulus industry and trade gradually expanded, cautiously feeling its way. The first effects were felt in increased employment as production and distribution increased and finally wage rates joined the upward movement. That was the sequence of events. It was a natural sequence and profit was its main-spring.

The New Deal set itself to change the sequence by placing increased employment and increased wages first and relegating profit to the last place. It invited capital to "invest in wages and in work," and wait for its profit as a final consequence of that investment.

Granted, for the sake of argument, that there was both justice and logic in the idea, the fact is that as human nature is constituted it was too violent a change of orientation to be accomplished in a hurry. The hope of profit as the *final* result of such a process has thus far been too dim and too remote to induce capital to activity.

Nor is this all. The New Deal includes yet another part equally disturbing from the same point of view.

That part is commonly described by the phrase, "redistribution of the national income." All that is necessary to note is that such redistribution will have as one of its principal features a notable diminution of the share allotted to capital and an increase of the shares of everyone else.

Not much need be said as to this particular complication. It is something that has long been preparing in the historical process by which the thing we so loosely call Democracy has come into being. The New Deal has merely brought a quickening of that process and has substituted for the slow and continuous progress of evolution a sudden and large change of a kind to which we give the name of "revolution."

Recognition of that change is percolating the consciousness of owners of capital with the inevitable result of increasing their already great perplexity and alarm. Not only do they think they see no *immediate* profitable opportunity for employment of their capital, but they visualize a yet greater re striction of their rights and their profits in the future, which takes on an appearance of something painfully like ultimate confiscation.

It makes not a hair of difference whether their fear is or is not reasonable. It is the *presence* of the fear as a *fact* that is important, for it constitutes another complication to be faced in dealing with our problem. It must be remembered that it is a problem in emotional psychology—and not in physics, logic or mathematics—that we are facing at this time, wherein, in fact, lies its chief difficulty.

The New Deal *must* have capital *if* it is to employ our people, and it *must* employ our people. Assume that it will not supply the motive necessary to induce voluntary enlistment of private capital, that is, that it will not offer the opportunity for a return sufficiently attractive for its direct investment in new "durable goods," what other source of the needed capital is open?

If capital itself will not assume the risks involved in the new sequence, the Government must do so. That means the use of Government credit for creation of that class of "durable goods" that we call public works. Government must borrow from the private investor the capital that he is unwilling himself directly to risk. It seems on its face a simple and practicable alternative. We have in fact already determined to employ it and are employing it as a part of our general plan.

But here, too, we encounter the same difficulty in another form. Can Government borrow from the investor upon reasonable terms the capital that will be needed if the *entire* burden of re-employment is to be laid upon Government credit? Here at once re-enters the fear of "inflation," and with it is coupled yet another doubt, that is, as to the ability of the Government to lay and collect—in any kind of money—the taxes necessary to make attractive the security that it offers. Whether that fear and that doubt are really warranted is irrelevant in face of the plain fact that both are present, to the mind of the private investor.

By whatever road and from whatever starting point we approach the problem we arrive at the same destination, and the same seeming impasse.

The New Deal *must* tap the resources of private capital—yet thus far it has, with the best intentions in the world, apparently tended to close up the very sources from which it must draw the one thing it most needs.

That is the fact which at this time confronts us. It must be squarely met. *October* 26, 1933

IV

Whether those fears are reasoning or unreasoning is totally immaterial so long as they in fact exist. The fact of their existence is plain even to a blind man. So long as they exist paralysis of private capital for permanent investment in new property will continue.

Not only does this paralysis prevent capital from assuming the risk of such investment on its own account, but it also brings sharply into question the ability of Government to borrow capital indefinitely and itself assume that risk. The consequence is that the specter of uncontrolled currency inflation instantly begins to arise in the investor's imagination at the end of the road of "public works."

Some may say—"If private capital will neither invest on its own account nor lend to the Government, let us draft it by a capital levy. That will relieve us from the need of using the printing press."

The answer is that this expedient is not open, and a simple analysis will make this clear.

It is *fluid, uninvested capital* that we need for employment of men. That exists in only two forms—currency and bank deposits. Cash is fluid. But bank deposits are fluid only to the extent that the assets which they represent are fluid. Stocks, bonds and mortgages are fixed and not fluid assets. Commercial paper is fluid in a sense, but only so long as the "cycles" of transactions which it renders possible work continuously. Profits are the final result of those cycles when completed. It is the capital generated by those profits upon which capital levy would have to be made to be of use in solving the problem.

The amount of such capital actually existing at any given time is not so very large. It is its *constant generation* by the uninterrupted operation of those innumerable "trade cycles" upon which dependence for its supply always has been and must always be based. Bank deposits are the main form in which this fluid capital is accumulated.

What would be the result of even a suspicion that a levy upon bank deposits was possible? Would it not be an instant run upon the banks by depositors in order that they might get cash and bury the cash? And in such case how much fluid capital would continue to exist at all? And what would probably be the effect upon the trade cycles from which new bank deposits accumulate?

The capital that we must have in order to put men to work must be either enticed to go to work for itself or borrowed by Government. It cannot be drafted.

"Very well!" someone may say, "If it cannot be drafted, why cannot we make capital by use of the printing press?"

One would suppose that any German, Austrian, Frenchman or Italian—not to mention others—could supply the answer to that question. It can, perhaps, be most succinctly put in the statement that the result would be to expropriate the holder of every bank deposit, every insurance policy, every Government bond, every corporation bond, every promissory note and every mortgage in the country. The owners of these constitute the vast majority of our people in these United States.

If history tells us anything, it tells us that for every man whom uncontrolled inflation temporarily puts to work it ultimately discharges at least two.

Use of the printing press in this way would be the last wild counsel of despair. It would be strictly analogous to the leap from the twentieth story of a burning building to the pavement below. There is no relief—no "way out"—in that.

No—the printing press will not serve, and no draft of capital—*the kind of capital we need*—is possible.

"Very well," it may be said, "Let it be Government public works. We know that these are possible, for we are building them all the time. Why not do it that way?"

It is not in itself a *good* way because it is not a *natural* way, and it can be justified only by necessity, and as the lesser evil. But, as already pointed out, the very circumstances of the case are such as to bring even its *practicability* into question. It depends upon Government's credit with the investor. There are under any circumstances quantitative limits to that credit and these limits tend to be swiftly contracted in the presence of doubt however slight in the investor's mind. Government is already committed to a scheme of relief upon a generous scale as well as to a large program of new work. To lay upon it, in addition, the main burden of remedying unemployment would be to raise a cloud of doubts which might well defeat the possibility of success at the very outset.

Government may perhaps safely bear a part of that burden, but the smaller that part is, the better.

The sum and substance of the whole matter is that if the premise with which we start is sound—that is, that only large-scale, permanent capital investment can return our idle men to normal employment—the conclusion is irresistible, that it can be done only by voluntary enlistment of private capital. By no other road can the goal surely be reached.

How can capital be brought to the recruiting stations?

It must at least be assured that there is to be no uncontrolled money inflation, and that it will have what seems to be at least a reasonable chance of making some profit.

Let no one for a moment assume that the *Wall Street Journal,* in saying this, either advocates or regards as possible a return to the old anarchic conditions of so-called "investment" and its concomitant excesses of wild "speculation." Those conditions should not be allowed to return. Such a return capital in its own interests could not tolerate.

But investment of capital in some form for production of durable goods we must have and, to the extent that modification of some of the laws, plans and ideas of the New Deal is necessary to produce that investment, such modification will have to be made—or else the men will not go back to work.

October 27, 1933

PROLETARIAN INFERENCES FROM THE ARTS

Professor Seymour's book, *American Neutrality, 1914-17,* is devoted to puncturing the theory that we were led into the war in 1914 by a mere desire to protect bankers' investments in loans to Allies and "profits" to big business, and so forth. He has little difficulty in showing that it was the German submarine that tipped the scales—which most intelligent people knew long ago. But that will not avail to change the views prevailing among the mass of people who are convinced that a conspiracy by the "money changers" instigated by Great Britain did the trick. Did we not allow our "bankers" to make loans to the Allies? Did not our industrial "autocrats" make large profits as a result? Well then—?

Quite so. And there will be no finality to the argument. The only interesting thing about it is that it is a demonstration of something which runs as a continuous thread through our entire social structure as a kind of *leit-motiv*, and is, this writer believes, a symptom of fundamental change in the structure itself. The attack on "wealth"—"concentrated" wealth, "entrenched" wealth—is, of course, evident in the political field, for it has been from the beginning the mainspring of the New Deal. On that fact, at least, there is no controversy, for New Dealers themselves make it their boast. The "wealthy" of today occupy the same position in popular execration that the French "aristocrat" did a century and a half ago. Maybe they should; maybe not. The relevant fact is that they *do*.

This is not by any means a wholly new phenomenon. When the yellow journalism came along some thirty or more years ago, we became well acquainted in the headlines with the misdeeds of the "wealthy clubman." The muckraking era, following rapidly on the shortlived worship of the "Captains of Industry," made "news" of anything to which the dollar sign could be attached, and the more ciphers that followed it the bigger the news. A million dollars in any connotation could always put its owner on the front page. The new thing in the phenomenon is the change in the emphasis of the news and the development of "proletarian" art, literature, drama and criticism. Money in bulk is still news, but now it places its owner in the public enemy class.

Mexican murals are today your only true art in painting; sculpture must reflect revolt (if against nothing else, against beauty, for mere beauty is bourgeois and reactionary); a novel that does not take for its theme the class-struggle is not literature at all; the proletarian play is today all the rage among the cognoscenti. Our book reviewers (those, at least, under forty years of age) exhibit extraordinary skill in drawing good proletarian inferences or morals out of almost anything printed, from metaphysics to gardening.

When a "movement" gets to the point of expressing itself in what we for the nonce may call literature, art and criticism, we may safely assume that something is moving, especially when at the same time politics exhibits the same characteristics. Particularly interesting is it to note that the "neutrality" debate is so concerned with the "big money" motif, which, indeed, is one reason for the confusion of thought and talk that has thus far characterized it.

Now this is significant of something, and this writer submits that it backs up his pet theory. That theory holds that we are engaged in working out the second stage of the thing that we call the French Revolution—namely, the demand for economic equality. As in the case of the first stage (which established political equality) the process naturally begins with dispossession of the top-dogs. We are doing pretty well with that already. But there is a difference between the transfer of political power from one class to another and the transfer of "wealth." The difference is that, while political power can be integrally thus transferred, has been in fact so transferred, it is most doubtful that economic wealth can be dealt with in the same way without a large loss in transit. It is comparatively easy to take it away at the top, but to keep it intact and pass it along to the lower brackets is the difficult job. That we shall, no doubt, find out in due time.

It is a habit with theorists, of course, to grasp at any fact which seems to support their theories, and this theorist knows quite well that in this respect he differs not at all from his kind. Nevertheless, it does not seem to him an accident or insignificant that preoccupation with the subject of money and wealth looms so large in the picture today. And, anyhow, he feels confident that the reader will not grudge him the satisfaction of spinning a little more theory.

January 7, 1936

ON ECONOMICS

CAPITALISM: INDIVIDUALIST VS. COLLECTIVE

I

Four years ago Lucien Romier published in Paris a small volume, *Si le capitalisme disparaissait* ("If Capitalism Were to Disappear"), in which he lucidly analyzed the present phenomena in the economic world with especial reference to the thing we call capitalism. Romier, like so many other cultivated Frenchmen, has a keen sense of history and has published several historical studies which have received respectful attention in France. His study of modern man *(L'Homme nouveau)* is a suggestive and illuminating work on the impact of the new politico-economic conditions on human behavior. The book on capitalism is equally suggestive.

What is capitalism? Romier's definition is simple: "the development of human enterprise by expansion of credit." Property, as such, is not necessarily capital; mere thrift, as such, is not capital. Capitalism begins and ends with the use of credit. If one disappears, the other vanishes. Capitalism of old *used* credit; modern capitalism *abuses* it. Capitalism's diseases are neither diseases of property or of thrift; they are diseases of credit. Attacks on mere property or thrift are strictly regarded as matters in the juridical order, not the economic; but as matters stand today the two orders are closely intermingled, for credit depends upon the confidence of property owners, savers and trustees.

Is *socialism* the alternative to capitalism? No, says Romier, for socialism's very principles are in contradiction. It professes to defend the working classes and provide for the material welfare of all. But as things are today, the working class depends upon capitalism, that is, on credit, for its existence, and in attacking capitalism socialism destroys confidence which is the foundation of credit. Socialism is feasible only under the forms of state socialism under either bourgeois governments or dictatorships, thus penetrating without destroying capitalism. But state socialism is not socialism. In fighting capitalism as such socialism is fighting against itself, for it needs the nourishment which capitalism alone can supply. If capitalism disappears, we should either have a system of forced labor and food cards or we should be forced to return to a primal form of patriarchal economy.

What has gone wrong with capitalism? What is the remedy? Romier's diagnosis, in broad outline, is something like this:

In former times capitalist operations were predominantly *personal*, and were conducted with *savings* made and in hand, as contrasted with *credit* borrowed. Capitalism was predominantly individualist rather than collective. During the last third of the nineteenth century a large emigration of European people to the new and undeveloped countries took place with a consequent emigration of European capital, owned by individual firms and later by large trading companies. The effect was to shift the power from a relatively slow *development* of existing enterprises to a rapidly growing *speculative* foundation of new ones, and the use of credit increased *pari passu*. After the war the pace of this process increased enormously. The war and its consequences, Romier says, "have widened and quickened as by a miracle the rhythm of overseas capitalist enterprise. They have changed the nature of European capitalism by substituting in Europe's economy a predominance of concentrated and anonymous bank-created capital for the former predominance of dispersed, individual capital created by savings."

Hence the rise of the banker to dominance, and the dependence, since the war, of states, companies and the majority of individuals on credit, together with a general tendency to speculation on prospect of future gains. Now the justification of capitalism is that it tends to enrich the material comforts of men by provision of more new products and services, and by industrializing the process of their production to diminish the burden of human toil. Modern capitalism has done this, but in doing it has, in its search for profit, engendered financial and economic anarchy and consequent disaster for all concerned. It has lacked all social consciousness, has been devoid of all moral restraint, and, of course, has lacked anything like intelligent foresight of the consequences.

That is what is wrong with capitalism. What is the remedy? The world needs capitalism if it is to keep and enlarge its living standards. Romier's conclusion is that it must develop a social consciousness, it must moderate its lust for profit, it must curb its speculative propensity, and it must cultivate intelligent foresight of the future. It must coordinate and correlate its plans and its operations with respect to the whole. It must have a philosophy, and it must have morals. It must have a directing power. *May* 21, 1937

II

Dr. Virgil Jordan, president of the National Industrial Conference Board, speaking at the annual meeting of the Chamber of Commerce of the United States, has touched the vitals of the matter of capitalism at a point somewhat different from that touched by Romier. Romier in the course of his argument fully recognized the material achievements of capitalism as represented by the greatly increased comforts enjoyed by the mass of the people and concerned himself mainly with the mistakes and defects. Dr. Jordan dealt with the thing that gave capitalism its life, especially in the United States. He called it *enterprise*, and he recognized it as "the vital principle underlying the accomplishment and character of the American people."

Its essence lies in personality. It is the principle upon which life and labor are so organized as to release the creative powers of the human person, for upon those powers exercised by individual persons depends the collective welfare. Progress is no doubt obtained by collective effort but not by collective creative power; that is strictly personal. Enterprise is personal, not collective. There must therefore be the utmost possible freedom for this power to operate. As Dr. Jordan puts it, "Personal freedom and responsibility are the twin moral roots of the enterprise principle." What it means in practice is that any person shall be free to work at any occupation, to save money, to acquire and own property, to enter any business, and to invest his savings as he pleases—all on his own judgment, on his own terms and on his own responsibility. All, of course, subject to the laws of the land protecting the common order and common justice, and all without the seeking of privilege at the hands of government and, by corollary, without unnecessary restriction by government. The function of government should be to protect the conditions under which the enterprise principle can fully function while preserving the rights of each and everyone concerned.

Now the problem that we face is, in the first place, to preserve social justice—that is, to prevent the imposition upon any group or class of living conditions which are not consistent with at least a minimum standard of living due to a human person as a person—and in the second place, to so manage the whole process as to avoid recurrent breakdowns causing large interruptions of employment and consequent suffering to many—and both with the maximum freedom for enterprise. Putting it in another way, it is to achieve a combination of progress and security.

Enterprise in practice is merely trial and error, and must always so be. Error involves casualties and the progress that we have made in the last hundred years has involved huge casualties. Hence D. C. Coyle's epigram: "A country can stand as much progress as it can stand bankruptcy." The practical question thus is how many casualties can we stand, or are willing to stand, for upon that answer depends the amount of progress that we can expect. Not that the casualty factor cannot be diminished by intelligence illumined by experience, for it can. That is what Romier means by his emphasis upon foresight and planning. Dr. Jordan, equally with Romier, rejects anarchy in individual effort. The question is: How shall anarchy be excluded? Whose task is it to be to correlate individual effort to collective results? In a word, who shall plan?

Romier's position is that civilization depends on capitalism, and that capitalism must have a philosophy and a moral system. At present it has none. Nor has the state. Statism cannot be capitalist, much less can a dictatorship. Capitalist philosophy and morals cannot come from the state or a dictator. Dr. Jordan points out that the state (in this country) has already largely established control of business and industry and is gradually asphyxiating enterprise. He calls on business and industry to resist its complete destruction. Romier believes the essence of enterprise (as Dr. Jordan describes it) to be practically incompatible with planning by business and industry themselves for the collective results. He wants it done by experts who themselves are neither officers of government nor in active business, but are convinced adherents of the principles of capitalism. Dr. Jordan believes that it is the job of business and industry, and the job of neither government nor experts. But he, too, is in search of "honest, enlightened and fearless leadership *from some source as yet unseen*" (emphasis supplied) to save the principle of enterprise for the American people.

"Some source yet unseen"; there's the rub! The truth on which we can all agree—probably—is that until we tap that source we shall have to choose between progress and security for we can't have both. Moreover, are we quite sure that we can have security, even at the price of progress, and keep our liberties? This writer is not. *May* 26, 1937

PERSONAL FORTUNES

I

Alfred P. Sloan's gift to establish an institute for research into "basic economic truths" is another illustration of the fact—indeed, without much exaggeration, one could call it a law—that large individual fortunes tend almost inevitably to return at the last to public service or benefit. That certainly is true of this country, at all events.

Lacking as we are in the tradition of continuity, which in the Old World has imposed a dynastic character on families in the upper brackets of wealth, especially where that wealth is rooted in manorial lands, there really is no place for the wealth to go other than back where it came from. Large wealth cannot be spent and it is a man's spending and not his possessions that are the measure of what he gets—for himself and his family—of the material goods of this world. "In meal or malt," as the Irish put it; the public, sooner or later, gets the rest.

That phrase, "basic economic truths," piques one's fancy somewhat. It is redolent of old times when we used to talk seriously and at great length of the *Economic Man*.

That imaginary being exists abundantly in fossil form in that nineteenth-century formation which appropriately might be termed the "automatic progress fault" in the general stratification of human thinking, immediately preceding the present seismic catastrophe. He was an interesting specimen while he lasted, for he constituted a complete mutation, which, however, did not result in a new species—probably because he was a flat contradiction of human nature.

In the first place, he was a standardized creation in whom the individual and the average were one and the same thing, which we know isn't so. In the second place, he was treated as a wholly determined thing helplessly responsive to external stimuli, whose actions and reactions could be predicted almost as closely as those of inorganic matter under heat, motion or pressure. In short, the *Economic Man* was not a person; he was a statistical datum.

This writer is well aware that in establishing the institute for the discovery of basic economic truth, Mr. Sloan is under no such delusion as to the matter with which it will have to deal. If there is one really hopeful sign in these times, it is the recognition by a rapidly growing body of intelligent thought that the rock-bottom cause of the present world-wide mess was the implicit denial by the nineteenth century of what Walter Lippmann correctly has called the "inviolable personality" of man and the consequent attempt to order human society on the basis of that denial by transferring the concept of personality to the State.

It is that transfer which is the vital principle in fascism and communism, in which it finds complete expression, but it is present under other forms of society, including our own. The ironical paradox is that it is among the leftist groups, which arrogate to themselves the label of liberal and progressive, that it is most clearly visible as an active principle.

Economics presumably signifies the field of human actions in supplying the needs of life on this earth. It is, therefore, a subdivision of general ethics, which deals with the conduct of rational beings—that is, *persons,* for it is reason that makes personality.

The first requisite for searching out the truth of economics is clear recognition of the fact that bad ethics cannot be good economics and that there is no body of laws in economics which can contravene the laws of ethics and produce anything but disaster. If the institute which Mr. Sloan has made possible by his munificence founds its study from the outset on that truth, it may render tremendous service to mankind. This writer suspects that it is this or something very like it which Mr. Sloan had in mind in making his gift.

December 20, 1937

II

The attitude of what we call the "public mind" toward "great fortunes" has been liberally exploited by a novelist or rather by our novelists and by that group of public social critics whom, forty years ago, Theodore Roosevelt (rather unfairly) labeled "muck-rakers." It has long seemed to the present writer that one aspect of these phenomena has been largely overlooked, notwithstanding the fact that it literally stares one in the face. The fact is that the American great fortunes return—and swiftly—to their sources as they do not, at least not nearly so swiftly, elsewhere in the world. It is true that the old proverb of "Three generations from shirt sleeves to shirt sleeves" momentarily squints in that direction, but catches only a partial glimpse of the important fact, namely, the return of the "wealth" to the place from whence it came—the public. The disposition of the Harkness estate reported last week is but one of a long series of similar instances. A sum of about $100,000,000 is involved, and even in these days that is a great fortune. It surprises no one very much that it is to go mainly to public institutions; we have been accustomed to that for a long time. What we have not seemed to realize is that there is, in fact, no other place for it to go. Nor have we further realized that before its final disposition it was already "in the public service," seeing that it existed in the form of "investments" in that service. As a matter of fact, great fortunes in this country must, willy-nilly, employ themselves in that way about as fast as they are generated.

But, someone will, perhaps, say: "How about a man who *holds* millions of railroad, or public utility bonds, or municipal securities or government bonds—he owns them, doesn't he, and he draws his interest from them?" Assuredly he does, but what does he do with the interest after he has paid his own family's living expenses? Even the richest man can use only a very small part of his income in that way. And all that he and his family *get for themselves* out of their fortune is what they can *use* in that way. What becomes of the rest? It can go only into more bonds and all those bonds represent *things* in the public service—to say nothing of endowments for colleges, hospitals and "foundations" for philanthropic purposes, which draw no interest. It appears that during his life Mr. Harkness "gave away" over $117,000,000 and that the total of these contributions, together with the remaining estate which will go the same way ultimately, will amount to $225,000,000. And that will be the end of the Harkness "great fortune," which from beginning to end will have covered but three generations of time.

"All right," one hears someone say, "that's the end, but how about its beginning? Where did it come from?" Very good; let us look at that side of it. Before doing so, let us clear the discussion of all questions of personal *behavior*, personal *motives* and of *methods* employed by the persons involved and look only at the *results* to the "public" of the process that produced these large rewards. The Standard Oil "trust" was one of the pioneer experiments in what we have come to call "integrated" industry, that is, an industrial process bringing together the principal operations in a single closely knit organization for manufacturing and selling. As a consequence, the use of petroleum and its products increased with remarkable speed as prices were reduced and access to profits made easy. Whatever else may be said about it, there is no doubt that the organization built up in the 80's gave the public an earlier, a cheaper, a more abundant volume of products than could have been supplied without it. This is not to say that it was the *best* of all possible organizations that could have accomplished the result or that the result was the best that could have been accomplished by any organization. It is merely to say that the result was better for the public than if no integrated process had been adopted. There is no known accurate methods of measuring in dollars and cents the resulting benefits to the American consumer so as to compare these benefits with the rewards to those who brought it about, for what "might, could, would or should have happened if something else had not happened" is both pure and empty speculation with no answer. But no one who remembers the early 80's and subsequent three decades will be disposed to say that the rewards look at least out of proportion to the achievements. But even were they twice too large, they had started flowing back to the "public service" about as fast as the "public" paid them.

All this is merely to say that these "great fortunes" (the same could be said with respect to all but very few of the others) were, in fact, in no sense parasitic upon the country's economy, either in their origin or their destination, but were essentially creative. Another point is worth noting which distinguishes them from Old World great fortunes; they seem to lack the "dynastic" quality of long continued possession in the same hands from generation to generation, and this was apparent long before the inheritance tax fastened its teeth upon their throats. As was said a long time ago by a French observer (this writer forgets by whom), the American fever to "get" is surpassed only by the fever to "give."

However all this may be, we now seem determined that if we can do it, we shall prevent more "great fortunes" being built amongst us, and the question arises, where in the future we shall look for the money necessary to keep our educational and philanthropic institutions in the "style" to which we have accustomed them to live. None of our postwar blueprints, so far, seem to touch this point.

January 19, 1944

BANK CREDIT

I

Fundamental in the classical (Aristotelian) metaphysics is the distinction between potency and act (or matter and form) and it is immensely fertile in content. The phenomenon of bank credit in these days perhaps is easiest to comprehend under the analogy of potency and act.

Bank credit exists potentially in the form of bank deposits owned by myriads of individuals and corporations. It becomes actual only when it is lent out to other individuals and corporations.

Never in the history of American banking has there been so large a potential of bank credit as there is at present—and this despite the fact that not in at least three-quarters of a century have the minima of legal reserves of commercial banks in the large cities been so high as they are now. It is important to note the process by which this potential becomes actualized.

The common impression seems to be that the banker *creates credit*—that is, that he lends money which he does not possess, getting it by some mysterious process out of thin air. Untrue. No bank president can lend money to anyone unless he has deposits on his books and a cash reserve in excess of the minimum which the law requires him to keep against those deposits.

The only money the bank *owns* is its own capital and surplus, which, in fact, is a main source of its reserve. The vast majority of the loans made by banks (and the investments purchased by banks) are made from the funds which the bank itself has borrowed from its depositors. In point of fact, the actual bank credit at any time outstanding consists of loans to individuals and corporations made (through the bank) by other individuals and corporations whose deposits are used for that purpose—in a word, loans *by* private citizens *to* private citizens.

If a banker cannot create credit, how does it happen that the volume of active bank credit can expand as it does in active business, generating more credit as it goes along? If that is not creating credit, what is it? The answer is that while *a banker* cannot create credit, the *banking system* can and does create it, after a fashion, as is seen readily from the facts.

Banker A (having plenty of excess reserve against his deposits) lends borrower A $1,000 by placing $1,000 to his credit in a deposit account and putting his note in the safe. Borrower A checks out the amount of his deposits to various people, B, C, D and E, either to pay for goods or services or to repay loans. These people deposit the checks with *bankers* B, C, D and E.

As a result, borrower A's $1,000 deposit with banker A disappears, but it turns up as deposits in the other banks, so that the banking system *as a whole* shows an increase in both deposits and loans of $1,000. Now, if we suppose borrower A, having completed the business for which he borrowed his $1,000, and collected from customers, F, G, H, etc. (who pay him with checks on their deposits), the proceeds of his sale or his services, pays off his loan to banker A, the whole position returns to where it started and the credit expansion has disappeared.

Expansion of credit occurs with active business because more and more people engage in operations such as that of borrower A. At all times there is in process a continuous stream of borrowing and repaying, so that the total volume of active credit is being refreshed continually and enlarged as the volume of business grows.

Growth can be stopped in either of two ways: one is the exhaustion of surplus reserves, which prevents bankers from making more loans; the other is the development of general doubt concerning the future of business as a result of any cause, internal or external, to business itself, which tends to shock confidence.

From what has been said, it follows that the power of the banker to grant or to withhold credit is unquestionably large and of great economic importance, but it also follows that it must be lodged in private hands. The reason is that credit is essentially *personal.*

No one has an "unalienable" right to borrow another's money; consequently, government is totally unfitted to administer bank credit, for it cannot discriminate between citizens, and discrimination of borrowers is the first law for the banker in dealing with the deposits entrusted to him.

There is no more complete—or pestilent—a heresy abroad today than that which classes bank credit as "money" in the constitutional sense and demands its nationalization and none that seems to be more widely current. To attempt to nationalize bank credit would be to abolish it altogether and it is as necessary to modern business and industry as is transportation itself. *February* 18, 1938

II

Some remarks printed in this corner a few days ago on the subject of actual and potential bank credit have brought to this writer mingled questions and remonstrances from correspondents which convince him that he was not entirely successful in establishing the points that he attempted to make. These points were as follows:

(1) Bank credit is not *money,* but a substitute for money in its least important function.

(2) Bank credit cannot be *created* by banks; it can only be *mobilized* and *activated.*

(3) The right to bank credit is not inherent; it must be established.

It may be useful to make another attempt to demonstrate these propositions for most of the present confusion of talk and thinking on the subject arises from failure to make the distinction above formulated.

What *is* money and why is bank credit not money? Money is a thing—a *tangible* thing—which we use for two purposes. One is as a unit of price measurement for all other things; the other is as a medium for making exchanges of other things. By all odds the most important of these two functions is that of furnishing the unit of price; in the modern world currency in fact makes but a few exchanges. Bank credit does not function as a unit of price measurement; it is measured itself in currency price units. It is not a *thing,* nor merely a *symbol* of a thing; it is a relation between two parties, lender and borrower, where one lends things to the other. (N.B.: things include services.) Only in so far as it enables exchanges of things and services has it any apparent kinship with money, and this kinship is only apparent, being lacking in the essentials.

A bank is but an agency between ultimate lenders and ultimate borrowers. It collects—borrows in fact—credit from its depositors and lends to others (or invests) this credit. It is compelled by law to keep a minimum money reserve against its deposits, and it can neither lend nor invest money when its reserve of cash is down to the legal minimum ratio. Thus it cannot *create* credit previously nonexistent; all it can do is to *activate* credit already existent in the shape of deposits on its books, and it can activate (by lending or investing) this credit only to an extent limited by its cash reserves. When a bank has cash reserves over and above the legal requirement, it possesses what we may call by analogy a credit potential, but it did not create this potential. What is true of an individual bank is true of the aggregate of banks. If credit can be said to be created at all, it is created by individuals who can only do so by saving.

Bank credit, therefore, is not money but is in fact the antithesis of money, in the sense that payment is the antithesis of borrowing and lending. Secondly, banks cannot create credit but can merely mobilize and activate credit already in existence as a potential. Surplus bank reserves measure and limit this potentiality.

No one in private life dreams of asserting that he has any right to borrow at will someone else's money; a would-be borrower, as the common phrase has it, must establish his credit in the eyes of the lender. A borrower from a bank is in precisely the same position; he must establish his credit with the bank as the depositor's agent. The right to credit is therefore strictly individual, not general as is the right to life and liberty. And from time immemorial the lender and not the borrower has been the judge of the borrower's credit, and there is every reason to believe that this will be true to the end of time.

Now, whether nationalization of banking is either necessary or desirable, or not, may be, and doubtless will be, discussed from many points of view. It is, no doubt, arguable, but in arguing it we should keep in mind precisely what the service is that it is proposed to nationalize and why it should be nationalized. And the first thing necessary is to clear the field of fallacies so that we know what we are talking about.

March 9, 1938

INFLATION

I

"Will you please tell me in words that I can understand what is meant by inflation and why we must avoid it?" So writes A. Y. L. of Reading, Pa.

This writer will try. "Inflation" as he understands it is merely a large and rapid rise in the *prices* of things and services. Prices are measured in *money*. When inflation is under way money buys less and less of everything, and therefore is *worth* less to its possessor. There are two classes of people who get hurt by inflation. One is the man who receives his income in salary or wages. He gets hurt because his salary or his wage does not increase as fast as prices increase, so that it does not "go so far" as it did before prices started to rise. His "purchasing power" is diminished. In periods of real inflation adjustment of his money salary or wage is always lagging behind prices. Thus for the worker inflation means reduced income. The other class which gets hurt is the possessor of notes, mortgages, bonds, savings-bank balances, unused bank deposits or any other form of *money debt* due to him. His money principal is fixed, his money interest is fixed, and he has no such protection, partial though it be, as has the salaried man or wage worker who from time to time has his money income increased. But these classes constitute by far the largest part of the population. Consequently, inflation is really a *national* evil. Anyone who lived during the last war has no doubts upon that point.

One class of people is not hurt in this way by inflation while it is in progress. This is the owner of *property*—not the owner of *money*. Theoretically, the money exchange value of his property rises with prices, as also does the money exchange value of the products of that property. *Stocks* represent property, *bonds* represent money. Dividends on stocks tend to rise with prices; interest on bonds does not. Prices of stocks tend to go up as dividends increase; prices of bonds do not. That is why people talk of stocks as "equities," because the worth of the property they represent is not diminished. There is a class in the community for which inflation is an opportunity—the speculator class. The speculator borrows money to buy property. As prices rise he can meet his money obligations by sale of only a part of the property he bought, the rest being pure profit. It was by this means that the late Hugo Stinnes accumulated a huge estate in the German inflation following the war. The speculator is the only class who profits by inflation; the property owner may save his skin; the wage and salary worker and possessor of money, in any form, lose. Nobody is much concerned over the speculator's fate, so the socially evil quality of inflation is clear.

What causes inflation? It should be clear that it results from a *surplus* of effective purchasing power operating upon a *limited* supply of goods and services, the consequence being a sharp competition for that supply, with the inevitable result of rising prices. Why are we apprehensive of inflation today? The reason is that the defense program on which we are engaged is creating a rapid increase in the country's purchasing power without a corresponding increase in the supply of goods and services. This increase in the supply of purchasing power results from government's borrowings of huge sums of money which, by spending it, it converts into active purchasing power in the hands of the individual. Furthermore, by its diversion of labor and material from ordinary peacetime purposes to military and naval uses, it diminishes the quantity of these things available for civilian use. Thus we have an increase in civilian purchasing power and a diminution of what we may call civilian goods and services to meet it. Here are the makings of price inflation. How can it be stopped?

It can be attacked in only two ways. One is somehow to increase the production of goods and services. The other is to prevent the increased purchasing power from reaching the supply of those things. The first is not easy to accomplish quickly. The second way is more promising. It consists in the recapture by government of the increased purchasing power that it has created, either by borrowing it, or by levying upon it by taxation, or partly by one and partly by the other. This keeps it out of the market for goods and services so that it does not affect prices, and is the only sure *way* to prevent inflation. All other expedients can be only partly effective and also likely to generate influences which may hamper production.

September 15, 1941

II

"In your discussion of inflation you referred to stocks as 'equities.' Will you please develop this idea further?" So telephones a valued reader (G.P.C.).

People who use the word "equity" in this connection really mean "property" as distinguished from "money obligation," such as a bond. Stockholders *own* the property of a corporation after payment of its outstanding obligations. During an inflationary period prices of property—things—rise. Securities which represent things necessarily rise. Common stocks represent things. Q.E.D.

That is the theory. As a theory it is quite sound. But in practice it is not quite so simple as all that. Let us analyze a little more deeply this matter of property and its money value or price. The real worth or value of property such as that represented by common stocks rests in its power to produce something by use and the price of property reflects the market's estimation of that power. The market takes into estimation both its present (actual) and its future (potential), power. In fixing the price for a stock it considers its present and future dividend-paying capacity—for dividends are the "product" of common stocks. Dividends come from earnings. According to the above-mentioned theory, earnings rise during inflation, thereafter dividends rise, therefore stock prices rise

But suppose there enter into the situation factors, social, economic, political, psychological, which affect the use of property so that either its power to produce is modified or the *cost* of its products materially increased—what then becomes of the theory? Government *regulation,* government *competition,* government *taxation,* government *labor* policies, all or any of these things may totally change the "equity" picture by reducing or preventing an increase in dividend-paying capacity. If dividends do rise, stock prices will not rise or if they rise temporarily they will not stay up, unless the market believes that dividends *will* come up to stock prices. In such cases common stocks are not "equities" in the meaning of the theory.

A little while ago the *Wall Street Journal* directed attention to the fact that common stocks had not risen in our markets as had common stocks in the European markets, nor was there activity in dealings here at all commensurate with dealings abroad. This notwithstanding the intense preoccupation in Washington with the danger of inflation. The fact seems to be that the market believes (whether rightly or wrongly matters little) that our national policy toward large industry and large business is now and will probably continue to be that our large corporations will be so restricted in their operations as to be unable to pay dividends at substantially increased rates. That is why one hears a good deal less talk in the financial district nowadays than one did in the days when we first began to talk inflation.

This writer had penned the foregoing sentences when he received the following from a friend (E.W.F., New York):

I do not know whether you share my view (held contrary to what I would like to see) that the "free" economy is a thing of the past, and that the future will see an ever increasing demand for the "controlled" economy. Under these circumstances, prices will be kept high. As a matter of fact, the government must keep prices high in order to have a somewhat rational approach to a balanced budget in the future.

If my premises are correct the outlook, without figuring even on a currency inflation which I do not anticipate, is exceedingly dark for those people that derive their income in the form of dividends and interest on bonds. I am certain that you could do a great service to your readers, if you could suggest something to them how they can keep their income from dividends and interest on bonds in line with the rising trend of the cost of living. I must admit that I am personally not able to give a satisfactory answer to this question.

Neither can the present writer! In former days when the economy was "free" it was generally true that interest rates tended to follow commodity prices, rising and falling—over a period—with them. To the extent that an economy is "controlled" this correspondence cannot be counted upon, for "control" will naturally be exerted to keep interest rates as low as possible. The tendency the world over is manifestly toward increasing control of major industry and commerce. The logic of this would seemingly point to such "free" industry and commerce as still can be found as the hope of the *rentier* for a rate of return commensurate with the rise in commodity prices. Discovery of suitable opportunities for investment in this field is, however, a rather difficult matter and the element of risk becomes important.

The conclusion seems to be that, being confined to this planet, we have to take all the planet's risks as they develop, and there is no sure way of eliminating one risk without accepting another or paying for "insurance." In a more or less controlled economy "insurance" means sacrifice either of "income" or "safety." There seems to be no way to have both.

September 22, 1941

III

The problem presented by the danger of "inflation" is, in principle, as simple as a sum in arithmetic, or an elementary proposition in the geometry of Euclid. The trouble is in the application of the principles.

The problem is to keep stable the prices of the commodities that we all use. Prices depend upon the relation of effective demand to effective supply. When this relation—or equation—is changed prices tend to change; when not, not. The problem is acute at present because, owing to the war, both effective demand and effective supply are undergoing a violent change, and both changes tend to cause an advance in prices. Effective demand is being increased by the creation of a large amount of purchasing power in the hands of certain classes of people, while effective supply is being diminished by decreased production of the commodities that we all consume in our daily lives. But government has of itself no purchasing power to distribute to anybody, nor can it *create*—in the proper sense of that word—any such power, or indeed anything. It can only *take* it where it can find it. It finds it already existing among certain classes of its people and it takes it from them either by taxation, or by borrowing, or both. If it were to take it from and distribute it to the same classes of people, then the price equation, other things being equal, would not be disturbed.

But it does not do so. It takes it mainly from certain classes and distributes it mainly to other classes. Nor is that all. A large part, the greatest part, of the purchasing power which it takes is *under normal conditions* not part of the effective demand for the commodities of which we are talking. It consists of *savings*, that is money not currently expended for current needs. On the other hand, it is distributed mainly to classes of people who *normally* are not in a position to save them, if anything, and among whom the tendency is—naturally—to use increased purchasing power to improve their living standards by increased consumption both quantitatively and qualitatively, thus increasing the *total* effective demand for consumable commodities. At the same time the war program operates to diminish the supply of these commodities by shifting labor and material to production of war material. All which, if allowed to operate without control, spells higher prices for the former commodities, higher "costs of living"—inflation. How can "control" be applied, on what principle?

The answer is quite simple *in theory*. All you have to do is to see that the increased purchasing power taken from one set of classes and distributed to another is recaptured from the other by the same process as that by which it was taken from the first. In this way there is no necessary increase in the total effective demand to operate upon the effective supply. The decrease in the effective supply then can be dealt with by rationing, that is, by dividing it equitably among *all* the people. When the effective supply is diminished by the war program the rationing process results in a corresponding diminution in the whole "standard of living" as measured by the commodity consumption. Purchasing power of all has to be diverted in a corresponding degree from consumption to saving, which saving must go to the government. Which being done, a final control of prices can be achieved by price ceilings. Nothing could be simpler—*in theory*.

The rub is in the application and the rub is *political*. It arises from the fact that the recipients of the increased purchasing power constitute a preponderant proportion of the population which is not accustomed to *saving* and that for two reasons. One is that its "margin" of income for possible savings has been relatively thin in itself and for many does not exist at all. The other is that it feels a strong natural urge to improve its current living standards by increasing and enlarging its consumption, and achieving the "social gains" of which we have in recent years heard so much. This being so, it is easy to see the difficulty of persuading it either to accept heavier taxation or to save and purchase government bonds. Being a "majority" it must be persuaded, it cannot be forced. All "politics" henceforth, here and everywhere, will be politics of the "mass"; that is the new thing in the world for the last couple of centuries. Moreover, mass politics has a natural tendency to generate dictatorships in form and totalitarianism in substance.

The special difficulty confronting us in grappling the problem of inflation is in the fact that for a decade at least the emphasis of our national policy has been upon the necessity of "social gains," that is upon improving the living standards of the "mass" and no one can deny that the objective is laudable. But the impact of this utterly unprecedented emergency requires a sudden halt in our "social" program, and may not improbably require a retreat, and that, politically speaking, is a most difficult task to accomplish quickly or smoothly. It is in this difficulty that the danger lies of the inflation of which we are all talking—a danger, by the way, which may be far greater after the fighting stops than it is at present. There is not the least doubt what has to be done to avert the danger; the difficulty is in doing it and the difficulty is *political*.

May 6, 1942

MONEY AND THE CAPITALIST SYSTEM

The other day this writer found in the London *Weekly Review* a definition of "money" that caught his fancy. (This paper, by the way, is the child of *G. K.'s Weekly*, which in its day, when Chesterton was running it—and writing a goodly part of it—made no small stir in the journalistic field. "G. K." is gone, but the *Weekly* still delights a small but sturdy clientele of readers who like forthright talk.)

The definition occurred in a letter to the editor signed Henry Meulen; it runs thus: "The classic definition of money is, I think, sound, namely, that 'money is a right or title to demand something from others.' " The present writer, being strictly illiterate in "economics" so far as "reading" is concerned, does not know who made the definition, for apparently Mr. Meulen borrowed it somewhere. He comments on it as follows: "Unless, therefore, money is issued as forced currency by the government, it indicates that the holder has provided goods or services, but has not yet received an equivalent." In other words, he has "saved it." Putting it another way, "money" in one's possession is the same as a *credit* on the community's stocks of goods and services against which one can draw at will. The *credit* arises from a previous *contribution* to the community's stocks of goods and services for which no equivalent in kind has been demanded or received by the creditor, or by some previous creditor or creditors who transmitted it to the present holder.

Thus "money" is "property," for it is convertible into property of any kind that exists which the owner is willing to "sell" and that, normally, means almost all kinds at all times. It is the life's-blood—literally the "circulating medium"—of the market. As "property" it can be acquired by legitimate or illegitimate means. The only legitimate source is *work* performed, i.e., goods and services rendered. There are various illegitimate means of acquiring it—robbing with violence, theft, fraud, deception, etc. The important thing is that only by earning or by gift is money legitimately owned. If these things are true, and if "property" is in itself a "good" (properly used) then "money" is also a "good" in the same sense.

If this seems self-evident, it should be remembered that

there are not a few earnest moralists who inveigh against "money" in terms which seem to imply that it is an "evil" thing *per se* and that it has corrupted the modern life beyond repair. Logically, this would be equivalent to branding "property" as an evil thing, but they do not state it in those terms. What they seem to have in mind is the "machinery" by which "money" is circulated through the economic body—banking, "finance," foreign exchange, currency and so forth—as largely a means of taking money from its rightful owners or preventing those who have rightfully earned it from receiving and owning it. This is merely the fallacy of confusing use and abuse. It is the origin of all the crazy notions concerning "bank credit" and "currency" which seem beyond possibility of eradication from many people's minds.

But there is more confusion about "money" than this; there is the debate over "capitalism"—the "capitalist system." There is a school of opinion which views the system as an evil thing in itself, just as our moralist extremists seem to view money. Yet "capital" is nothing but money (or property) and the capitalistic system is nothing but the use of "money" for purposes of producing things other than goods and services for immediate consumption or enjoyment. If it be not morally wrong to use "property" for such purposes—and no one seems to assert this in definite terms—what is morally wrong with the capitalist system as such? Incidentally, Bolshevist Russia was in its "five-year plans" an extreme example of that system in that it stripped the backs and starved the stomachs of the most "approved types!" Here we have the same fallacy, the same confused thinking on use and abuse. The fact is that in the present state of technology, i.e., applied science, "money" and the "capitalistic system" are essential to modern economy.

The real debate between "left" and "right"—the real conflict—is over who is to exercise the "power" to govern the "system" and who is to receive the "money" that results from its operation. Merely that. And another fact is that jealousy over another's share of the product seems to be as strong a source of conflict as a desire for a large share for one's self—sometimes stronger! We attempt sometimes to cover it up by assuming that these "inequalities" must be the result of chicanery somewhere, that they cannot represent "value received" by the community. It may be, probably is, true in cases, but it is obviously not necessarily true when one considers what technology combined with someone's imagination has produced. It is this which clouds the aura of "justice" in which we like to conceive these emotions. Which is doubtless at bottom the reason why Artistotle noted the incompatibility of great economic inequalities with the form of society that we call "democratic."

But this is not to be understood as suggesting that we have yet attained a condition in which justice can be said generally to reign. We are far from it. It is merely to suggest that even had we attained it, there would in all probability be the same "right-left" conflict powered by the same emotions.

December 20, 1944

SPECULATORS AND INVESTORS

For many a long year the present writer has been interested in what we may call the "official" state of mind on the relation of the "speculator" to the "investor" in the case of the securities markets, and the relation of the "futures" markets in staple commodities to the various producers and the "trades" which are concerned with the processing and distribution of these commodities for consumption. In general this "mind" has disliked "the speculator" wherever found and has regarded him as the enemy of the "investor" in securities, and of the producer, manufacturer and distributor of commodities. It regards him as a parasite pure and simple, who levies a toll upon others for no service rendered, and, as such, an evil thing to be wiped out as far as possible. In this writer's opinion this is a badly mistaken deduction from the facts, as a very simple analysis will demonstrate.

Let us simply define an "investor" in securities as one who pays cash for the securities that he buys and puts them away in his safe-deposit box or in the custody of his bank, and a "speculator" as one who buys on margin. The definitions are sufficiently close for our purpose. Now there was one indisputable fact about the stock market prior to a few years ago, and before trading on margin was greatly restricted by regulations at the hands of the Federal Reserve Board and the Securities and Exchange Commission. That is that the class of "speculators" who traded in brokers' offices and paid commissions invariably lost money on balance. Any broker of long and large experience will confirm the facts from the record in his own books of account. Furthermore, its truth can be demonstrated in another way. We have had for some time records of brokers' borrowings at the banks. The amount of these borrowings always reflected the volume of speculation on margin in progress at any given time. These loans were always at a maximum at the climax of a "bull market" and at a minimum at the bottom of a "bear market." Putting it in another way, brokers' offices were always "full of stocks" after a large rise in prices and bare of stocks at the end of a long fall.

Where did these stocks come from and whither did they go? They came from the strongboxes and they went back to them. There was no other whence or whither. That much is evident. Equally evident is the fact that their owners sold on rising markets and bought on falling ones. It follows that if the speculators who bought on the rising markets and sold on the falling ones—as they obviously did—and lost money in doing it—must have given the investors from whom they bought and to whom they sold an opportunity to sell for more money and buy for less than would have been possible had there been no speculators. In short, the losses of the stock-speculator class have always inured to the benefit of the investor class.

Some five and thirty years ago this writer made a short course of lectures at a university "school of business" on the movement of security prices. He devoted a good part of his time to impressing on his audience the difficulties and the dangers of stock speculation, and pointed out that the fundamental principle of successful speculation is the assumption that the great mass of speculators will continue to make in the future the mistakes that they have made in the past. This writer will aver that in the fifty-odd years that he has been an observer in these matters that assumption has proved itself entirely reliable and never more so than in 1929. The reason is simple: All these mistakes are the result of men's hopes and fears which only a few men can successfully control. The speculator is his own worst enemy, but he is assuredly no enemy of the investor. It would be useful if the official mind could absorb that simple fact.

As for the markets and commodity futures, another simple fact is evident. The function of these markets is to provide the processors and distributors of these commodities with insurance against losses resulting from price fluctuations in their raw material during its conversion for use. This insurance is furnished by speculators who stand ready to buy or to sell the materials at fixed prices at a future date. A processor can thus exclude by "hedging" all uncertainties of price risk and relieve himself of the need for buying and storing all his material at one time. He can "hedge" his actual holdings by a sale of "futures" or he can provide himself with material by a purchase of "futures" so arranged as to dates as to suit his needs. In both cases he relies upon the speculator for the insurance. Now there is a strong probability that the "speculator class" in the commodity markets fares as a whole in its net results much as does his "class" in the stock market, that is, that it "loses money" on balance. In which case the "trade" gets its insurance not only free of cost, but with a "bonus" thrown in. But what of the producer of the commodities? Is the speculator his friend or his enemy?

The official mind has always held to the "enemy theory"; it has always supposed that the speculator lowered prices when the raw material was coming to market and when they had it in their hands put prices up. All that can be said on this point is that this has not been demonstrated by the visible facts. Such studies as have been made of "seasonal" price movements in, for instance, wheat and cotton, are not conclusive of any such continuing effects. Moreover, who can tell whether or not the producer would do any better for himself if there were no "futures" markets at all, and he dealt directly with the "trade"?

It seems to be clear that speculation and "markets" are inseparable and that speculation is unprofitable to the vast majority of those who attempt it. But it is equally clear that men never have been and probably never will be deterred by anyone else's experiences from trying it for themselves and will always find new ways of doing it when the old ways are closed.

March 16, 1945

CRISIS: WAR AND PEACE

THE AUSTRIAN CRISIS

Long before these lines are in print the Austrian crisis will, doubtless, have been resolved in one way or the other, for good or for ill. This writer will not presume to offer his own views as to what is going to happen now, for, in the first place, he does not know, and, in the second place, if he did know, it would probably have happened before he could make his prediction known to his readers. He will venture, however, to record some of the impressions he has received in the past forty-eight hours.

It happened that in these closing days of July, twenty years ago, he was in London, and witnessed the sudden breaking of the great storm which has so profoundly changed the face of the world. The events of the last two days have vividly recalled those crowded hours during which we vainly strove to realize what was happening, while all that we could do was vaguely to "feel" that it was the end of the world.

Now, twenty years after, we know that that feeling was prophetic. There appears a deadly logic in the course of events, and a singularly dramatic concentration of destiny upon Austria—*Austria felix* as she used to be called!—which to future historians should be of the greatest interest. It would almost seem that Clio had set herself to the building of a great drama around that unfortunate nation, sparing no pains to make it complete in every detail—even to reproducing something of the Atridae curse upon the House of Hapsburg. There is an appalling symmetry in the drama's construction, wherein the vengeance of destiny upon the remains of the Holy Roman Empire was coupled with the chastisement of an age that had become drunk with the *hybris* of material achievement, and was bankrupt of statesmanship.

From beginning to end, the Austrian red thread runs through the drama's texture, unbroken from Sarajevo in 1914 to Vienna in 1934. The malign spirit that dictated the treaties which committed the fatal error concerning Germany, so as to perpetuate instead of ending the war, deliberately dismembered the Austria of 1914 so as to make its remnant a rodent ulcer, economically and politically, in Europe, and thus ensure a perpetual reminder that there was neither peace nor prosperity. Of Vienna, long a center of culture, science, good manners and of that thing the Germans call *gemütlichkeit*, it made a city of poverty, of misery and of the bitterest class hatred—literally a beggar at the doors of the League of Nations. And today it is from Vienna that the same sardonic spirit invites the world to note that the play is not yet finished. There is something Greek about it—as if Thespis and Clio have collaborated!

The leading article in the London *Times* today opens with the following words:

> There has been nothing for centuries like the vogue of political assassination which threatens, if it goes any farther, to submerge the civilization of a continent. The ordinary decencies of public life, the conventions which raise human society above the life of animals, the bonds of family relationship—all these are being swept away by political desperadoes who respect no laws and recognize none of the common obligations of humanity, but who choose to consider

that their own particular purpose may and should be achieved by any methods, however barbarous and inhuman.

Quite so! But whence and why has this come about? What has loosed these forces? Why *is* Hitlerism? What has driven a people like the German people into what is literally the kind of madness that set Ajax to slaughtering sheep?

We all know the answer. It lies plain for history to read on the face of the treaties. Of all whose signatures are on those documents only old Clemenceau seems to have known what he was about and to have been frank enough to say it. He knew that the Treaty of Versailles was war in a permanent form and he meant that it should be. What he did not know, and what none of the others knew, was that in the end it would wreck them all, victors and vanquished. Today we are just beginning to find out. Perhaps that one fact may mean that the drama is entering upon its last act; at least there is that much hope—slight as it is! *August* 6, 1934

THE LAST OF THE LEAGUE

If anything were needed to bring home to the imagination the present state of world affairs, this morning's (Sept. 13) London newspapers should be helpful. Upon an *inside* page one finds a report of the session at Geneva of the League's national assembly, representing over fifty nations, at which a presiding officer retired and a successor was duly elected. The former in his valedictory address congratulated the assembly upon its holding to the faith in "international coöperation" and the latter called upon the League "to lend its moral support to all those who, no matter what their nation, strive to find a just and peaceful solution here or elsewhere for the immediate international difficulties with which we are surrounded." Spread all over the *front* pages—and the theme of all the leading editorials—are columns of print reporting the speech of a single human being, who last evening for some two hours or more held the attention of the whole world, as it listened anxiously for the word that might unloose the ultimate forces of destruction. To this ironical impasse has come the nineteenth century's vision of "the Parliament of Man, the Federation of the world!" One's lips involuntarily achieve a wry contortion that may pass for a smile, but one of the *risus sardonicus* order.

Opinion here is almost unanimous that Europe has a respite, and that the crisis remains unsolved. The opposing forces have if anything stiffened their lines and there is no abatement of the fundamental tensions. The great tragedy of the matter is, first, that the things we have learned to call ideologies are the source of these tensions, and, second, that neither of the opposing ideologies has as its vital principle an element of the kind that we commonly call *spiritual.* The sad truth is that the "democracy" of the European "democracies" is at the root a doctrine of power as much as is the Nazi doctrine; neither doctrine is at its root firmly planted in the zone of strict morale. Each is totalitarian in its ultimates, and totalitarianism is *per se* unmoral. Neither is compatible with civilization in any true sense of that word.

The Nazi philosophy as stated by its official representatives constitutes a formal and complete apostasy from all the elements that made the Western civilization—Greece, Rome and Christianity. No question as to that. The European democracies of the "left" (which are the backbone of the democratic "front") all talk the liberal language of the nineteenth century, and profess that century's liberal principles. But those principles are but the etiolated survivals of a spiritual unity which has vanished, and having no present roots are mere empty phrases. By no possibility can the Western culture and the Western civilization be renewed merely by conflict between these two camps, no matter which may be victorious.

It is remarkable how many minds of utterly divers habit, training, environment and experience nowadays find their thoughts converging to a common point, the necessity for Europe's recovery of its lost spiritual unity. Mr. J. Middleton Murry *(Heaven and Earth)* is the most recent voice in this swelling chorus, and, because of his various adventures in search of a philosophy, one of the most interesting. The instinct that inspires these expressions is authentic, for as Christopher Dawson has so clearly shown (in those two notable works *Progress and Religion* and *The Making of Europe*) Christianity was the vital element in creating the European culture and civilization and enabling it to gather into itself all the best that the Hellenic and the Roman civilization ever contained. The Nazi philosophy definitely rejects Christianity. The European democracies of the "left" either fight it, as do the Communists, or ignore it, as do practically all their other component groups. Whichever wins in the present conflict, it seems, Europe must lose.

Nuremberg's tumult and shouting dies, the torches are extinguished and, for the moment, the danger has passed. But nothing is changed and we still are in a world which can neither afford a war or make a peace.

September 21, 1938

THE SOVIET-NAZI ALLIANCE

I

Whatever else may result from the Hitler-Stalin alliance in the domain of arms and politics, and whatever may be the "power picture" at the end of the fighting in

Europe, it seems that the cause of Communism as a philosophy, a doctrine and a religion has received a serious, perhaps a fatal, blow as an enduring force in the world. Its true home and source was Russia. It was from Russia that there came its real impetus. Now it has become plain to all with eyes to see that Stalin's Russia is at bottom an Asiatic imperialist despotism, headed by a man bearing all the stigmata of Napoleonic will to power, to whom Communist mysticism is as foreign as Byzantine Christianity and who is quite prepared to use either form so long as it is helpful to his purpose. Where are those people left who until a little while ago were captivated by Soviet Russia's "democracy" and who made up the membership of the "innocents clubs" here and in Europe?

How, for instance, do the groups of the British opposition party feel about it? None but the extreme wing would have any truck with the Communists as such, but all were strong for Czechoslovakia a year ago; all were strong for Soviet Russia, and it was Soviet Russia which was the key to the other two loyalties. What chance is Communism now likely to have in Great Britain? And what in France? The time may come when the "left" may come to power in both countries, but whatever may be the banner under which it marches to victory, it does not seem likely that it will bear as its chief symbol the hammer and sickle.

From the first, the great vitality in Communism was in its genuinely mystic core, for the hatred of religion professed by its leaders was of such an intensity as to call forth missionaries and martyrs for the cause. It was this very real fervor which distinguished the Russian movement as it flourished before the Great War. The latter was essentially political and, except for a few individuals, quite devoid of real fanaticism. Where is that Communist core to be found today? It is true that between the Nazi war on Christianity and the Communist war on the Almighty there was no vital difference in results, but there was all the difference in the world between a purely synthetic cult and a cult with a core. Today that difference has disappeared, and between Hitler and Stalin there is no likelihood of the *odium theologicum* disturbing their pleasant relations.

So far as this country is concerned, the whole importance of Communism was and is wrapped up with the strategy of the Trojan Horse. Our left intelligentsia—save for a few instances—were much in the same state of mind as that of the British Opposition groups, that is, indifferent to the mystic doctrine of the original Bolshevists but much in love with the "democracy" of the Stalin regime. That the "front," which it was the object of the Trojan Horse strategy to build here, and in the building of which notable success had been achieved, is seriously weakened by what has happened is most probable. We shall know more as to this next year, when the lines of the campaign are drawn.

But the result in the "intellectual" field is more interesting and probably in the long run more important. What it has disclosed is the pathetic shallowness and "atomistic" character of left-wing thinking in this country, which has held it in a blind worship of forms as distinct from substance. It is here that the effects of the "naturalistic" philosophy have been most plainly observable, for, in so far as the left intelligentsia have a philosophy at all, it is derived from that school of thinking. The essence of that philosophy—which is professedly wholeheartedly Darwinist—is a complete negation of the Declaration of Independence. The consequence is that its concept of democracy is necessarily totalitarian, with the whole emphasis upon "society" as against the individual person—a complete contradiction of the central principle of our American theory of government.

October 11, 1939

II

More than ten years ago—his book, *Défense de l'occident,* appeared in 1929—Henri Massis definitely foreshadowed the Russo-German alliance, and with a wealth of evidence culled from both German and Russian writers pointed out the fundamental bond of union between Bolshevist Russia and postwar Germany. This bond was no more and no less than an attack on all the essential elements that made the Western civilization. Read ten years ago, his book gave the present writer a mild nightmare, with, however, a comfortable sense, after its perusal, that it was the stuff of which nightmares were made. Re-read today, it takes on the stature of prophetical clairvoyance and it seems to light up the deep significance of current events as do none of the present-day moralizings and attempts at exegesis. If anyone wants to see the European scene of today in full historical perspective he will find in Massis' book a most suggestive and convincing exposition of its roots and backgrounds.

Beginning with Fichte, and tracing it down to modern times, through names well known to the generation of today—Keyserling, Curtius, Spengler, Thomas Mann and other lesser lights—he shows that the German mind has ever hesitated between a certain Asiatic mysticism and the Latin spirit, so that it has seemed to be in a state of perpetual protest against the latter. Under the shock of defeat in the Great War, this protest took on fresh vitality. Shortly before his death, Rathenau wrote: "Evening falls on Europe. More and more everything forces us to turn our eyes to the East. For us Germans it is a question of life and death." For a while Keyserling enjoyed great popularity with his Orientalizing philosophy, and the names of Tagore, Gandhi and Rolland were much upon the air. There was a flood of books dealing with Asiatic art and philosophy. Dostoievski's works enjoyed a special boom. Thomas Mann and Ernst Curtius visualized Germany as a sort of mediatrix between East and West. Romain Rolland pointed to China and India as having the answer to the West's chaotic consciousness, and as having the nourishment that Germany's famished spirit needed. Spengler's doctrine of fatalism released it from all sense of responsibility to the past. Mann said that a policy of "hands free" between East and West was for Germany the way to form itself and civilization.

So much for Germany. As for Russia, Massis says that its historical mission has been to bring face to face for final conflict the elementary principles on which East and West have built their ideals of life, their metaphysics and their beliefs. "The painful questions, the enduring anguish of Russia uncertain of its ways now becomes the problem of human-kind." Such, he says, is the consequence of the Bolshevist revolution; it constitutes an "historical fracture," the most serious that our civilization has known. Rousseau, Bonald, Renan, all recognized in Russia a tremendous reservoir of barbarism, which, as Keyserling pointed out, had nothing to do with Marxism. The essence of Bolshevism is its anti-Western, antihuman principle which is the logical enemy of the great spiritual European tradition. As Herzen said, modern Russia's point of departure is the negation of all tradition. "We are all nihilists," said Dostoievski. "We are Scythians!" said Block. Massis collects many more similar utterances.

In this combined attack from the German spirit and the Russian spirit upon the spirit of the West lies the danger, as Massis saw it ten years ago, to the future of the West. It is a conflict of fundamentals and a conflict *à l'outrance*. And it is this which invests with a sinister significance the return of Russia to European territory in what was Poland, probably never again to be dislodged. Viewed in such a perspective, it seems fatuous to talk of the present conflict as one of "dictatorships or democracies," or as if Hitler's elimination would end it, or as if peace were a question of colonies or exports. True, the book does read like a nightmare, but we have seen it strikingly verified in broad daylight in one most important respect. Massis does not pretend to impartiality in this matter; he is spiritually of the Old Europe. But with all allowances for that, it is a book which gives the reader furiously to think, and this writer commends it for that reason.

For it is all-important for us in America to understand the nature and the causes of the conflict that has opened and what must happen before it is ended. It cannot be ended by battle of arms, for at bottom it is a war in the spirit of men.

November 15, 1939

WHAT IS PRUSSIANISM?

I

Everyone will wish Mr. Sumner Welles success in his European search for a basis of European peace, and will credit the President who had dispatched him on his voyage of discovery with the highest motives and most generous impulses. But it is doubtful that people generally in this country recognize or fully understand the real nature of the present conflict or the character of the forces that are loose, and what, if anything, this country can contribute toward the return of a durable peace. So much emphasis has been laid on the economic aspect of the dispute—"haves against have-nots"—that the deeper aspects of the conflict have escaped attention. It is these that offer the real problem of peace, and it is absolutely necessary to take them into account in considering our course.

So many factors are present in the situation that in the attempt to make anything like a complete picture there is danger of over-simplification and consequent error. But at the risk of this, it must be pointed out that the rationalization of the German phenomenon in terms of *Lebensraum,* colonies, raw materials, and so forth, covers something much more serious, the roots of which grow deep in history and have no fundamental economic character. For a full understanding of the spirit which has seized the German nation as it faces the rest of the world today, one must go back to the history of Prussia as it began early in the thirteenth century and follow the growth of "Prussianism" from the "colonization" of Prussia by the Teutonic Knights of St. John down to the present day. It is not oversimplifying the picture to say that the "spirit" of Germany today is the essence of *Preussenthum* directed curiously by an Austrian, in whom there is incarnated a certain *daemonisch* element which is at one and the same time logical and irrational, the whole constituting an utterly un-European force, a totally "foreign protein" in the European body. Against this, Europe's body is reacting powerfully in a manner which is analogous to the reaction which doctors of medicine call anaphylaxis.

What is "Prussianism"—*Preussenthum?* It is a strange compound of good and bad. As some writers point out—Foerster, for example—it is a mixture of solid virtues conscripted for evil ends. The virtues are order, discipline, sense of duty *(Pflicht),* self-sacrifice, heroic ideals, endurance—the things that originally characterized the *Ordensritter* of the thirteenth century. The evil ends are first and last *conquest,* unrestrained by any moral considerations whatever and carried away with an unqualifiedly inhuman savagery, utter ruthlessness and an undescribed cynicism which is otherwise unparalleled in history. Conquest has been the distinguishing *motif* in Prussian history since the days of Frederick II, as has moral cynicism, and the conquest of Germany by Hitler is but the prelude to an attempted conquest of Europe—as indeed the Nazi leaders frankly inform us. To suppose that the spirit can be exorcised by economic concessions is totally to misconceive the nature of the struggle. The problem is to redeem Germany from the spirit of *Preussenthum* and revivify the moral consciousness that may still remain in that part of its people which was once part of the culture of the West. The unholy alliance between Nazi Germany and the inhuman Soviet power is a complication of the problem much as pneumonia complicates typhoid fever, but it is not an essential part of it, nor is it permanent.

The real problem is the result of the seizure of the German "split personality" by the evil partner and it can be solved only by the elimination of Mr. Hyde. An indispensable preliminary is—apparently and unfortunately—the *forcible* suppression of that gentleman. But that is merely the preliminary; after that is the question what to do next, and how to do it. All we know at present is that the final solution cannot be reached by force or by economic concessions. It can come only in one form and by one route; it must be in the order of *morals.* In that is the appalling difficulty of the business. It is of the greatest importance that we in this country should keep that clearly in mind, if we hope to aid in the building of a peace. Unless we can bring effective reinforcement of a moral kind, nothing else that we can do will be of much avail.

Moreover, just as mere economic concessions will not suffice to heal Europe, neither will a change of mere governmental forms. It is, for instance, very much more than a fight between "dictatorships" and "democracies." The cure will have to go to the substance. We will do well to overhaul our own medicine chests to see if *we* possess in our own moral pharmacopoeia anything which we can contribute to the cure.

February 26, 1940

II

This writer has received some comments and criticism of his remarks some days ago on the spirit of *Preussenthum* as the ruler of present-day Germany and the consequent difficulty of establishing an accord between Germany and the rest of Europe. The burden of these criticisms may be summarized about as follows:

It is a dangerous mistake to push the Jekyll-Hyde analogy too far, or, for that matter, the metaphor of German split personality, if it leads to the conclusion that a disappearance of the evil partner is within the early possibilities. While it is true that the Nazi movement is in its essence a return to the essence of *Preussenthum* in all its primitive savagery of theory and practice, it is not safe to assume that its resurgence in Germany has not bitten so deeply into the German "soul" as to leave but a small residue in that soul which is still in tune with the Western culture, and to which the rest of Europe can look for an ultimate understanding and accord. In a word, "Prussia" (i.e., Nazi) and "Germany" are today much more nearly one and the same thing than we commonly like to think. Not merely is Nazism not a temporary psychosis (as this writer had somewhat rashly assumed), but it has long been markedly inherent in the Teutonic psyche.

It was there before the religious wars of the sixteenth century. A friend (Mr. Louis Gallantière) a few days ago read for this writer's benefit an address by a German, one Heinrich Bebel, to the Emperor Maximilian at the very beginning of that century, which in substance and style might pass today for an utterance of Dr. Joseph Goebbels himself, and would make Fichte and Euston Stuart Chamberlain sound like sober historical commentators. The wars of the sixteenth century and their final crystallization in the Thirty Years' War prepared the ground for *Preussenthum* to take visible form in the kingdom founded in 1701, and—according to this critic—it has been steadily enlarging its influence upon the German people as the years have passed.

One hundred and ten years ago the Frenchman, Edgar Quinet, wrote:

> Out of Prussia is arising against the old cosmopolitan objective spirit a wild and raging nationalism. In this the *Volkspartei* finds itself, and strikes hands with the ruling power. Prussian despotism is intelligent, subversive and full of initiative. All it needs is a man who will recognize his star. . . . National unity is the deep-rooted idea which irresistably and tirelessly works in and permeates this land. . . . What Germany evinces today is the overthrow of the spiritual. . . . Let us be clear about it; it is precisely this impetus of conscience, this emptiness of morals, this collapse of real intelligence in Europe which permits the rise of Prussian brutality. . . . Up to now Europe has relied on open war, the moment of decision will first come when power makes its mean alliance with the lie. . . . When this marriage comes then say good-bye to the Germany you have not known—the Germany of spiritual frankness, thoroughness, inner greatness and praiseworthy genius.

Almost fifty years later (1777) Constantin Frantz wrote: "The new Reich issued from the barracks of Berlin. Instead of forming the keystone of European peace, it has become the cornerstone of a system of European wars."

The gist of the matter is that Europe has to deal with a threat probably as great as—perhaps in reality greater than—that of the Goths, the Huns and the Mohammedans, and that no terms can be made, no treaty of peace negotiated with the enemy that has arisen in its midst, while the spirit that animates that enemy remains unexorcised. So seem to agree the friends who, out of an abundance of historical scholarship, have sought to supply the present writer's lack in that field and warn him against jumping too fast to unsafe conclusions. As, however, the purpose of the same writer in his earlier remarks was to point out the terrible difficulty of achieving anything like a durable European peace, the deficiencies in his own historical scholarship do not weaken that conclusion, which is strengthened by what his critics have had to say in correcting his error and supplying his deficiencies. They will please accept his hearty thanks. *March* 11, 1940

III

Several weeks ago there came for the first time to this writer's hand a book published—or at least dated—about three years ago, which seemed to him the most important book on the sources and the nature of the present war and on the phenomenon of "Hitlerism" that has so far appeared—*Europa und die deutsche Frage*—by the well-known German publicist, Friedrich Wilhelm Foerster. It will be issued in translation here in the coming spring or early summer and should be read by all who are acquainted with *Mein Kampf* and the two books by Rauschning, for it describes the historical sources and the real nature of the Nazi phenomenon in such fashion as to enable the reader to see it in true historical perspective and appreciate its full significance. So it seems, at least, to the present writer, for whom the book sheds a flood of light upon the events of today. Written before the rape of Austria and what followed, it reads like a commentary on all that has happened since its publication. Not all readers, perhaps, to whom the Nazi phenomenon is wholly hateful, will agree with Foerster's thesis in all its details, but it has the solid merit of accounting for all that has happened both before and after the author put pen to paper. For that reason our readers may be interested in the thesis, which is, in summary, as follows:

It may best be stated as the author himself gathers it up at the conclusion of his book in the answers to four questions: (1) What were the fundamental mistakes made in dealing with Germany after the surrender? (2) What is Hitler's

Germany? (3) Where is Germany going? (4) How shall Europe protect itself in face of the German threat?

(1) The fatal mistake made at Versailles by the Allies was in failing to recognize that they were dealing with people who did not *mean* an enduring peace, to whom agreements meant nothing and to whom the determination to *revanche* was dominant. They totally misunderstood the German mentality and built a peace on the shifting sands of Geneva—a "pacifist" peace that had no foundations. As Foerster puts it: "When people discuss the question of guilt in the next world war they will surely name as one of the war's essential causes a certain Genevan-spirit, that is, the false and mistaken pacifism of many League men." The next peace will have to be built along sterner lines and upon more stable foundations.

(2) Hitler's Germany is the Germany that broke away finally from the Western world in the Thirty Years' War, since which time the spirit of *Preussenthum* has by degrees captured the German soul and rules it absolutely today. Of Hitler, Foerster says that he "comes out of the dust heap of the Thirty Years' War," he is the "resurrected Ferdinand II who again picks up the quarrel with Richelieu," but in a new phase, this time to overthrow once and for all the Western world; he is "starting" another Thirty Years' War; the old one was never expiated, the World War was never expiated; it is all to do over again; Germany of today cannot be "converted" peacefully and led back into the European fellowship. Hitler can claim to have led the German people "to a willing departure from all reason, all truth and all right." It is interesting to note that three years ago in this book Foerster wrote a warning to Europe not to take seriously Hitler's propaganda against Soviet Bolshevism, and said: "Germany will be the Bolshevist center. German Nazi Bolshevist totalitarianism will bring all the consequences that the indestructible realism of the Russian peasant has successfully resisted."

(3) Writing in 1937 (be it remembered), Foerster asks where German arms will strike first. He does not undertake to answer it definitely, but he warns us that the irrational element that Hitler has aroused in German life has power enough to coerce the army to its will for any external adventure—as we now see!

(4) How shall Europe protect itself? First and foremost—*arms*. Germany's neighbors must convince Germany that the risk of war is too great. Next, propaganda in the true sense of that word. Next, a clear recognition of what Europe is defending. Is it merely so-called "modern civilization" which is no more than a whitewashed barbarism, or is it that most deep Christian tradition which alone is capable of rescuing both Europe and Germany, the splintering of which threatens both?

These are Foerster's conclusions, to which his book leads through a background of detailed historical facts covering seven centuries, all strung upon one continuous thread of reasoning. The present writer finds that reasoning completely convincing; it is certainly entitled to the attention of American readers who wish to see the present world picture in its proper proportions, its relation to the past and its implications for the future. Agree with it or disagree with it as one pleases, one cannot afford to neglect it. *March* 18, 1940

AN OPEN WINDOW AND IMPERIALISM

A correspondent (E.H.G., New York) writes: "I have thought of bringing to your notice a remarkable parallel between one of the Orations of Demosthenes—the third,

I think—and the Hitlerian method of waging war. "You think," he said to the Athenians, "that he [Philip of Macedon] will be content with the few poor villages that he has taken. Not even if he were at your gates would you believe that he intends to make war on you."

This writer is always tempted—despite his indifferent scholarship—to seek analogies in history. It is not to be denied that a surface analogy—not to be pushed too far—can be discerned between the Athens of the middle of the fourth century B.C. and the Britain of the years immediately preceding Munich. Macedon might stand for Germany and Demosthenes for Churchill. Difficulty arises when one attempts to read Philip for Hitler any further than in the similarity of their dreams of conquest. Philip was no such person as the Fuehrer. A French historian thus characterizes him: "An astonishing person this Macedonian, subtle and intelligent, brutal and charming, a great administrator, a general beyond compare, perhaps the only man of whom one could say that from the very beginning of his life he had the clear notion of what he had to do to give his country the place that he wanted for her in Hellas." What he wanted was "a window opening on the Aegean."

Now at that time Athens did not believe that Philip's operation in the North presented any real danger, and there were plenty of highly respectable leaders in the city who were as pacifist and appeasing as the Baldwins, Churchills and the Chamberlains of yesterday. Demosthenes was not popular when he started his warnings to wake up and prepare for battle. Philip had started to move south and west in 349, when Demosthenes began his great series that we knew in school as the Philippics. But Athens woke up too late and tried a "Munich" of its own by sending a mission to Pella to talk with Philip and Demosthenes was of the mission! Philip reassured the other members, but Demosthenes kept his fingers crossed.

The second embassy—the same personnel!—tried it again

and got some promises from Philip which satisfied the popular assembly, but not the council. Philip's successful raids on Phocian cities and then on Delphos finally gave Demosthenes his chance. But—and here is an analogic touch—Athens had a chance to make an alliance with the Persian king (Britain-Soviets) but passed it up, whereupon Philip grabbed it (Hitler-Stalin) and Athens' goose was cooked.

In 337 Philip had all the states of Hellas under his hegemony. The following year he was assassinated, but not before he had proposed to the Greeks that they should make war on the Persians. His son Alexander (pupil of Aristotle!) was awarded divine honors by Athens not long before he died. Following his death, Athens made a shortlived attempt to arouse the Greek cities to revolt, but it failed and Demosthenes died self-poisoned in exile. From which facts it is assuredly to be hoped that the partial analogy will fail to hold throughout. But it will do no hurt to remember that Alexander's conquests fell apart rapidly after his death and Athens ended under Roman rule. (Might Rome perhaps stand for a Federation of European states?)

Broken promises between states were assuredly no novelty in those days, but it is doubtful if so many were ever crowded into so short a time as have been squeezed into the last three years. This phenomenon is a distinctly modern development in international relations and, even though it has not become accepted as a diplomatic practice outside certain nations, it adds another difficulty to the already appalling set of difficulties in getting a peace. Talleyrand remarked of Metternich (or was it the other way around?) that Metternich never told the truth yet deceived no one while he, Talleyrand, always told the truth and people did not believe him.

There is an anecdote of a famous Chief Justice in Dublin who flourished sixty years ago. A friend mentioned the name of someone to the Justice, saying: "That man's an awful liar, isn't he, Chief Justice?" To which the Justice is said to have replied: "Liar is he? Ye only know when he's telling the truth by the greater embarrassment of his manner!"

Thus far, at all events, no embarrassment has been observable in the manner of the principal promise-breakers.

August 28, 1940

VITORIA ON A JUST WAR

Apropos Attorney General Robert H. Jackson's address to the International American Bar Association at Havana late last month and his references to Hugo Grotius and the "scholastic" writers in the formative period of the law of nations, the reader may be interested in the views of one of these writers, of whom Dr. James Brown Scott has written exhaustively in his book, *The Spanish Origin of International Law (Francisco de Vitoria and His Law of Nations),* and whom he called "the founder of the modern law of nations."

There came to this writer's hand shortly before he read Mr. Jackson's address an article in the *Dublin Review* (January, 1941) on Francisco de Vitoria's teaching on the law of war, in which the whole subject is treated from the point of view of natural law. This was done in a lecture delivered at the University of Salamanca in 1539, which has been regarded by scholars as one of the most masterly treatments extant and profoundly influential upon all subsequent thought. The reader may be interested in a brief summary of Vitoria's doctrine, borrowed from the Dublin article.

(1) A Christian nation may lawfully make war to defend itself against aggression or to punish an injury received; the purpose of a just war is to bring about peace and security.

Every state has the right to make war in defense of its own welfare.

(2) The only just cause for war is a wanton wrong received from an enemy, and the wrong must be such as to necessitate war as the only remedy. Diversity of religion is not a just cause, neither is desire for aggrandizement of territory, nor desire of a ruler for personal glory or advantage.

(3) In war, whatever is necessary for public order—recovery of lost territory, the securing of due compensation for injuries received, and for such punishment of the enemy as will prevent him from renewable attack—is just.

(4) The ruler of the state must be positively sure of the justice of his cause before declaring war. His *subjects unless positively convinced that the war is unjust* should serve in it, and they are not bound by mere doubts to abstain.

(5) A war cannot be just for both sides; one must be wrong.

(6) War may not be levied upon innocent parties, but accidental damage to them may not always be avoidable.

Vitoria summed up his lecture in three "canons" which read as follows:

Canon 1. Assuming that the prince has the authority to declare war, he should first of all never seek occasions and reasons for so doing but should wherever possible endeavor to remain at peace with all men, as St. Paul writes to the Romans. He must bear in mind that our fellow man is a neighbor whom we have to love as ourselves; that we all have a common Lord, before Whose Tribunal we shall appear to render an account of our deeds. It is moreover the height of cruelty to seek occasions for war, and to rejoice when they are found and thus to massacre and destroy men created by God, and for whom Christ died. Recourse must be had to war only as the very last remedy, when all others have failed.

Canon 2. If for just reasons war has been declared its aim must not be the ruin of the enemy, but the righting of the wrong suffered and the defense of the country, with a view to securing a lasting peace.

Canon 3. When the war is won the conqueror must use his victory with Christian moderation and equity, remembering that he is acting as a judge between two states, the one injuring, the other injured. Hence he must give his verdict in the spirit not of an accuser but of a judge, making reparation in deed to the injured state, but inflicting the least possible harm on the guilty state, limiting the punishment as far as may be, to the truly guilty—and this especially because among Christian people the whole guilt usually rests with the rulers. Subjects are in good faith when they fight for their rulers, and it is most iniquitous that the follies of Kings should, as Horace wrote, be paid for by their peoples.

By the way, in condemning the making of war by a ruler for his own glory or advantage, Vitoria significantly observed, "*For the King has his authority from the state.*"

As the writer in the *Dublin Review* comments: "We call these words startling; for it should be remembered that Vitoria wrote in the sixteenth century, at the very time when a crowd of servile philosophers, chiefly in northern Europe, were defending the divine right of kings in matters temporal as well as spiritual." And yet there are those today who suppose that the "divine doctrine" was medieval.

April 11, 1941

THE SWASTIKA ON MT. OLYMPUS

The Swastika on Mt. Olympus! Not that there was much that was sacrosanct about the mythical denizens of that spot as the classics report their doings. As between Zeus, Hera, Mars, Aphrodite and the rest of the crew and Wotan and his companions in Valhalla there is little to choose. Both are a pretty squalid collection of gods. But that is not the essence of the matter. There was more to Olympus than its gods and goddesses of mythology, as Socrates well knew, when with his last breath he reminded Crito that a cock was owing to Aesculapius, and as Aristotle knew when he bequeathed a couple of monuments to two gods—this writer forgets which they were, but they were Olympians. The Swastika is the symbol of everything rotten in the paganism of Greece or Scandinavia, without a trace of the redeeming qualities of either of these "creeds outworn." It is most appropriate, too, that it symbolizes a broken cross—the rejection, lock, stock and barrel, of Christianity. Peter Wust in a short essay (it can be found in *Essays in Order*) entitled "The Crisis in the West" brings out the point in striking fashion. The classic man (of Greece) he says, was more than *homo sapiens,* the pure rationalist. He was primarily the *homo naturaliter obediens.* "Man naturally submissive to the sacred sanctions of being."

> All modern attempts [he says], to resuscitate the spirit of antiquity have never achieved more than a temporary or superficial success. For it is precisely the objective piety of the classical outlook that is essential to the success of all such attempts at resuscitation. And that outlook cannot be so easily recaptured. . . . I would like to inform sophisticated twentieth-century freethinkers that the pagans of old had at least this "natural piety" and we have lost it. "Yes," they may reply, "but they prayed to Zeus and Poseidon and to a multiplicity of gods and that was folly." Of course it was folly, but the actual prayer itself was not folly. On the contrary, it was the ancient supreme act of childlike wisdom. Their whole life was fashioned to a liturgy, and thence it derived its sheer greatness and monumental quality, and that character of sacredness, before which we still find ourselves obliged to linger in reverence. For from the flame of that unique consecration a spark yet glows. Classical humanity still stood for a realism that was naturally religious, at any rate before skepticism and profanity had as yet made their appearance, and before the noble unity of a civilization based upon natural religion had dissolved in decay and corruption.

Wust calls this the "*naturalis pietas*" of the ancients. The same thing can be found in the Icelandic saga upon which Wagner drew for his *Ring*. There is no trace of it in the Nazi idea. Strange that this has not dawned upon the "cultural" authorities of Hitlerdom! (To say nothing of *Parsifal!*) Modern paganism first departed from the ancient in its complete secularization of life, and in its Nazi development it has almost formally brutalized it. It is not merely paganism, not merely secularism; it is virtual animalism. And beyond that man cannot go in separating himself from his past. Wust likens the modern man to the *steppenwolf* man of Hesse's famous novel (so entitled),

> roving ruthlessly hither and thither in the endless and loveless desert that is Western civilization, and hideously crying his hunger and thirst for Eternity . . . the howling of the wolf that we hear today is . . . the distinctive cry for help of a man who feels by instinct that he has lost both the classical and the Christian piety. The cry for help of a man who, as a metaphysical being, now feels himself really cheated out of the ultimate reason for his existence.

The man of the Swastika is of the authentic *steppenwolf* breed.

April 30, 1941

THE WILL TO PEACE

The April number of *International Conciliation* (published by Carnegie Endowment for International Peace) is an unusually interesting document. It contains "Preliminary Report and Monographs" of the Commission to Study the Organization for Peace, established in 1939 under the chairmanship of Professor James T. Shotwell "to study the reorganization of the world for peace, in preparation for the vast work of reconstruction which will face the world upon the termination of this conflict." The monographs are twenty-eight in number, under seven heads, all related to the problems of a new world order and "the tranquility of order which is peace." This writer will say for those few which he has examined that they are worth reading.

The preliminary report is relatively brief but comprehensive. It boils down to a simple conclusion which can be simply stated. Modern war between nations has become impossibly destructive—thanks to the misuse of science—and the civilized world can no longer tolerate it. Nations must, therefore, exclude it as an instrument of international relations. This can only be done by establishing an international juristic authority to which international disputes must be referred, and an international force to back that authority's decrees. In turn this will require a partial surrender of national autonomy. A federal system is the logical form for the world organization of nations. The only alternatives to this are a so-called "balance of power" system or a single power domination of all nations. Balance of power is essentially unstable; a single power world hegemony is unthinkable. There is no escape from the logic of the facts; it is as terrible as it is simple. All that is needed is the *will* to put it into effect.

Psychologists in medieval days had a word for *will;* they called it *voluntas* and it meant the resolve to achieve an end and to take the *means* necessary for its achievement. They had another word of etymological ancestry—*velleitas,* which meant a desire for an end, but without the will to take the means by which alone the end could be attained. For more than a generation men of the civilized world have desired peace, as it had not been desired before that time, that is, if one may judge by the general preoccupation of thought everywhere on the matter. But Emile Boutroux in or about 1911 stated in a public discourse in Paris that, judging from all the talk in the world about the necessity of peace, he would conclude that the very near future would be unusually bloody! And, nearly forty years before that, Jacob Burckhardt had declared that the years of "deceptive peace" were over and we were entering on an era of great wars! In short, the world was indulging in an unusually violent fit of pure *velleitas.* Is there yet any sure sign that *voluntas* is in the making?

The "Preliminary Report" recognizes the need. "The reorganization of peace," it says, "must have back of it the force of a unifying ideal." Most true. But it must be a *moral* ideal. Moral ideals cannot be generated by expediency or experience. War cannot be eliminated from human relations merely because it hurts, no matter how much it hurts. Experience can prepare the ground for the reception of a moral ideal, but it cannot, of itself, provide the ideal. That must come from another source, and that source is natural law, which rests upon a religious foundation. Now the unfortunate fact is that for some two centuries or so the whole trend of modern thinking has been away from religion as such, from natural law as such, and from morals as such. What prospect is there then for the recovery of the necessary "unifying ideal" by the world today, in time to avert the general catastrophe which we all recognize as possible, if not indeed imminent?

No international courts, no leagues, no collective security, will avail unless there is substituted for the *velleitas* upon which all have so far been founded a *voluntas* which must have its principles of life from religion. And there can be no *peace* until then.

May 9, 1941

THINKING IT OVER

THE PROBLEMS OF LASTING PEACE

I

In *The Problems of Lasting Peace* by Herbert Hoover and Hugh Gibson we have an orderly and carefully thought-out attempt to envisage and analyze the elements of the tremendous problem that confronts our civilization. Whatever critics may find in which to disagree with the conclusions of the authors, they must be credited with an excellent piece of work, deserving of study by all who feel concerned with the question. The method they have followed is a good model for others to follow, and is in sharp contrast to the disorderly and emotional treatment of the subject with which we have been surfeited.

They begin by seeking to isolate what they term the "dynamic forces" which run through history and make for peace and war, and find that they fall in seven categories as follows: (1) "Ideologies," (2) "economic pressure," (3) "nationalism," (4) "militarism," (5) "imperialism," (6) "the complexes of fear, hate and revenge," and (7) "the will to peace." These, they say, are not arranged in their order of importance. Having done this, they divide their analysis into three main parts, corresponding to three historical periods, studying each in the light of the above seven dynamisms. The first in the period from the American Revolution to the outbreak of the World War in 1914, the second the World War and the peace-making 1914-1919, and the third the twenty years 1919-39, gathering up in a final summary the conclusions suggested by the study as to the foundations for enduring peace and the method of preserving that peace. It is all done with a notable restraint of emotion, with complete absence either of Utopian blueprints or high-sounding abstractions, and with a logical continuity in treatment which makes the reading attractively easy, yet productive to the reader.

The present writer's immediate purpose is to recommend this book to his readers, and, this being so, he will neither summarize all its contents and conclusions, nor enlarge upon such differences between his own points of view and those of the authors as detailed study develops. Two important conclusions may be noted as among the "foundations" for peace. One is that "representative government" all around is a primary requisite and must be accepted by the enemy nations. The other is that "freedom" rather than government "planning" must be the dominant factor in the world's economic processes, subject, of course, to inhibitions upon abuse. Peace, they believe, cannot be preserved in the absence of either. On the matter of representative government Messrs. Hoover and Gibson have this warning to offer:

> There are some profound lessons to consider, however, in any attempt to force personal liberty and representative government on nations. Ideologies of personal liberty and free will cannot be imposed by machine guns. Wrong ideas cannot be cured by war or treaty. They are matters of mind and spirit. The lasting acceptance of any governing idea lies deep in the mores of races and in their intellectual processes. Liberty does not come like manna from Heaven; it must be cultivated from rocky soil with infinite patience and great human toil. . . . Yet there is an instinctive craving of man for personal freedom. . . . If we were wise enough in the peace-making we might start the rebuilding of freedom in some form. Probably not in our exact form for every race moves in the orbit of its own mores.

On "economic freedom" they have this to say:

> To be free, men must choose their callings, bargain for their own services, save and provide for their families and old age. And they must be free to engage in enterprise so long as each does not injure his fellow men, and that requires laws to prevent abuse. And when we use the terms "Fifth Freedom," "economic freedom" or "free enterprise," we use them in this sense only, not in the sense of

laissez-faire or capitalistic exploitation. Such freedom does not mean going back to abuses, it in no way inhibits social reform and social advancement. . . . It would be ironical if, having fought a war to establish freedom, we should have fastened any form of collectivism on our own country.

There is much more that could be said of the merits of this book but the present writer will content himself with his general recommendation above, promising the reader that the time spent in reading it will not be without at least some profit. He has his own reservations concerning the treatment of the "ideologies," but passes them for the present.

June 19, 1942

II

Nothing in the visible world scene more vividly demonstrates the tremendous scope of the change that is sweeping over the earth than does the Anglo-Russian-American agreement reached a few days ago when taken into account with Russia's military effort. These two things open a vista of possibilities affecting the future course of the Western world that both excites and swamps the imagination. More than twenty years ago this country flatly refused to "recognize" the Union of Soviet Socialist Republics. It is worth while to read over the statement of our reasons, prepared by Mr. Bainbridge Colby as Secretary of State for President Wilson. Some nine years ago we "recognized" the Soviets, but with a good many mental reservations. Since then, Soviet Russia has risen up in arms against the common enemy of civilized Europe and of ourselves and is fighting with a courage and tenacity that has surprised not only that enemy but the whole world, and has held off at an enormous cost in blood the Nazi horde which, but for that, would have blotted out what remained of civilization in Europe, and, perhaps even in the whole world. Finally, it has formally accepted the Atlantic Charter in which

Great Britain and ourselves laid down the principles on which we conceive our civilization to be based.

Whatever may be the course of events between now and the final destruction of the Nazi hordes and their allies, it is clear that Russia's contribution to that result will have been a main determinant of the conflict. It is likewise clear that Russia will henceforth play a most important part in Europe's councils of the future. And the great question that remains yet to be answered is—what kind of Russia have Europe and ourselves to deal with? Is it the Bolshevist Russia with which we gingerly came to terms a few years ago? Is it the Russia that stood wholeheartedly for three years behind the last of the Tsars in the last war, and behind Alexander against Napoleon? Is it a Communist Russia? Or is it something far more primitive, a Russia of Berdyaev, of Soloviev, of Dostoievski, of Turgeniev? A Russia profoundly "religious" and deeply infiltrated with Christianity? It will make a great difference to the future of Europe (and of ourselves) which of these is the Russia with which Europe (and ourselves) henceforth must reckon.

Here an important distinction must be observed. It is a distinction between what Mr. Hoover and Mr. Gibson call the "ideologies" and the "material" forms of society. The Communist "ideology" is one thing, and the Communist "form" of society is something quite another. It would be quite possible for something very like the Communist industrial and agricultural structure to exist in a community whose ideology was fundamentally Christian. All appearances at present support the belief that the collectivist principle has received a foothold in Russia, not, perhaps, in its extreme form, but in a greater degree than in Europe proper. The chances are that Russia's economic structure will, in the future, be definitely State-Socialistic in character. But so far as the orthodox Communist ideology is concerned, there is little in sight to indicate that it has made any important impression upon the mass of the Russian people. Not only is this the case, but there are abundant signs to the contrary. Can anyone suppose that this people is fighting for it, and not for something very much more elemental? Is it not clear that they are fighting for the "Russia" that their imagination identifies with the steppes, the forests, the rivers in which all their memories are rooted, and of which they feel themselves part? How else explain the fury, the tenacity with which they meet the hated enemy? And the fact that not only is the Communist propaganda visibly smothered, but the old religion is openly abroad in the streets?

Yet another thing is apparent. The Russia of today shows no more sign of imperialistic designs on its European neighbors than did the Russia of Alexander or of Nicholas. That its attitude toward the small so-called Baltic nations on its Northwest frontiers is defensive in motivation rather than aggressive is now clear. As to Poland, Stalin has convinced the Poles that they shall have their country back and so they fight for him. In the Southwest they claim no more than that which was theirs before the last war.

In sum, it is manifest that while the liberated Europe will have on its Eastern borders a new Russia economically speaking, and one whose social structure may differ in important respects from those of the Western nations, it may be a Russia more spiritually akin to the Western soul—or what remains of it—than has seemed possible in the last quarter-century, and this is of the very greatest importance to Western civilization and culture. Furthermore, should it so turn out, the influence of both Europe and the new Russia upon the Far East awakening from its long sleep may be as great as it is difficult now to foresee. Finally, what is likely to become of Communism as a world-ideology, if it shall prove to have withered in Russia where it had its great experiment station?

It may be for some of us, as Sorokin says, a "privilege" to live in times such as these when events so portentous are following each other with such baffling rapidity, but for full enjoyment of the privilege we should have to be immortal on this earth—and does anybody *really* desire that?

June 24, 1942

III

Messrs. Hoover and Gibson, in opening their discussion of *The Problems of Lasting Peace* have this to say of the "ideological forces" which they list first among the seven "dynamic forces of peace and war":

"The importance of religious faith, of social, economic, political, artistic and scientific ideas, in shaping the form of the world and the making of its wars and peace is not to be estimated as less than that of other forces. Over the whole range of history they are the determining factors in civilization. One thing is certain: that is, the ideas which involve human belief and faith contain a militant crusading spirit. Within them is inherent aggressiveness. Great and revolutionary ideas have within them at least a period when they are borne aloft by military action. Christianity, the Divine Right of Kings—with all its armour of feudalism—Mohammedanism, the Protestant Reformation, and Liberalism have all marched with the sword. Now new ideologies—Communism, Fascism and Nazism—are on the warpath—ideologies can also make for peace. For these nineteen centuries Christianity has been unique among religious faiths in its preaching of peace and compassion. Personal liberty and representative government as a political concept have also preached the gospel of peace. Both, at times, have sought to impose their beliefs with the sword, but their final purpose is peace. And so long as men have beliefs, they will strive to protect and expand them.

About a dozen years ago the historian Guglielmo Ferrero delivered a lecture on "*Paganisme et Christianisme,*" which is included in the small volume *La Fin des Aventures.* Its theme is the conflict of two great forces during the last four centuries as bearing upon the question of war and peace, and Ferrero's analysis offers an interesting commentary upon Messrs.

Hoover's and Gibson's thesis. Briefly summarized, it is as follows: Pre-Christian civilization in the political order virtually divinized the State, sometimes even in the person or individuals as in Egypt and later Rome. The resultant social order was a strange mixture, with its artistic and intellectual achievements and its hardness, violence, rapacity and ferocity toward persons. Above all the ancient state was totalitarian and militarist. Christianity was neither. Socially regarded, its essence was the dignity and the sacredness of the person, and the ideal Christian state was the servant of man and not his master. That, at least, was the spirit of the Western civilization, after its Christianization, up to the coming of the Renaissance. Of the Renaissance Ferrero says that it was not, as so many believe, a mere revival of ancient literature and art. The Middle Ages, he reminds us, were rich in both. It was much more than that; it was a return to the political and military ideals of the ancient state, which Christianity had to a considerable extent obliterated. By the sixteenth century Europe was "nationalized" and the nations were organizing themselves politically and militarily. The ancient state furnished the model, and the "absolute state" was reborn. That was the theme of Ferrero's *La palingenesi di Roma,* which antedated the lecture we are discussing by a decade.

There was, however, no formal break with Christianity. Paradoxically, the humanitarian influence of Christianity on family life, manners and customs continued to grow, while the paganization of politics, law, literature, philosophy and art proceeded apace; and today's confusion of the two ideals is the consequence. The fundamental question of society today is: What is the state? A *means* or an *end?* For the ancients it was an end; for the Christian it was and is a means. But the question has not been clearly envisioned by the moderns, not even yet, despite the resurgence in its most brutal form of the ancient paganism in the Axis assault upon Christianity itself.

Curiously enough, the existence of these two contradictory currents in our more recent civilization, while they were more or less in balance, operated to enrich in many particulars that civilization in many respects. As Ferrero says: "Thanks to that permanent conflict the nineteenth century could create a civilization in which order and liberty supported each other, and the individual's highest development balanced with the development of the state's power such as no epoch ever saw equalled." But this equilibrium has been broken and the pagan state has risen in its most terrible form, backed by a power for destruction such as the world not only never saw but never even dreamed. War is and must be its main business so long as there remains a possible opponent, and no peace can be made with it that will be a peace. In a word, we live today in a world which cannot afford war and is unable to make peace, so long as the pagan state exists among us. Only in a world in which the Christian spirit again rules is there hope for peace. Christendom, as Rosalind Murray says in *The Good Pagan's Failure,* has never been fully Christian; there has always been a strong pagan leaven in Europe, and it has never been more active than it is today. When all is said and done on the question of peace, the sole hope for it is in Christendom becoming again predominantly Christian.

June 26, 1942

THE THIRD REPUBLIC

"Why are you so rough on the French 'Third Republic'? What was wrong with it? It was democratic, wasn't it? France never had a dictatorship after the Empire fell." So demands a reader (H. G. S., Pasadena, California).

This writer will be quite frank in answering his correspondent's question, being quite conscious of the fact that the grounds of his dislike of the Third Republic regime as a whole may seem to others not merely insufficient as grounds for criticism but no grounds at all, indeed the reverse. It is the predominant orientation of the regime as a whole that he objects to, that is, the underlying philosophy or philosophies that informed its general policies. These may be summed up briefly under two heads. One was *money*. The other was *laicism*—that is, hostility to religion as *religion*. The thread of both dominate the warp and woof of the structure throughout its history.

The swift, peaceful and easy transition from the Empire of Napoleon III to the Republic of Thiers was a remarkable phenomenon which must have surprised even most of those who were concerned in it. In this it differed sharply from the experience of the First Republic. The collapse of the monarchy was sudden and complete and found no group or even body of opinion prepared to take over the task of organizing a civil order. Order came first with Napoleon and the *coup d'etat* of 18th Brumaire after several years of what was little better than anarchy, and the First Republic went under for many years. Not so the Third Republic. It came into being almost spontaneously and swiftly snuffed out the anarchy of the Commune. It managed to secure the acceptance of enough of the monarchist-minded, as well as of the revolutionary left-wingers, to settle it securely in power with a solid center of "moderates." Behind these moderates was the solid and stolid mass of provincial France which wanted only peace and to be left alone, with its possessions and its daily routine of industry and thrift. It was mainly the creation of Thiers, and "conservatism" was his watchword. He was French middle class from top to toe. It was not that he was a Republican at heart. As he said himself, he was for a Republic because "it is the regime which least divides us." He learned from the Napoleonic regime that there were no dangers in universal suffrage, because the mass of the electorate could be depended upon so long as its elemental rights to till its fields and keep and transmit its possessions were guaranteed. Therein lay stability. And therein lay the seeds of the *money* worship which seized upon French public life after the recovery of France that swiftly followed upon the payment of the indemnity in the early Seventies and the liberation of French territory.

The greed of money grew with the growth of riches, and permeated French society, public and private, to an extent quite unmatched elsewhere in Europe. The depth of its penetration is best evidenced by the fact that, notwithstanding sordid public scandal after scandal, the Republic survived unshaken. Cynicism of the most complete kind and venality, barefaced and unblushing, marked it from beginning to end. As early as the eighties Renan characterized French public life in blistering terms as dominated by third-class men and "*declassés*," with "intrigue, vulgarity and charlatanism the road to prominence." Twenty years later Labori (the defender of Dreyfus) said that things had reached a state of moral anarchy unmatched in half a century, as a result of the prevailing money madness. In his sketch of the Third Republic (1935) Jacques Bainville summed it up in a closing passage quoting Livy's introduction to his great history in which the Roman historian, speaking of the moral debacle of Rome, characterized his times as those "in which we can neither endure our vices nor their remedies." There were, of course, always clean men in France even in public life, but never enough to dissipate the dense money-miasma that shrouded the regime.

So much for that factor. The policy of *laicism* is not so simply describable. It must, if it is to be understood, be sharply distinguished from the thing which is called *anti-clericalism.* Laicism signifies an orientation opposed to all religion as such; anticlericalism signifies an attitude not formally anti-religious as such, but one professedly opposed to what it deems to be clerical interference in the strictly secular domain of "politics," and that is quite another thing. The Third Republic inherited from the First a strong anticlerical instinct as was, all things considered, quite natural. Early in the days of the Third Republic Gambetta's famous slogan, "*Le cléricalisme—voilà l'ennemi*" ("Clericalism!—that's the enemy!") was taken up by the Center and the fight opened with Ferry's laws (1879) removing education from the hands of the Church. He was convinced that the "*Ecole laic*" was the means to a high "democratic" morale. A dozen or so years later Viviani could boast that "We have extinguished the lights of Heaven!" The Sorbonne was immensely powerful in the field of higher education and was completely soaked with Positivism. French Free Masonry (Grand Orient) was openly antireligious (in contrast to the older British Masonry) and was immensely powerful in politics and in the armed services. Gradually, what was originally anticlericalism developed into definite laicism and *L'Affaire Dreyfus,* in the nineties, gave a tremendous impetus to that development. The important thing for Americans to bear in mind is that French laicism was not simply a matter of separation of Church and State and French education was not merely "neutral" to religion, as is our school system; it was definitely *hostile* to it.

Believing, as the present writer believes, that "democracy," as we more or less understand the word, which is devoid of a basic foundation in religion is no *democracy,* and is incompatible with human liberty because it must be totalitarian, the French Third Republic seems to him to have been no democracy, for all its elaborate machinery. Coupling that with the general putridity of its "moral concepts," the last thing he wants to see is its re-establishment after the war has been won. He cannot believe that it will "come back." And he does not see how Americans who believe in the principles of our civil system can want to see it do so.

June 5, 1942

MADARIAGA ON SPAIN

I

Salvador de Madariaga has recently published a third edition of his important book on Spain first issued in English about thirteen years ago and, shortly afterwards, in a slightly abridged edition in Spanish. It was a sketch of Spanish affairs as they stood just before the abdication of Alfonso XIII, with studies of the three principal Spanish institutions, the Monarchy, the Army and the Church, also the agrarian question, the labor question, the Catalan question, the Moroccan, and the South American questions and Spain's foreign relations. It provided a good background against which to set the tempestuous scenes that followed Alfonso's exit. A second edition was issued in 1934. And now there has appeared a third edition with an important added series of chapters which bring the story up to the outbreak of the World War and contain a careful study of the founding of the Republic and the Civil War and an important summing up of Madariaga's conclusions in the final chapter as to Spain's future. As in the case of the first edition, the third is issued in English and Spanish. A few copies of the Spanish text have just arrived from South America; copies of the English text do not seem to be as yet available in the country but they should very soon arrive. A cursory examination of the South

American volume persuades the present reader that the book is important to anyone desirous of informing himself as to the facts of present day Spain and the causes leading to the facts, and he hopes that the English text will be widely read as soon as it is available. Madariaga is well known to English-speaking readers and audiences both here and in England. He is one of the group of Spanish intellectual "liberals" who have stood outside of strict party lines, such as Unamuno, Ortega y Gasset, Marañón, Costa, etc., and have generally been absent from Spain during the stormy years following the outbreak of the Spanish War. Republican, antimilitarist, anticlerical—all in moderation—an ardent lover of Spain and Spanish culture, he is also gifted with the observing eye as his studies of France and England amply demonstrate, and he has also a keen instinct for personalities.

He was an eyewitness of the circumstances attending the formation of the Republic and was a member of its first Cortes which made the constitution of 1931. His account of the proceedings and his studies of the "left" and "right" groups and individuals is interesting in the highest degree, and seems to explain the course of events. The present writer is, of course, unable to determine the degree of accuracy in Madariaga's statement of facts, and the correctness of his judgments, but he finds the story intelligible as a story, and the sequence of events seems to him logical. There is, moreover, at least one fact in support of its general correctness. What he has to say will please adherents of neither side of the hot controversy that has raged and still rages in this country over Spain. Both will object to many of his judgments and conclusions. In all such controversies, agreement by both sides and disagreement by both sides to an account of the conflict have about equal weight in support of the truth of the account.

The present writer will not attempt to summarize either Madariaga's story or the conclusion that he draws from that story. His purpose is to point out that the book as a whole throws much light on many facets of a situation which is infinitely more complex than most of us suppose and which is also important for us to understand more thoroughly than we do today. If it does no more for us than to give us a more intimate picture of the Spaniard as he actually is, it will repay the reading. It is a lamentable fact that as a people we do not have real "cultural" contact with the Spanish "genius," that is, with the way the educated Spaniard "looks at life," and still more lamentable that we do not, for the most part, even suspect the lack, much less regret it and try to supply it. A century of "neighborhood" with the republics to the south of us leaves us both still largely devoid of mutual understanding. Moreover, and of more immediate importance, there is the "post-war" problem, in which the future of Spain is an awkward angle in which our sympathies are already as strongly engaged as our knowledge is limited.

April 12, 1943

II

What might perhaps be termed the "scouts" or "skirmishers" of our "liberal" forces in their enthusiasm for freedom for all peoples seem to believe that our main "war aim" is to impose *our* system of government upon the oppressed peoples of Europe—President, Senate, House, Supreme Court and adult suffrage, lock, stock and barrel—and call it a day. There is no doubt that it would be an excellent thing if it could be done—and when done, stay put. In Madariaga's recent book, the third edition of *España,* there are some considerations which are worth bearing in mind, and, having in mind that they are those of a Liberal Republican Spaniard, identified with no party and known to all the world as a patriot. This writer will borrow a few sentences:

The case of Spain is one that must put to the proof the political sense of those who will direct the world that is to be. If they are at pains to impose upon Spain political institutions, born and grown in other countries of different psychological habitat we are headed for a certain smash. Direct and universal suffrage is a concrete example. Everything concerning elections, representative bodies and executives and in general the machinery of the state must above all be construed with eyes fixed on order and continuity. Without order and continuity all the rest imaginable as desirable cannot succeed. . . . In this omission the constitution of 1931 was, as we have seen, a tragic mess which brought Spain to disaster, swinging from extreme right to extreme left by the combined play of direct suffrage, an absurd electoral law and the lack of a senate. This above all is what Spain must defend itself against in the future. . . . The statesmen whose business it is to guide the soon-coming creative years will have to concentrate their efforts in safeguarding the essentials of democracy without wasting them in the small details which the devotees of the Holy Democratic Church still are defending with singular tenacity despite their failure in almost all the countries of the world. Respect for man's person, liberty of thought, and government by consent of the governed, are the three things on which there is no yielding. All the rest is machinery and, therefore, it must be adapted to the human metals at hand.

Madariaga is speaking for Spain, but his general theme might be any liberal in any one of the European nations. In no two of these is the human metal of precisely the same composition and in none of them is it the same as our own. It seems to the present writer that our own "liberals," actuated as they are by the best intentions in the world and the noblest desires of all men, lack a sufficient appreciation of the cultural differences distinguishing these European nations from each other and all of them from our own. The political polarization of any country will be determined by its specific culture, which in turn will be the result of many causes operating over a long time. Take, for example, the countries that make the western border of the European peninsula from north to south. What similarity is there between the specific culture of the Scandinavian nations, the Belgian, the French, the Dutch, the Spanish and the Portuguese? How could a uniform "machinery," as Madariaga calls it, fit them all, let alone *our* machinery, and give each the "freedom" that it wants? And what about eastern and southeastern Europe, whose peoples are culturally far more remote from us than the nations just mentioned? Our "messianic complex" is in its way a natural product of our history and our environment and there is in it a genuinely fine idealism for which we need apologize to no one. But it needs to be infused with a liberal dose of humility —intellectual humility—if it is to be helpful to those whom we desire to help. The truth is that as a nation we are far more remote, culturally, from these European nations than they are from each other and the pity is that we do not seem even to suspect that fact. It would be a good thing to call in our "liberal" scouts and skirmishers and look over the situation in something of the spirit in which Madariaga has looked over his own land. *April* 21, 1943

THE TRUCE OF GOD

It has been said that the devastation wrought upon the Germanies in the Thirty Years' War was such that complete recovery took a hundred years. It was after that experience that there gradually developed the movement toward minimizing the generally destructive character of warfare, which resulted in armies beginning to carry the supplies they needed instead of "living off the country" after the manner of locusts, and it finally culminated in the eighteenth-century concept of war which the late historian Ferrero described so interestingly in his small volume *La Fin des aventures* published a dozen or more years ago. The essence of that theory was the recognition of the fact that the true end or purpose of a *war* was to achieve a *peace* which could not be achieved by negotiation. Consequently, the aim was to *limit* the process of war-making as far as possible, to avoid making the achievement of the peace more difficult by what was done in war. It was in fact a chessboard concept in which actual combat was excluded as far as possible, and one of the greatest eighteenth-century generals declared that a really great soldier could make a successful war all his life without a single battle.

Napoleon's idea was different; he believed in a *"bonne bataille,"* followed by a triumphal entry into the conquered capital, a banquet, a gala theatrical performance and a treaty. He planned his Russian campaign on that principle, but never could get his *"bonne bataille"* and the desired sequel. Finally, his enemy got the desired result at Waterloo and Vienna. With him vanished the eighteenth-century theory of limited war-making and today we are back to the conditions of the Thirty Years' War in the matter of destruction of populations, only on a much greater scale. And the one thought of the United Nations now is how to banish war itself from the earth. Once started, war cannot be "limited" for, in the first place, it is now a *national* affair, and in the second place, it has become fantastically destructive. The only recourse is to banish it altogether.

There is but one way to banish war, namely to substitute law for force. We are all agreed as to that. Law to be effective must be generally accepted by those who live under it; it cannot indefinitely function if it rests primarily upon force—although, behind it, a sufficient force must be always potential to deal with the recalcitrant residuum. This acceptance must have a *moral* foundation; if it be merely based upon fear of the alternative, or upon considerations purely in the order of expediency or even of refined hedonism, it is a house built upon sand, certain sooner or later to fall. It is here that the final world problem lies—how to evoke the moral force on which alone world peace can be securely founded.

The last time that the West found itself in the ruins of a great civilization was some fifteen hundred years ago when the Western empire went down. Then Christianity took over and Christendom arose. Christianity was never wholly Christian, but for a time, in the Middle Ages, it was Christian enough to keep the Christian peoples together in a sort of family relation with each other, at least, in recognizing, however vaguely, a common spiritual ancestry. There was even a time when the feudal combatants recognized the *Treuga Dei*—the truce of God. But today it is not a pagan civilization which is sick; it is a civilization which was Christian that is fighting for its life. Can a civilization which once was Christian and is sick almost to death find any other soul to give it new life? Can Christendom live again without Christianity?

Every great "culture," as Christopher Dawson reminds us (in *Progress and Religion*), has been vitalized by some form of religion. History shows us no trace of a completely secular culture, nor has anthropology yet found any tribal group of human beings entirely devoid of dependence upon the transcendental. Men have always in their own fashion and time sought the Absolute. In the Western civilization they reached the highest concept of the Absolute in the intuition of Pure Being. Beyond that it seems the mind cannot go. Can a great "culture" which has ever attained that summit ever settle back to any lower concept and remain great?

The sickness of Christendom might be described in many ways, but these might be summed up in the statement that it has almost lost its hold upon the Absolute. It is not accidental that an almost passionate rejection of all "absolutes" is the heart of modern "philosophic" thinking. It is not thinkable that Christendom would return to any of the earlier attempts to reach the Absolute and there rest and renew its cultural life. It is often said—and truly—that Western society is largely "paganized," but the modern "paganism" lacks the *pietas* (as Wust calls it) which underlay the old pagan systems—all of them. If these things be true, the conclusion is that Christendom can recover from its sickness only by again becoming Christian, and, if this be true, there is no other hope than that for world peace and world civilization.

October 8, 1943

THE QUESTION MARKS OF EUROPE

In last Sunday's magazine section of the New York *Times* the leading article written from Paris by that uncanny person, Mrs. Anne O'Hare McCormick, bears the caption: "Europe, Landscape of Question-Marks—A reporter looks beneath the surface and finds a challenge for Americans." "A reporter," forsooth! Doubtless Mrs. McCormick *is* a "reporter"; so is Kreisler a "violinist," Rachmaninoff a "pianist," Beethoven a "composer" and Dickens a "novelist." But the present writer, who has been avidly reading Mrs. McCormick's "reports" since she made her debut in print, will unashamedly declare that she has been for him *the* "reporter," who in traveling the civilized world has delivered to him, as none others have done in that field, those harmonics, flavors, colors, lights and shades of events and personalities which bring the picture she presents to that completeness which gives it the final touch of life and actuality. No derogation is here suggested or implied of her able and earnest men co-workers; there has never been better "foreign corresponding" as a whole than there is today. So, at least, this writer will testify from his own experience of nearly sixty years of newspaper reading. It is not that their work is inferior, as work, to Mrs. McCormick's, so much as it is a difference in *genre* of work. Anyhow, this writer's opinion and "taste" in the matter are irrelevant and uninteresting to anyone, so enough of both. Let us look at the nature of the challenge that Europe, as she sees it, offers to us in America.

The word is that of the caption writer; it does not occur in her text. The nearest she goes to the notion is in her opening paragraph, where she states that what she has to say is based upon three conversations—one in Italy, one in France, and one in an American Army mess, and that the drift of these talks seems "to pose some pertinent questions for Americans to answer." Now there are two sets of questions in the matter. One is the questions which the "liberated" peoples are *silently* asking themselves as the tumult and shouting dies down, questions as to themselves, their government and their futures which have not yet become articulate. The other is the questions that our fighting men are asking themselves. Out of the two sets rises the question what we—America—are thinking and likely to think about Europe and ourselves. Are we going to relapse into a new "isolationism"? As Mrs. McCormick puts it: "The American people have paid a fabulous price to learn that isolation is a chimera; can they afford to let a narrow nationalistic outlook prevail again at home or abroad?" That is the challenge implicit in her articles and it is a challenge.

But there are overtones in her piece which it seems to this writer should not be missed, for they are important. The significance of the "silent questioning" that she had detected among the liberated peoples is in its bearing upon the special danger that she sees in the sentence just quoted. That danger lies, not so much in the order of intention, as in the order of intelligence. No country entertains any better or higher intentions toward the world than does our own—or ever has. We have always felt toward it a messianic mood. The trouble is that our people as a whole are deeply, massively—mainly inculpably—ignorant of the peoples who make up that world, ignorant of their histories, their traditions, their cultures and their souls. We are also so enamored—rightly so—of our own history, tradition, culture and soul that we think it is the only remedy for the troubles of other peoples—we concede the basic world conflict as one between democracy and dictatorship and we conceive democracy as synonymous with freedom and exclusively expressed in our own civil order. It does not seem to us that other peoples may possibly conceive freedom in other forms and terms than those expressed in our own order. Nor are we aware of the crucial differences between the concepts of these things existing in the various peoples and the countries of Europe. Take the Western nations of the Continent—Portugal, Spain, France, Belgium and Holland; no two are fundamentally similar in characteristics. The Portuguese differs radically from the Spaniard, the Spaniard from the Frenchman, the Frenchman from the Belgian, the Belgian from the Hollander, and each and all differ from the Scandinavian. Each of these peoples has its own picture of its freedom and the means to achieve and protect it. No two are really alike, and all pictures differ from our picture of our own freedom. There are several dangers in this. One is the tendency to an oversimplification of the problem of Europe as a whole and of its component parts. Another is the danger of completely misunderstanding each of these component parts as a result of partial information and definite propaganda by refugees from countries where the internal polarizations are many and sharp, as has happened notably in the cases of France and Spain, not to mention others. It is these internal polarizations indeed in which our ignorance is deepest and the consequences of imperfect or incorrect information and actual propaganda are most deadly.

It seems to this writer that one of the most important implications in Mrs. McCormick's "piece" is the necessity for us to approach our share in the stupendous task that lies before us in a spirit of *intelligent humility,* to recognize the scope of our ignorance, and the need for us to learn before we undertake to teach. It may not be the easiest thing to do, but to do it will be the best preventive of the danger that Mrs. McCormick referred to in the phrases quoted above.

November 17, 1944

CHRISTMAS AND RESENTMENT

Not in many a long year, if ever, has the "Christmas spirit" found itself so much a stranger on this earth as it does this year, for, probably, never has the earth nourished so large and so deadly a brood of hatreds as it harbors today. It is not the temporary "hatreds" of warring peoples that are the matter, although these are deeper and fiercer than usual. The terrifying thing is the hatreds within the peoples themselves, especially the "occupied peoples," the "group" hatreds, and worst of all, perhaps, the personal hatreds of man for man in these countries, the hatred of the "patriots" for the Quislings and the "collaborationists" who live in their midst. These are of the cold murderous type which waits only an opportunity to wreak total vengeance. This sort of thing has existed before, sporadically, locally and temporarily, but never on today's scale. Today it wraps the European continent in a thick lethal miasma, that like poison gas has soaked deeply into the very earth and water of life. How shall the Christmas message of "peace and good will toward men"—or if one prefers it—"Peace on earth to men of good will" penetrate that pall, which seems to have all the stigmata of a direct exhalation from Hell itself? If any reader thinks that this is wild and whirling rhetoric all he has to do is to listen for five minutes to any one of the refugees among us from those countries speaking out his full mind.

We have, thank Heaven, nothing amongst us nearly approaching this sort of thing. But we have even here a perceptible sharpening of edges in our more or less routine group disputes that carries unpleasant possibilities. A new "flavor" seems perceptible in some of these, a flavor which is none too easy to describe. The French seem to have a word for it—*ressentiment*. English has not, for the word "resentment" does not carry its full freight. German also lacks an equivalent; Spanish takes it over as *resentimiento* and Dr. Marañón's study of Tiberius is centered upon the thing. Perhaps more curious than all, the Russian writer Berdyaev borrows the French word directly in treating the idea; it is found in his Russian text, as his translator (French) notes. Now the thing is best described, perhaps, by starting with the English word "resentment," and noting wherein *ressentiment* differs from it. A resentment can be temporary, however hot it be; *ressentiment* is lasting and tends to deepen and grow with time. There is in it a cold bitterness, a sense of deep-rooted grievance, a desire for something more than mere removal of the cause of grievance, the whole making a state of mind that can only be described as an unsatisfied gnawing desire for vengeance, that is, for that measure of *vindictive* justice which goes beyond the bounds of the human "anger which sins not." In all these things it is the opposite of the thing which the Apostle calls "charity" and violates the Evangelist's endlessly repeated counsel: "Little children, love one another"—which last is the essence of the Christmas message.

The "left-right cleavage," the world over, has taken on a degree of *ressentiment* greater than ever *before;* that element was always in it to some extent. In our own country there was always less of it than in the Old World but it is increasing here, and is beginning to be observable in the increased acrimony appearing in the outgivings of our intelligentsia where urbanity has been more or less the rule. Here is an example from the pen of one of the most "urbane" exponents of the "intellectual left," describing the "enemy":

I think he knows he is helping to destroy the New Deal and the whole democratic effort. I think he knows he is not helping the war in the process. . . . These political fellows are out to wreak their frustrations on the New Deal and wrest political power from it—no matter what happens to their party in the process. And some of the press and business groups are out to do the same, no matter what happens to the business system in the process. Why do they do it? They do it out of a deep irresponsibility. For a decade these men have had to dam up in themselves the frustrations of men who see the world going the wrong way—not theirs. In their hearts have raged many of the same emotions which the men of Europe learned to recognize as fascist. They find themselves now in the midst of an anti-fascist victory they have not willed. They see rising around them the framework of a world which may become the house of the democratic nations. Do you wonder that they are desperate—that in their hearts is a death-wish, and deep in their blood is a death instinct? . . . I think they are so bitter that they are beyond the reach of reason.

There is in these words a new note, having in mind their source, and no elaborate chemical analysis is needed to disclose the fact that it is in the order of *hatreds*. This is bad business, for there is no place in democracy for hatreds either of persons or of groups. The Spanish have a proverb: "Love requites love" *(Amor con amor se paga)*, and equally, hatred requites hatred, and we have hatreds on both sides. No good can come of that. No good can come of it anywhere or any time it enters into any human relations, for it is the very contrary of the primal Love which is the Source, the Law and the Purpose of the created universe. That man has now completely lost touch with it is proved by the fact that once a year he responds in a vague instinctive way to the call of the

"Christmas spirit." In that response is the only visible ground for hope for the kind of world of which we are all talking.

December 24, 1943

PANDORA'S BOX OF BARBARISM

Last week's revelations of what has happened to our war prisoners in Japan has shocked us beyond our powers of expression. It is as if there had been suddenly opened at our feet a new bottomless gulf of horrors beyond not merely anything that we had already experienced, but also beyond our wildest fears of horrors to come. One word springs naturally to almost everyone's lips—*devilish.* It is the only word in our ken that fits the facts, for it is the only word that implies something at once unhuman and wholly evil, and the presence amongst us of that something has startled us as nothing else has done in the long catalogue of horrors of the last five years. Anger is merely a vehement passion for justice and never in our history has it so possessed our hearts. Never, so far as history can tell us, has a whole people been so swiftly stirred to a white heat of anger as have we, and our allies, in these last few days. It is something quite new in the modern world and it forecasts a coming world-assize of a character and of a scope entirely unprecedented in human experience, the consequences of which are beyond our capacity to foresee.

It is difficult for us in our present mood to still our passions and to try to understand what has happened, and how it has come about. But the effort is not merely worth making but, indeed, is necessary to make. In making it, the first step is to look back over the facts in as cold a spirit of analysis as we can muster, and try to discern when and where this diabolism first clearly made its appearance in the dealings of men with each other in these our days. Let us draw a line at the end of the last war and forget all the atrocity stories of that time.

A few years ago, Mr. Maurice Hindus published a book here entitled *Humanity Uprooted,* dealing with Russia in the formative years of "the Bolshevist Revolution." Stripped of all possible exaggeration, the story is one of cold-blooded extermination of millions of human beings who had committed no crime other than that of being innocent obstacles to a political reconstruction of their country. Also, for the first time in recorded history, the rulers of a great people formally declared war upon Almighty God. That *did* startle a good many of us here and a good many in other countries where it was going on. But we did not clearly recognize it for what it was, and it is to be feared that it was the economic revolution of the Bolshevist regime, rather than that regime's treatment of human beings, that had much to do with the attitude of other nations beside our own to the Soviet Government. With the advent of Hitler and Nazism, the smell of brimstone seemed first to be discerned by our nostrils. Perhaps the reason was that whereas a good many of our people had viewed the economic side of Bolshevism with sympathy, indeed with approval, the Nazi deviltry was devoid of this or any other adventitious attraction and the facts of that deviltry were more clearly observable in detail. The story of the Warsaw Ghetto, for instance, lacked little, if anything, of the infernal characteristics of the Bataan story. It shocked us, yes; but not as Bataan has shocked and angered us. We have witnessed the process of extermination as applied to the European Jews—as truly devilish in its character as anything that has so far happened—with nothing like the excess of angry heat as that in which we are today.

Perhaps this is natural, in a way, as men are so constituted. Now it is not the Russian kulaks or the European Jews who are the victims; it is our own people. But if we are bent upon analysis, we must discard as best we can all the emotional elements from the equation and look only at the remaining fundamental facts. The one fundamental fact that stares us in the face is this: After a good two centuries of "humanitarian" progress—as we imagine it—we find ourselves suddenly confronted by the spectacle of something which is more, much more, than a reversion to something which we call "barbarism." It is something much worse. It is "barbarism" stripped of all its youthful freshness and vigor, which contributed to European civilization (as Count Coudenhove-Kalergi has reminded us) the idea of "chivalry" and not merely stripped of these things, but infused with a positively evil spirit. The question that faces us is: How did this happen? What has gone wrong? We had a "civilization" that in its *mores* was by all odds the most "humanitarian" in all history, yet there has appeared this monstrous thing which, in its negation of human nature, itself makes the Aztec human sacrifices look almost like a noble conception.

What opened the door to the thing? Through the centuries what men have called the law of right and wrong has underlain men's *mores*. It has remained for our day to furnish its first formal *denial*. That law barred the door to the spirit of evil. If that does not point to the answer to the question, where else are we to look for it?

February 4, 1944

ON WAR AND PEACE

THE CHRISTMAS MESSAGE OF PIUS XII

The Christmas Eve utterance of Pius XII is a statement of the origin, nature and purpose of democracy, more complete (so far as the present writer is aware) than can be found in any other single statement from the same source in the past. As such it should interest those who, while they do not accept the Vatican's teaching authority, are deeply concerned in the subject itself and recognize the care taken by Pope Pius to present his view. The present writer will attempt to summarize in a few "propositions" the essence of that view to exhibit its logical structure, that the reader may judge it for himself and compare it with his own.

(1) The starting point is the nature of man himself as the creature of God in the image and likeness of his creator. In this all men are equal, and in nothing else. Man is a *person.*

(2) He is *social* by his nature and human *society* exists for the good of the persons who live in it. As a *social* person man is also an *individual.* As a person he enjoys *rights* against society; as an individual he owes to society certain *duties.* Rights and duties are correlative, but the rights are paramount in importance as being personal; nevertheless, his duties as an individual are necessary for the proper functioning of society.

(3) *Government* is necessary in any society for the preservation of *order,* for order is necessary to secure *justice* in social relations, and government connotes *authority* to secure the individual's performance of his duties. Authority connotes *power* to enforce its devices.

(4) As society is a necessary provision for man's personal good, government is inseparable from man's natural life, being ordained by God as a *means* to that good. Society is thus the *means* to the person as the end.

(5) The *scope* of government authority is, therefore, *limited;* government may not be *absolute* (totalitarian). As all persons are equal in personality, no person has any *inherent right* to govern others. Thus the persons who constitute a society may, as a society, determine for themselves who shall exercise the authority and powers of government. This is the essence of *democracy,* as the word etymologically implies. This they do by choosing *representatives* for the necessary offices of government. This is democracy *in action.*

(6) These men should be chosen for *character.* (The Pope's message has a long passage describing the qualities that they should possess.) However chosen—it rests with each society to determine the *form* of the civil structure and the details of the distribution of governmental powers—these men must represent *all the people* and not merely a *party* or a *class.*

(7) Governmental bodies must make a large number of *positive* laws in the preservation of social order and justice. None of these laws may contradict the demands of the *natural law,* and *moral law,* the divine law of right and wrong inseparable from the nature of man as a person. So long as they do not offend in this way the individual is bound to their observance.

(8) "Mass government"—that is, government by "popular fronts" out of which grows the single-party state and the "leader"—is not democracy, but its perversion, for it is inherently *totalitarian* and sinks the *person* in the social group. Democracy is necessarily *pluralistic*—that is, it must reflect *all* classes and groups, and respect their rights. Any government, *which is accepted by the people as a whole, whatever its form,* and fulfills these requirements is *democratic;* no government, *whatever be its form,* which does not can properly be so called.

(9) Thus, the whole notion of democracy as Pope Pius sees it rests upon the notion of man's *moral personality* as the

ultimate *end* for which civil government is the proximate *means* and, therefore, on the notion of the *moral law* which forbids the violation of that personality by society. At the end it rests upon acceptance of God the creator of all things.

The structure of the papal thesis is severely logical if one accepts these basic premises. Not all men accept them in a real sense and draw out the conclusions implicit in them. Some, perhaps many, have never thought about them. Some, a relatively recent phenomenon, deny them *in toto*—our "Instrumentalists," for instance. The problem for those who do not accept the Pope's premises is to discover a principle other than one rooted in moral law which will exclude governmental totalitarianism, for it is this that under any and all forms—and it can assume all forms with equal facility—is the eternal enemy of human liberty. *January* 3, 1945

YALTA: MORALS AND PEACE

I

There are two "perspectives" in which to view the Yalta agreements as they settle themselves into the record—the "short" view and the "long" view. In the "short" view, they seem to give us a reasonable hope for an armistice which may last a fairly long time, possibly even a decade or even two. That would be in itself quite a notable achievement. Taking the other view, they seem to have produced nothing of consequence representing *real* progress to the *peace* that we are all talking about.

All the conditions for this armistice seem to be present.

With the destruction of Nazi military strength (we may leave Japan to one side for the time being), there will remain in being only three "great powers" capable of making war in Europe on any large scale—Soviet Russia, Great Britain and the United States. With Nazism smashed, there will remain no immediate burning issue in dispute between the three, which might lead to immediate conflict—that is, conflict in the next decade or less between them. Britain and Soviet Russia, moreover, will need not a little time to recover from their exertions, and neither is looking for new territorial gains; Russia has already collected much spoil. All things considered, the "Big Three" should be able to live together without fighting for a while, and prevent anyone else from starting trouble.

Taking the long view, the picture is different, and *peace* is not in it. In the first place, there can be no *peace* for the world with the German people in indefinite "receivership" of the kind specified at Yalta. The program in this matter is tantamount to a confession of despair. There is no precedent for it in modern history. If history proves anything, it proves the impotence of mere force to break the human will. Yet that is what we are going to try to do with the German people. Unless that people is, as a people, fundamentally different from other European peoples, it can be no more forced to submit its *will* to its conquerors than, as conqueror, it could force its victims to submit their will to it. In the second place, there is Poland still pointing stubbornly at the Atlantic Charter and asking whether its fine language means anything—to say nothing of the other small Baltic nations already swallowed up in the Soviet Union's capacious maw. The Charter is supposed to map the *peace* that we are attempting to make by laying down the principles, and principles are not compromisable. The *peace* we are talking about rests upon a *moral* foundation; so at least we say. We are learning to manipulate nature's molecules in our laboratories, but morals are not manipulatable. The lamentable fact is that the moral foundation for the peace is not in sight. Europe and Christendom were once synonymous terms, as indeed were Christendom and "the West." But in the last century and a half Christendom has in part ceased to be Christian; it has in fact become *secularized*, especially in its thinking. There has indeed developed in it a wholly secularized philosophy of life and of morals. Nor is this the worst of it. In face of this common danger to Christianity as the vital principle of the "West" there have flamed up the conflicts within the Christian bodies themselves which threaten to be more acute than in a long time. If there were ever a time when Christian unity were needed it is now and it finds Christians bitterly divided. This would be bad enough in itself, but the geographical distribution of these groups is such as to endure the maximum of difficulty in achieving even a temporal stability of social order.

If the foregoing remarks should strike the reader as unwarrantedly pessimistic, the present writer would suggest that they so seem only by reason of the extravagant hopes that so many have permitted themselves to entertain under the influence of much impassioned rhetoric. The world has never known the kind of peace that we have been envisioning. Europe has never had anything more than successive armistices of varied duration. Perhaps the nearest that it came to controlling war was in feudal days by the "Truce of God"—and that was not very near—but the "Truce" *did* work while it lasted. And so far as the evidence of history tells us anything, it suggests that if we desire a "truce" from wars now, it is in the direction of a "Truce of God" that we had better look, rather than in the direction of a "truce of trade," a "truce" of stable currencies or—even!—a "truce" of democracy.

February 23, 1945

II

This writer does not know whether in the days when Abailard was warring with William of Champeaux and Bernard of Clairvaux men were in the habit of tagging each other with descriptive labels, as we do nowadays, and letting it go at that. We don't take much time or trouble in actual dialectics; we simply dismiss our opponent as a "fascist" or a "red baiter" or as a "labor baiter" or as a "Roosevelt hater" and Q.E.D. Not that the three twelfth-century champions above mentioned were unskilled in or averse to invective in argument; far from it, but at least they did deal in argument and they did join issues in argument. Listening, as this writer occasionally does, to discussions and debates on topics these days, he rarely comes across a debate where this happens. The disputants seldom get to real handgrips. But they frequently revel in tags. Two new ones have recently appeared in connection with the Yalta Conference which may get into general use. One is a simple label—*perfectionists;* the other is a distinction offered to the House of Commons by no less an authority than Mr. Churchill himself, when he pointed out in reply to an opposition member that the Atlantic Charter was a "guide" and not a "rule." Who first coined the word "perfectionist" this writer does not know. But its meaning is apparently a person who in the present case regards the Charter as a "rule" and not merely a "guide." (Mr. Churchill's questioner, by the way, missed a nice dialectic "opening" in not then asking Mr. Churchill whether the Ten Commandments were "rules" or "guides," but one cannot think of everything at the moment. The best retorts as we all know come to us only in the homing taxi.)

The implication is that a "perfectionist" is a person who demands impossibilities by unreasonable interpretation of words—in this case the words of the Atlantic Charter—instead of being "practical" and recognizing that the essence of statesmanship is "compromise." It is quite true that compromise is the essence of statesmanship, but are we to conclude that compromise is regarded by the United Nations as extending to *principles?* The Atlantic Charter is in form and substance a declaration of principles in which the signatories believe. These principles are stated in plain terms without any qualifications or reservations, including that concerning the "freedom" of small nations. There is no obscurity in language. The thought is therefore as clear as a postulate of Euclid, that is, as a "rule." When does a "rule" of this sort cease to be a "rule" and become a "guide"? When does a "principle" in the moral order cease to be a "principle" and when can it be discarded for the "greater expediency"? Can anyone who asks these questions be reasonably waved aside as a "perfectionist"?

Admittedly Mr. Churchill and Mr. Roosevelt—and their respective countries—are in a difficult position with respect to their partner in a gigantic task. He holds the trumps in his hand and he knows it. They also know it and the cards must be played out as they lie. But that is no reason for misrepresenting the state of the game. Much less is it a reason for juggling with the meaning of words. Happily there is no reason to doubt that Soviet Russia is as determined as are the United Nations to smash the German military power. But who in his senses supposes that Mr. Stalin's picture of reconstructed Europe bears any real likeness to our own concept of a "democratic" society, or to that of Great Britain and the British Commonwealth, much less to the picture sketched by the Atlantic Charter? Some keen observers in Washington point out that Stalin's idea of what are the "democratic and anti-Nazi parties" who are to be permitted to reorganize the "liberated countries" under the Yalta agreement may differ sharply from the ideas of the peoples concerned. Moreover, "free elections" in principle and "free elections" in practice may turn out to be far from the same thing. They not infrequently have done so.

If it is impossible for the world in its present state to put into practice now the principles of the Atlantic Charter—and this writer believes that it is—it is for lack of the necessary moral conviction and moral purpose which alone can generate the will to do so. But why should we try to deceive ourselves into believing that we *are* doing so when we are not? Moral principles—the Atlantic Charter's principles are moral or they are meaningless—are *rules,* are *laws,* and calling them "guides" does not alter that fact. Why not be honest about it, admit the truth and drop labels?

February 26, 1945

SAN FRANCISCO HOPES

I

To appraise the result of the San Francisco Conference which is ending its two months' labors, one must view it in its true perspective and in its broad outlines, remembering always what was its purpose. That purpose was to draw the charter for a world organization for the preservation of peace by substituting international arbitration for international war in the settlement of international disputes. The Conference was not charged with any other duty. The terms upon which the war, now half concluded, would be settled, were not its concern. The task was to construct "machinery" for use when those terms were settled. This it has done; the "machine's" blueprint looks, on the whole, reasonably logical.

Naturally it does not in every particular satisfy everybody, but it does seem to contain the parts essential to the purpose in view.

But that is not the really interesting feature of the whole affair. Let us go back a very few years, say to 1939, and note the tremendous change that has taken place in the thinking of the American people in those six years. Six years ago, the "isolationist-interventionist" debate was in full blast. Of that debate it can be said with truth that the most passionate advocates of intervention could not have contemplated the possibility of that which has in fact been accomplished at San Francisco in this spring of 1945. Who then could have supposed that American public opinion would accept the tremendous responsibilities for participation in world affairs expressed in the new charter only six years later? What are the causes which here operated to make our American people abandon the tradition of a century and a half?

For one thing we were suddenly dragged into the war by Japan, followed by her Axis allies, and from the first we recognized that it was to be an "all-out" war for our national life. But we were "forced" by events of World War I to take up arms and we promptly dropped them at the end of it, and declined responsibility for what followed. As World War II developed, we quickly discovered that warfare had become vastly more destructive in weapons than in World War I, and, even more important, that the enemy had not only dropped the "civilized" restraints that had remained through World War I, but had adopted a policy and method of action in war-making of which all that can be said is that they constituted a comprehensive and scientifically refined attack on the most elementary decencies of human life itself. As the war progressed, its destructiveness took on new dimensions, in fact, new horrors, literally diabolic, in the enemy's conduct, which brought into play on our side two powerful motives for a change in our traditional view of our policy.

One was a vivid realization that modern warfare has reached a point of destructiveness which threatens the very continuance of civilization itself and could not longer be tolerated among civilized men. Here the motive may be called fear. The other was a deep moral revolt against the open and deliberate jettisoning by the enemy of the last shreds of morality itself. Combined, the two motives may well account for our national *volte-face* and we need not stop to ask which played the major part in bringing it about. But one thing is certain so far as the future is concerned. That is that the fear motive is not likely to be permanent. We are now learning that our enemies had devised new engines of destruction, even more terrible than any yet employed, but the end happily came before they could be put into action. We have adequate scientific warrant for their appalling efficiency. World War II began where World War I left off. If there is to be a World War III, it, too, will begin where World War II stopped, and that contingency is intolerable even to contemplate. Granted all the obscurity surrounding everything else, it is impossible to believe that any one of the United Nations is now directly or indirectly planning for future war. It is hard to believe that it will come unplanned long in advance.

Strong as is the fear motive, it is, however, a transitory thing, and as time passes and generation succeeds to generation, it naturally, unless renewed, slips from men's minds. The only sure road to the elimination of war is the moral road and that road ends in religion, just as it starts there. War between nations as nations are today can never be securely banished by purely material considerations with "utilitarianism" as the only principle. So this problem is a problem of conscience and not merely of the intellect. Until Christendom recovers its faith in what for centuries was called the natural law and a conscience which accepts the rule of that faith, there can be no enduring peace. Our real hope for that peace is in the stirrings, faint as they are, of that old faith and that dormant conscience.

June 20, 1945

II

For two months, the present writer has been removed from circulation by what we like to describe as an indisposition, but which, in this particular case, has prevented practically all activity from the collar button down. Nevertheless, although deprived of continuous reading and during hospital experience from contact with the outside world except for a few friends, the tremendous events of the last few weeks have burst into his secluded consciousness and driven him irresistibly to an effort to express himself upon them.

Passing for a moment the whole question of the atomic bomb which, as a matter of fact, still dwarfs all other considerations, this writer was interested in the argument that for a little while absorbed the attention of not a few people. This was whether what was going on at San Francisco was "realistic" or mere "idealism." Curiously enough, there has since come up another highly interesting question in connection with the coming trial of war criminals—whether, as in the case of the atomic bomb, men have come up against something hitherto outside their consciousness which suddenly places them upon a precipitous spot.

Obviously the proceedings at Dumbarton Oaks and San Francisco were devoted wholly to constructing a piece of machinery to be applied to the preservation of world peace. Machinery does not work by itself. No doubt, a machine is a realistic thing in itself, but devoid of power and guidance, there is not much realism left in it. Now the fact of the matter was at all times clear and is equally clear today, namely: that the United Nations Charter could only work if behind it there stood a definite intention and unqualified determination on the part of the nations, themselves, to make it work. Many people have supposed that such determination could be reached by the road of fear, fear of war and its consequences. Others, as this writer believes, more correctly view that men would have to go deeper by a good deal than this particular emotion. Peace is a positive thing, not a negation of conflict. It must rest upon something in the spiritual order. It must rest upon a conviction in men's minds that there is such a thing as a law of right and wrong which must be obeyed by all people at all times, by nations as by individuals. A law of this sort transcends all questions of balancing consequences.

Modern man has virtually forgotten the existence of natural law—as people for many, many centuries called it—the law recognized, alike by pagan and Christian, as fundamental in human nature. To those who criticize Dumbarton Oaks and San Francisco as unrealistic, the whole thing turned upon natural law. There was a time when nations recognized, at least more or less, the existence of such a law, even though they broke it or evaded it. It was not until the last century, or so, that its very existence passed out of their consciousness. Now the interesting thing is that it comes up again in striking fashion in connection with the trial of war criminals. The fact is that the Allied nations find themselves somewhat at a loss to determine precisely the nature and extent of the criminality of these chief culprits. The report of Justice Jackson to President Truman originally, after preparations for war trials and the test of the four-party agreement as to their set-up, indicates the perplexity of men who find themselves face to face with actions which today have become revolting to human nature but which, or many of which, have not hitherto been questioned. It has been said that the courts that will hold these trials will have to manufacture the laws *ex post facto* under which some of these criminals, notably those at the top, are to be brought to punishment. No one until now, for many a long year, has really suggested the indictment of the head of a state merely for making an aggressive war. There probably has not been a single war in Europe of any consequence for centuries that was not an aggressive war on somebody's part. The canons of a just and unjust war have been laid down for centuries for all to see and there is no dispute about them, but the whole structure of international law has disappeared into a maze of vaporous nothings in the last two centuries. This is another aspect of the destruction brought upon human society by the abandonment of belief in the natural law.

Not only to lawyers will the forthcoming trials be of the greatest interest; the whole represents the reappearance, at least, of something which had virtually disappeared from modern jurisprudence. Just as return of the natural law to honor among men is absolutely necessary for international peace, so, too, it is absolutely necessary, if we are to have an orderly structure of human society. Here, again, men seem to have reached a great and tremendous turning point.

August 20, 1945

A LAST WORD

America should again proclaim our faith. We should proclaim our resolution to hold it. We should cease to apologize for it. Our first postwar purpose should be to restore it." *(From Mr. Hoover's birthday speech on his 71st birthday a few days ago.)*

Mr. Hoover is not a person whose habit it is to make overstatements. Nor does he deal in empty rhetoric. He uses a word in the above quotation that should, however, be hammered into the consciousness of the American people. That word is faith. No doubt most of us feel a sort of comfortable sense that we have a vague faith in something which very few of us probably, if challenged, could state in clear and definite terms. This is an astonishing thing, because the fact is that we have a clear and definite creed stated for us at the very founding of our nation, by men who knew exactly what they were doing and stated it in the plainest terms. The American idea is no mass of cloudy, fanciful, pleasant, high-sounding generalities. On the contrary, it is a definite, coherent, tightly-linked mass of the most important possible affirmations. We have it in the Declaration of Independence. The Preamble to that document is literally a form of credo in terms exact enough almost to satisfy an Athanasius. These affirmations are all-embracive. How many of us ever stop to examine them? They begin with a positive statement of belief in God as the Creator of men. They point out that the Creator definitely singled out His human creatures from the great mass of living beings by clothing them with a tremendous importance. He endowed them with something that no other living being on this earth possesses, namely, rights. The whole purpose of civil government, so our creed points out, is to secure these individual creatures in the possession of these rights. It states definitely this purpose in unmistakable terms. Now the implications in these statements are enormous. The important point is that they all rest upon the unique value of a human being. It is in this unique value that human beings are equal; in every other respect they are wholly unequal.

The Founders, moreover, did not say "we believe" or "we opine" that the truths which they enunciated were true. They boldly stated them as self-evident. Technically, the expression is faulty, for in the strict sense of the word extremely few things are self-evident. They regarded them, however, as being so plainly evident on the face of the facts as to admit of no denial. If one unpacks the implications contained in them, there arises what is substantially a fundamental religious doctrine. Man has these rights because God created him to have them.

If the creed thus contained in the Declaration's Preamble be not a complete series of fundamental affirmations all resting on a Creator and a divine purpose, words have no meaning. Moreover, in that creed lies the whole theory of what we like to call our democracy. Its essence is that the least important human being possesses a right assuring his liberty against all the world. That right is to justice, and freedom is inseparable from justice. A curious thing in the pagan mind was that it sensed the principle of the non-totalitarian state but never carried it through. "Let justice be done though heavens fall" expressed its essence. The lowliest human being was entitled to justice—that is, to his due, as the old definition had it—no matter what the consequences were to all the rest. The Greek and the Roman states, set up as they were by a sort of democratic process, were in fact treated as absolute, omnipotent and totalitarian. Yet the philosopher who uttered that phrase about the heavens was a step beyond that notion. We, for the first time in human history, set up a nation based upon a complete creed of human freedom.

Now, what Mr. Hoover says and rightly recognizes as a terrible danger is that we have lost, or rather many of us have lost, our faith in our creed. The truth of the matter is that democracy as we understand it depends upon that faith and faith in its entirety. Its first principle must be the right of the individual to justice against the world. The present writer will venture the statement that that notion of justice to the individual is essentially a religious notion and can live only with a live religion. He is convinced that, where religion has been weakened, the democratic values at once lose their efficacy and proceed to disintegrate. Disintegration may be slow at the start, but once it sets in, it is but a short step from freedom to despotism. In calling, therefore, for a renewal of faith in our American ideals Mr. Hoover is sounding a note that needs to be heard far more widely and clearly than it has been heard of late years. We need it for ourselves, but we need it additionally for our dealings with the rest of the world. We represent to the nations the idea of democracy at its best. We need to take care that the picture we give them is true and clear and that we ourselves believe in it. Surely our great parties ought to be able to agree on a thing like that.

August 27, 1945

INDEX OF NAMES

INDEX OF NAMES

INDEX OF NAMES